MW01505224

The Devotion of the Holy Rosary & the Five Scapulars

Fr. Michael Müller, C.SS.R.

Loreto Publications
Fitzwilliam, New Hampshire
Anno Domini 2011

First published by Benzinger Bros., 1878

Reprinted: March 1998
               March 1999
               July 1999
               January 2003

Published by:
Loreto Publications
P. O. Box 603
Fitzwilliam, NH 03447

www.LoretoPubs.org

603.239.6671

Printed and Bound in the U.S.A.

CONTENTS

CHAPTER 1

INTRODUCTORY

Some years ago, a traveler visited the famous ruins of Palenque, in Central America. While rambling alone one day through the forest, in the neighborhood of the ruins, he heard the song of a bird. The notes were sweet and clear and full of wondrous harmony. The traveler, resolved to secure a specimen of so rare a bird, cautiously approached the thicket from which the sweet sounds proceeded. On arriving at the spot, he found that the bird had already flown to a neighboring hill. He ascended the hill, but now the song rose up from the valley below. So eager was the traveler to secure the bird that he followed it without heeding for a moment the direction in which he was going. He followed on and on, from hill to hill, from thicket to thicket, from glade to glade. Sometimes the strange, weird notes seemed just above his head, sounding clear and loud, like a song of triumph and again they were heard far away, as if dying in the distance. The pursuer gradually became possessed with a feverish anxiety to secure the coveted prize. He searched for the bird on every tree, on every branch. At times he raised his fowling piece to fire at it, as it seemed only a few yards distant, but suddenly it again disappeared, and was nowhere to be seen; and so he continued to pursue it, till at last he found himself, alone and bewildered, in the midst of a dense forest.

Then he began to retrace his steps. He went on for some time without the least anxiety, diverted by the curious flowers and insects that beset his path. After a while, however, he noticed that the scenery around him was altogether strange and unfamiliar, and, growing alarmed, he hurriedly ascended an eminence hard by. He gazed anxiously in all directions, but could see nothing, save the foliage of the great forest – could hear nothing but the beating of his own heart. With all the energy which terror inspires he climbed a lofty tree. He now looked once more around him on all sides, but his heart sank within him as he saw nothing but an ocean of verdure that spread far away to the distant horizon, and seemed limitless. The unhappy man descended from the tree, and shouted for his companions; but no answer came back. He sat down at the foot of the tree, and, pressing his head with his hands, tried to devise some means of escape from his dreadful situation. But he could not collect his thoughts. The blood rushed to his brain; all his faculties seemed paralyzed. After brooding thus for some time in the most cruel agony of mind, he arose full of the worst foreboding, but yet with a fixed plan of action. Choosing the spot where he was standing as a point of departure, he marked a gigantic tree, and piled up stones around it so that he could recognize it even at a distance. He then resolved to walk in a straight line in every direction from this central point till he should at last reach some sign of the ancient ruins where he had encamped. He walked on for hours. He tried one direction after the other, but everywhere he was met with the same waving vegetation, the same large shining leaves filling up the space with their wild luxuriance, and shutting out the horizon from his view. As he was struggling on feebly, well-nigh overcome with terror and despair, he suddenly heard from the neighboring thicket the clear, musical note of the strange bird that had lured him away into the depths of the forest. A thrill of superstitious terror shot through his whole frame as he heard this wondrous melody. It now seemed to him indeed like the ironical voice of an evil spirit mocking him in his distress. He determined, however, not to be misled this time, and continued his course without heeding the invisible bird that seemed to tempt him with its sweet but delusive melody. He traveled over hill and dale, through open plains and almost impenetrable thickets, till his face and hands were covered with blood. Daylight was now fading fast, and, as the darkness began to gather around him, the thought of spending the night alone in the heart of the vast unknown forest, infested with wild beasts and poisonous serpents, filled him with indescribable sadness and terror.

At the thought of being condemned to perish alone in the forest a death-like shudder passed over him; the perspiration started through every pore; his very breath seemed suspended. As he continued to struggle on feebly, not knowing whither to turn, he spied through the gathering darkness a conical-shaped hill. He went towards it, and found at its base some stones that seemed to bear the traces of human industry, although defaced by age. They had evidently formed part of some ancient structure that time had leveled to the ground. A ray of hope suddenly flashed upon his despairing soul. Perhaps these stones were connected in some way with the ruins from which he had strayed away. His first impulse now was to fall on his knees and, with swelling heart, to thank God for this unexpected help when all seemed lost and utterly hopeless.

Advancing with renewed courage, he soon came upon other ruins, but they were still unfamiliar to his eyes. Other remains which he again discovered encouraged him to keep on in the same direction. By degrees the shape and style of the ruins began to grow familiar to him. He kept on, with ever-increasing hope, till, finally, as the last ray of daylight had faded away, bruised and bleeding, and completely worn out with fatigue, he reached his companions.

We are all, like this young man, travelers here below − poor pilgrims on our way to heaven, our true home. The unhappy condition of the traveler, deprived of all human aid, represents vividly to the mind the unhappy condition of those who, in the pursuit of the fleeting pleasures of this world, have lost sight of the end for which God made them. The few stones and traces of ruins that at last led him back to the place of safety represent the truths which God has revealed, scattered here and there over the world, left to linger in neglect, but which we must follow if we would reach the bourne to which we all turn and if we would be happy for ever. The untiring efforts of this poor man to reach again the place from which he had strayed, serve as a model to all those who sincerely wish to reach the end for which they were created. The bird in the story represents Lucifer, who sends his infernal companions all over the world to lead men astray by the enchanting song of their subtle temptations, as God one day showed in a vision to Blessed Mary of Jesus d'Agreda. This great servant of the Lord saw how Lucifer, after the death of Christ, called together the chiefs of the infernal legions, and spoke to them thus:

"Companions, you see that we have lost the empire which we so long maintained over the world, and have been overthrown by the death of the Man-God upon the cross, and crushed beneath the feet of his Mother. What shall we now do? How shall we ever re-establish our fallen empire? How shall we be able to draw men to us? Will not every one follow and imitate the Incarnate God? They will walk in his footsteps, give him their hearts, practice his law, observe his precepts, and no one will ever listen again to our deceitful promises. They will reject the riches and honors with which we try to allure them! No doubt, after his example, they will love poverty, obedience, purity, and ignominy, and thus attain to that eternal kingdom which we have lost. In order to imitate the Redeemer, they will humble themselves to the dust and suffer all things with patience. Nevertheless, my pride fails not. Courage! let us confer together on the means by which we may still make war against the world, redeemed by the Man-God and protected by his Mother, our terrible enemy."

To this difficult proposition some of the most cunning of the infernal chiefs replied: "It is true that men now possess a very mild law, very powerful sentiments, the new example of a divine Master, and the efficacious intercession of this new Woman. But human nature is always the same, and things pleasing to the senses have not changed. It is a condition of human nature that when occupied with one object, it cannot pay attention to another which is opposed to it."

Then they resolved to maintain idolatry in the world, so that men might never attain to the knowledge of the true God or of the mystery of the Redemption, and that, should idolatry be overthrown, they would introduce into the world new sects and heresies, such as the erroneous and infernal doctrines of Arius, Pelagius, Mahomet, Luther, Calvin, Henry VIII, John Knox, and others. All these plans were approved by Lucifer, because they aimed at the destruction of the foundation of the blessed, eternal life.

Other demons pledged themselves to devote all their energies to cause parents and heads of families to be careless and negligent in the education of children, and send them to godless state or public schools. Others promised to sow discord between husbands and wives, thus to raise hatred and quarrels between them. Others said: "Our office will be to destroy piety and all that is spiritual and divine, and to prevent men from understanding the power of the sacraments, so that they may receive them either in the state of mortal sin or in a state of tepidity and indevotion; for, as the benefits which flow from them are spiritual, those who wish to receive the fruit of them must be fervent in spirit. If they have contempt for the remedy, they will be careless about their salvation, and thus become too feeble to resist our temptations; being blinded, they will not perceive our snares and deceits, they will not appreciate the love of their Redeemer, or the intercession of his Mother, that powerful Woman and great enemy of ours."

They unanimously resolved to devote all their zeal and energy to cause the faithful to forget the Life and Death of Jesus and Mary, and to neglect prayer, by tempting some to pursue, with blind eagerness, the riches and pleasures and honors of this world; others, to gratify their passions; others, to embrace false doctrines and erroneous principles; others, to take special delight in licentious and infidel literature and novel reading; others, to establish secret societies, and introduce by their means godless, infidel education all over the world. "Thus," they said, "men will be led to forget the pains of hell and the danger of eternal damnation."

The truth of this vision is apparent from the experience of all ages. Satan is constantly engaged in doing all in his power to entice men away from God, and to have himself worshipped instead of the Creator. The introduction, establishment, persistence, and power of the various cruel, revolting superstitions of the ancient heathen world, or of pagan nations in modern times, are nothing but the work of the devil. They reveal a more than human power: God permitted Satan to operate upon man's morbid nature, as a deserved punishment upon the Gentiles for their hatred of truth and their apostasy from the primitive religion of the holy patriarchs and prophets. Men left to themselves, to human nature alone, however low they might be prone to descend, never could descend so low as to worship wood and stone, four-footed beasts, and creeping things. To do this needs Satanic delusion.

Paganism in its old form was doomed. Christianity had silenced the oracles and driven the devils back to hell. How was the devil to re-establish his worship on earth, and carry on his war against the Son of God and the religion which he taught us? Evidently, only by changing his tactics and turning the truth into a lie. Satan is called in Holy Scripture the father of lies. From the beginning of the world, he has tried to misrepresent every religious truth. He practiced this black art in Paradise, and so unhappily successful was he in it that ever since he has practiced it in order to propagate error and vice among men. He has practiced this black art even in the presence of Christ himself. By malicious men, the ministers of Satan, Christ was contradicted and misrepresented in his doctrine; for, instead of being believed, he was held up to the people as a blasphemer for teaching that he was the Son of God, as the impious Caiphas declared him to be, saying: "He hath blasphemed; he is guilty of death" (Mt 26:65). He was misrepresented in his reputation, for he was noble, of royal lineage, and yet was despised. "Is not this the carpenter's son?" (Mt. 23:55). He is wisdom itself, and was represented as an ignorant man: "How doth this man know letters, having never learned?" (Jn. 7:17). He was represented as a false prophet: "And they blindfolded him, and smote his face . . . saying: Prophesy who is this that struck thee?" (Lk. 22:64). He was represented as a madman: "He is mad, why hear you him?" (Jn. 10:20). He was represented as a wine-bibber, a glutton, and a friend of sinners: "Behold a man that is a glutton, and a drinker of wine, a friend of publicans and sinners" (Lk. 7:34). He was represented as a sorcerer; "By the prince of the devils he casteth out devils" (Mt. 9:34). He was represented as a heretic and possessed person: "Do we not say well of thee, that thou art a Samaritan and hast a devil?" (Jn. 8:48). In a word, Jesus was represented to the people as so bad and notorious a man that no trial was deemed necessary to condemn him, as the Jews said to Pilate: "If he were not a malefactor, we would not have delivered him up to thee" (Jn. 18:30). The reason why those malicious men misrepresented Christ to the multitude, reporting light to be darkness, and God to be the devil, was that thus they might frighten the people from embracing the truth and following the Son of God. The disciples of Christ everywhere met with the like treatment. The people were stirred up against St. Stephen by misrepresentation, because they were told that "he had spoken blasphemous words against Moses and against God" (Acts 6:11). They were also stirred up against St. Paul because they were told that he was "a pestilent fellow, and a mover of sedition amongst all the Jews throughout the world" (Acts 24:5). Neither did those calumnies, those wicked misrepresentations, stop here. Jesus Christ said: "The disciple is not above the master. if they have called the master of the house Beelzebub, how much more shall they call them of the household?" (Mt. 10:24).

In these words our Lord not only foretold what was to happen to his followers then present, but also to the faithful who were to come after them, and to his Church in future ages; so that, though they should be ever so just to God and their neighbor, upright in their ways, and live in the fear of God and the observance of his laws, yet must they be reviled and hated by the world, made a by-word to the people, have the repute of seducers, and be a scandal to all nations. Has not this come true in all ages? See what was the state of Christians in the primitive times. Their lives were holy and pure; and yet it is almost impossible to believe in what contempt they were held. Tertullian tells us that so malicious were the scandals scattered about concerning the manner of their worship – their whole religion being described not only to be mere folly and foppery but also to be grounded on the most hellish principles, and full of impieties – that the heathens believed a man could not make profession of Christianity without being tainted with all sorts of crimes, without being an enemy to princes, to the laws, to good manners, and to nature itself. Thus the Christian religion was made wholly infamous amongst the heathens, was condemned and detested by the greater part, and most bloody persecutions were raised against the Christians, whilst they were guilty of no other crime than that of adhering to the truth. And those calumnies, those false accusations, were invented to cry down the Christian religion. Hence Tertullian was driven to write his "Apology," wherein he showed to the world that Christianity was nothing like that which the heathens imagined it to be; that idolatry, superstition, impiety, cruelty, treachery, conspiracy, etc., were views condemned and detested by their doctrine. He showed that these crimes were only the malicious inventions and reports of the heathenish priests, who, being unable to withstand the force of the Christian religion, had no other way to preserve themselves in repute and keep the people in their error, than by an ugly, odious, and most horrible mask, a damnable scheme of religion: and then, holding this forth to the world, cried out: "This is the religion of Christians; these are their principles; behold their ignorance, their stupidity, their profaneness; behold their insolence, their villainies – a people insufferable in a commonwealth, enemies to their country and their prince!" Thus representing the Christian religion as monstrous as they pleased, they brought an odium upon as many as owned that name and condemned them for follies and crimes that existed nowhere except in their wicked imagination.

As the darkness of the night is expelled by the light of the sun, so also was heathenism at last overcome by the light of Christianity. But the mouth of malice was not closed; the calumnies which had been invented by the heathens were taken up by such Christians as had fallen away from the faith. No one ever left the Church without trying to make her infamous and blacken her with such crimes as were best calculated to make her hateful to all. To justify their apostasy from the faith and gain to themselves the character of orthodox Christians, apostates have invariably painted the Church in all possible anti-Christian colors, and represented her as hellish as wickedness could desire to make her.

St. Augustine tells us that the Manichees and Donatists did all in their power to raise prejudices in the minds of the people against the Roman Catholic Church. They told men that the teaching of the Church was unsound and profane doctrine, that it was full of wicked principles and human inventions, instead of divine faith; and all these calumnies were spread abroad among the people in order that they might not think of going to the Church to learn the truth, or even suspect her to be the Church of Christ. "The chief reason," says St. Augustine, "why I continued to live so long in the errors of the Manichees and impugned the Catholic Church with so much violence, was because I thought that all I had heard against the Church was true. But when I found out that it was all false, I made known this falsehood to the world, in order to undeceive others who were caught in the same snare. I mingled joys and blushes, and was ashamed that I had now for so many years been barking and railing, not against the Catholic faith, but only against the fictions of my carnal conceits. For so temerarious and impious was I that those things which I might first have learned from Catholics by inquiry, I charged upon them by accusation. I was readier to impose falsehood than to be informed of the truth." This he did, deluded and deceived by the Manichees. Alas! this has not been the case of St. Augustine alone, but of almost as many as have given ear to the deserters of this Church; nay, it is at this very day the case of infinite numbers who, following St. Augustine in his errors, do not inquire how this thing is believed or understood by the Church, but insultingly oppose all as if so understood as they imagine. They make no difference between that which the Catholic Church teaches and what they think she teaches. Thus they believe her guilty of as many absurdities, follies, and impieties as the heathens did of old. They are impious enough to make liars of Jesus Christ, of the Holy Ghost, of the Apostles, to blaspheme the Mother of God and his saints, to slander the Spouse of Jesus Christ – the Roman Catholic Church – in every possible manner.

Jesus Christ says: "Hear the Church." "No," says Protestantism, "do not hear the Church; protest against her with all your might." Jesus Christ says: "If any one will not hear the Church, look upon him as a heathen and publican." "No," says Protestantism, "if any one does not hear the Church, look upon him as an Apostle, as an ambassador of God." Jesus Christ says: "The gates of hell shall not prevail against my Church" "No," says Protestantism, "it is false; the gates of hell have prevailed against the Church for a thousand years and more." Jesus Christ has declared St. Peter, and every successor to St. Peter – the Pope – to be his Vicar on earth." "No," says Protestantism, "the Pope is the Antichrist." Jesus Christ says: "My yoke is sweet, and my burden is light" (Mt. 11:30). "No," said Luther and Calvin; "it is impossible to keep the commandments." Jesus Christ says: "If thou wilt enter into life, keep the commandments." (Mt. 19:17). "No," said Luther and Calvin, "faith alone, without good works, is sufficient to enter into life everlasting." Jesus Christ says: "Unless you do penance, you shall all likewise perish" (Lk. 3:3). "No," says Protestantism, "fasting and other works of penance are not necessary in satisfaction for sin." Jesus Christ says: "This is my body." "No," said Calvin, "this is only the figure of Christ's body; it will become his body as soon as you receive it." Jesus Christ says: "I say to you, that whosoever shall put away his wife, and shall marry another, committeth adultery, and he that shall marry her that is put away, committeth adultery" (Mt. 19:9). "No," says Protestantism to a married man, "you may put away your wife, get a divorce, and marry another." Jesus Christ says to every man: "Thou shalt not steal." "No,"said Luther to secular princes, "I give you the right to appropriate to yourselves the property of the Roman Catholic Church."

The Holy Ghost says in Holy Scripture: "Man knoweth not whether he be worthy of love or hatred" (Eccl. 9:1). "Who can say, My heart is clean, I am pure from sin?" (Prov. 20:9); and, "Work your salvation with fear and trembling" (Philip. 2:12). "No," said Luther and Calvin, "but whosoever believes in Jesus Christ is in the state of grace."

St. Paul says: "If I should have faith, so that I could remove mountains, and have not charity, I am nothing" (1 Cor. 13:2). "No," said Luther and Calvin, "faith alone is sufficient to save us."

St. Peter says that in the Epistles of St. Paul there are many things "hard to be understood, which the unlearned and unstable wrest, as also the other Scriptures, to their own perdition" (2 Pet. 3:16). "No," says Protestantism, "the Scriptures are very plain and easy to be understood."

St. James says: "Is any man sick among you? Let him bring in the priests of the Church, and let them pray over him, anointing him with oil, in the name of the Lord" (James 5:14). "No," says Protestantism, " that is a vain and useless ceremony."

Being thus impious enough to make liars of Jesus Christ, the Holy Ghost, and the Apostles, need we wonder if they continually slander Catholics, telling and believing worse absurdities about them than the heathens did? What more absurd than to preach that Catholics worship stocks and stones for gods, set up pictures of Jesus Christ, of the Blessed Virgin Mary, and other saints, to pray to them and put their confidence in them; that they adore a god of bread and wine; that their sins are forgiven by the priest without repentance and amendment of life; that the Pope or any other person can give leave to commit sin, or that for a sum of money the forgiveness of sins can be obtained? To these and similar absurdities and slanders we simply answer: "Cursed is he who believes in such absurdities and falsehoods, with which Protestants impiously charge the members of the Catholic Church."

Satan's kingdom in this world originated in the denial of truth. Succeeding as he did in making our first parents believe his lying tongue, he sustains falsehood by the same means. His friends and agents, the enemies of our religion, are now making war upon its dogmas more generally and craftily than at any former period. Their attacks, being wily and concealed, are all the more pernicious. The impious rage of a Voltaire or the "solemn sneer" of a Gibbon, would be less dangerous than this insidious warfare. They disguise their designs under the appearance of devotion to progressive ideas and hatred of superstition and intolerance, all the better to instill the slow but deadly poison. By honeyed words, a studied candor, a dazzle of erudition, they have spread their "gossamer nets of seduction" over the world. The press teems with books and journals in which doctrines subversive of religion and morality are so elegantly set forth that the unguarded reader is very apt to be deceived by the fascination of false charms, and to mistake a most hideous and dangerous object for the very type of beauty. The serpent stealthily glides under the silken verdure of a polished style. Nothing is omitted. The passions are fed, and the morbid sensibilities pandered to; firmness in the cause of truth or virtue is called obstinacy; and strength of soul, a refractory blindness. The bases of morality are sapped in the name of liberty; the discipline of the Church, when not branded as sheer "mummery," is held up as hostile to personal freedom; and her dogmas, with one or two exceptions, are treated as opinions which may be received or rejected with like indifference.

Nor is this irreligious tendency confined to literary publications; it finds numerous and powerful advocates in men of scientific pursuits, who strive to make the worse appear the better cause. The chemist has never found in his crucible that intangible something which men call spirit; so, in the name of science, he pronounces it a myth. The anatomist has dissected the human frame; but, failing to meet the immaterial substance – the soul – he denies its existence. The physicist has weighed the conflicting theories of his predecessors in the scale of criticism, and finally decides that bodies are nothing more than

13

the accidental assemblage of atoms, and rejects the very idea of a Creator. The geologist, after investigating the secrets of the earth, triumphantly tells us that he has accumulated an overwhelming mass of facts to refute the Biblical cosmogony and thus subvert the authority of the inspired record. The astronomer flatters himself that he has discovered natural and necessary laws which do away with the necessity of admitting that a Divine Hand once launched the bodies into space and still guides them in their courses. The ethnographer has studied the peculiarities of the races, he has met with widely different conformations; and believes himself sufficiently authorized to deny the unity of the human family. They conclude that nothing exists but matter, that God is a myth, and the soul "the dream of a dream."

In a word, it is by heresies, revolutions, bad secret societies, and godless state-school education that Satan has succeeded so far as to bring thousands of men back to a state of heathenism and infidelity. "Beware of false prophets," says our Lord. " Yes, yes," said our Holy Father Pope Pius IX, in his address to the representatives of foreign colleges in Rome, "*beware* of all those who enter not by the gate of the fold; beware of those who are the masters of lies, as the Prince of the Apostles called them; *beware* of those who are carried away by unbounded pride, as the Apostle says. Pride stands upon a weak foundation, and easily falls, as, in fact, so many proud men have been hurled to destruction. *Beware* of them, for they are impious; and not only are they impious, but the Apostle St. Jude Thaddeus characterizes them by a series of epithets the very perusal of which causes a shudder of horror. These are the men who preach in the pulpit, and who, instead of being disciples of truth, are the masters of error and falsehood. *Beware* of them."

The devil has stationed his false prophets in every part of the world. His kingdom is becoming wider every day. The number of those who listen and follow the false prophets of error, of their passions and unruly appetites – the number of those who follow the false prophets of wicked companions, of the allurements of the flesh, is daily increasing. "It is our duty," says our Holy Father Pope Pius IX, "to fight them with all the means at our command – science, purity of life, and patience, because God sends us as lambs among a pack of wolves.

Among those whom we must oppose in their errors, so as to enlighten them and bring them back into the fold by means of divine grace, are some who are deaf to all warnings. 'Children of darkness' as St. Peter would say, they are the blind and leaders of the blind, and we should abandon them to themselves. *'Preach not to those who will not hear you.'* There are also many others who are misled, and these we must recall by every means which ingenious charity can suggest, and, if possible, lead them to the feet of our divine Redeemer. We must employ every possible means; but all means are not at the command of every one. Those among us who are gifted with great minds and with great learning will be able to battle against the giants of unbelief. Others, whom God may have endowed with less penetration of mind, will also contribute to the triumph of truth by making good use of what talents they have received from him. Look at David. He was so confident of his ability to slay the proud Goliath that he did not hesitate to present himself to Saul to fight the threatening monster, against whom not a single Israelite had the courage to march forth. Saul hesitated, but, after hearing the story of the young shepherd's exploits, of his victories over the bears and the lions, he began to feel reassured, and ordered the beardless warrior to be vested with the royal alms, with the helmet and all the royal armor. David therefore, dressed himself as the king desired, but he soon felt the weight upon his shoulders, and, in attempting to walk, found that he could scarcely move. Then he exclaimed: 'I cannot go thus, for I am not used to it.' From this I conclude that all are not fitted to encounter certain kinds of giants of unbelief, because they have not the right kind of armor for it. But if they cannot directly encounter them, they can overcome them with the effects of an exemplary life, by instruction, by relieving the poor" and, I add, especially by using that kind of armor against unbelief, heresy, and vice which the Blessed Mother of God gave to her great servant St. Dominic – the Devotion of the Rosary; for, as we shall see in the next chapter, the Devotion of the Rosary was given by the Blessed Virgin as a most powerful means of dissipating heresy, extinguishing vice, spreading virtue, imploring the divine mercy, and obtaining the divine protection. " I desire," said the divine Mother to St. Dominic, "that this manner of prayer shall be perpetually promoted and practiced."

CHAPTER 2

THE ROSARY: THE GREAT GIFT OF THE BLESSED VIRGIN

It is now over one thousand eight hundred years since a poor, meanly-clad wanderer entered the capital of the ancient world – the great, wealthy, magnificent city of Rome. He passes its gates and threads his way unobserved through its populous streets. On every side he beholds splendid palaces, raised at the expense of ruined nations; he beholds stately temples, dedicated to as many false gods as there were nations represented in Rome; he beholds public baths and amphitheaters, devoted to pleasure and to cruelty that had become a pleasure; he beholds statues, monuments, and triumphal arches, raised to the memory of the vilest tyrants, deified by the victims of their tyranny and lust.

He passes warriors and senators, beggars and cripples, effeminate men and dissolute women, gladiators and slaves, merchants and statesmen, orators and philosophers – all classes, all ranks, all conditions of men, of every language and color under the sun. Everywhere he sees a maddening race for pleasure; everywhere the impress of luxury; everywhere crime in its fullest growth, side by side with indescribable suffering, diabolical cruelty, and barbarity. This poor, meanly-clad wanderer was St. Peter. Oh! how the noble heart of the poor fisherman of Galilee must have bled when he observed the empire of Satan so supreme; when he witnessed the shocking licentiousness of the temples and the homestead; when he saw the fearful degradation of woman, groaning under the load of her own infamy; when he saw the heartrending inhumanity which slew the innocent babes and threw them into the Tiber; when he saw how prisoners of war, slaves, soldiers, were trained for bloody fights, entering the arena of the amphitheater and striving whole days to strangle one another, for the entertainment of the Roman people.

Here, then, was St. Peter's great mission. Into this foul mass, into this carcass of a rotten society, he was come to infuse a new life, to lay the foundation of a new Rome – a Rome which, instead of paganism and depravity, would spread abroad the truth and the blessing of the Christian religion to the furthermost ends of the earth. In those days the blind would cry for light. Men could no longer see their way. Why are we here? who created us? whither are we going? whence the evils of the world? why have we a thirst for immortality? why does nothing on earth satisfy us? Why our yearning for perpetual happiness? – such were the questions that resounded everywhere, in the schools of philosophy, in the forum, in the market place, in the temple, at the fireside. No one could answer; and yet the social, domestic, and religious happiness of the world rested then, as it now does, on a right answer to these questions. What remedy could be applied to heal such inveterate evils of the mind and the will? Pagan philosophers, poets, and orators had tried their best to elevate mankind, but all their efforts were in vain. They could not give what they had not to give. Then the light shone into the darkness, and Jesus Christ was this light. His divine doctrine and example were the light of the world. St. Peter and the other Apostles, and their lawful successors, the Roman Catholic bishops and priests, became the bearers of that light. Christ had said to them: "As the Father hath sent me, I also send you. Go ye into the whole world, and teach all nations, baptizing them in the name of the Father, and of the Son, and of the Holy Ghost. Teach them to observe all things whatsoever I have commanded you. He who heareth you, heareth me; and he who despiseth you, despiseth me; and he despiseth me, despiseth him who sent me. Behold, I am with you all days, even to the end of the world. Amen I say to you, whatsoever you shall bind upon earth, shall be bound also in heaven; and whatsoever you shall loose upon earth, shall be loosed also in heaven" (Acts 6:4).

St. Peter laid his hand to the plough, and never once looked back. For twenty-five years he prayed and he preached the life and doctrine of Jesus Christ, from whom he had learned that it is neither philosophy nor theology nor eloquence alone that moves the hearts of men; that mere human industry will only injure our work if God's blessing is not upon it by fervent prayer. Christ himself was not satisfied

17

with preaching, laboring, fasting, nor even with the sacrifice of his blood and life. To all this he added incessant prayer. He needed it not for himself. It was on our account that he prayed so much, in order to teach us to do the like – to pray not only for ourselves, but for those also whom we wish to convert to him. Hence, St. Peter writes: "But we will give ourselves continually to prayer and to the preaching, of the word of God" (Acts 6:4).

Thus by constant prayer and the preaching of the life and doctrine of Christ, St. Peter succeeded in establishing in Rome, in that center of every excess of which the human mind and human heart could be guilty, a congregation of Christians, to whom St. Paul could address an epistle, and state in it that the fame of their faith had already spread over the whole world. "I give thanks to my God through Jesus Christ for you all, because your faith is spoken of in the whole world" (Rom. 1:8).

The foundation of a new world had been laid by St. Peter, the first Pope and Vicar of Christ, and cemented by his own blood. This deep and everlasting foundation he laid, not by means of eloquence or the assistance of monarchs, but by prayer and sacrifice, and by relating to the people what Jesus Christ had done and taught for the redemption of the world. Since then, Pope has succeeded Pope in spite of persecution and death, in spite of the opposition of pagan philosophy and of pagan intrigue, of pagan hate and of pagan enmity. It was through the Popes and the Roman Catholic bishops and priests that Jesus Christ crucified was preached everywhere, so that, at the end of the third century, the light of the Roman Catholic religion was spread over the whole of the then known world. The Capitoline temple, and with it the many shrines of idolatry; the golden house of Nero, and with it Roman excess and Roman cruelty; the throne of the Cæsars, and with it Roman oppression and Roman injustice, had all passed away and there stood the Rome of the Fathers of the Church, the Rome which was yet to do such wonders in the world. Two hundred and fifty-eight Popes have till now succeeded one another in the See of St. Peter. Of these, seventy-seven are honored by the Church as saints, and twenty-seven, in imitation of St. Peter, sealed their faith and work with their blood.

"And the light shone in the darkness." Pope after Pope sent forth to the nations bishops and holy missionaries, enamored with Jesus Christ and devoted to his religion. They preached Christ crucified, and year after year gained new tribes, now nations, for Christ. Thus, St. Austin preached Christ crucified in England, St. Patrick in Ireland, St. Boniface in Germany. The Frieslanders, the Moravians, the Prussians, the Swedes, the Picts, the Scots, the Franks, and hundreds of others, were brought to the bosom of the Church because Christ crucified was preached to them by holy men, filled with love for Jesus Christ and enkindled with ardent zeal for the salvation of souls. One of the greatest blessings, therefore, God can bestow upon a nation is to give them zealous pastors, who constantly preach to them Christ crucified, and teach them how to pray and what to pray for. The more deeply the life and doctrine of Christ are impressed upon the minds and hearts of the people, the more lively is their faith, the purer are their morals. But take away from the minds of the people the remembrance of our Lord's life, sufferings, death, and resurrection, let them forget his saving doctrine, and see how well he then may say: "Of what utility is my blood?" Whenever this remembrance vanishes, faith is dead, hope becomes languid, charity grows cold, and into silence lapses that great cry of his blood for mercy. It is to forgetfulness and ignorance of the life and doctrine of Christ that we must attribute, in great measure, the many heresies that arose and carried off so many sheep from the flock of Jesus Christ after Christianity had been established all over the world.

Our dear Savior, however, incessantly watches over the welfare of his Church. He tells us in the Gospel that he is the Good Shepherd. Jesus is indeed a good Shepherd. He knows his sheep in general and in particular. He instructs them by his word, he strengthens them by his grace, animates them by his spirit, and enriches them with his merits. He does not, like other shepherds, nourish himself with their flesh, or clothe himself with their fleece; on the contrary, he gives them his flesh to eat and his blood to drink. He watches over his sheep with a special providence; he never abandons them; he defends and protects them against the foe who would devour them. When he prowls about the sheepfold and would enter, Jesus comes to their assistance to drive him off and save them. Hence, in every century, he has provided chosen vessels – Saints – to defend and edify his Church and to supply her wants. Just as a good general, when the battle is begun, observes from a rising ground the state of the combat, in order to send reinforcements wherever they are needed; so, also, Jesus Christ, who is the general of the Christian army, beholds from the heavens above the state of his Church in the different combats which she has to sustain, and, in proportion to her necessities, he sends, from time to time, new reinforcements of holy men to aid her and fight her battles. Such holy men are invariably endowed by God with those graces and gifts which are necessary for the healing of the world and the victory of the Church.

God raised up St. Athanasius and St. Hilary of Poitiers to confound the Arians. He sent St. Cyril to oppose the Nestorians; St. Augustine to beat down the Pelagians; St. John Damascene to fight the Iconoclasts. In the decline of the Roman Empire, and to counteract the vices of the decadence, God sent St. Benedict and his legion of toiling monks. When the world became Christian, and Catholics grew rich and forgot the poverty of our Lord Jesus Christ, St. Francis was called by God to teach the love of Christian poverty to voluptuous Catholics. Heresy and ignorance then followed; and finally, as the last consequences of heresies, infidelity and impiety boldly raised their heads, and permeated society from the nobility to the lower classes.

In the twelfth and thirteenth centuries the Albigenses, a set of heretics in the south of France, denied the most vital articles of the Roman Catholic faith. Not content with filling their own country with terror and desolation, they overran several other provinces in troops of four, five, or eight thousand men, pillaged the countries and massacred the priests, flaying some alive and scourging others to death. They plundered the churches, broke and profaned the sacred vessels, and sacrilegiously converted the ornaments of the altars into women's clothes. To stem the torrent of these evils, God was pleased to send St. Dominic, as the instrument of his grace, to strike the rocks, and to soften the hardened hearts of many which even the thunder of St. Bernard's voice had not been able to move.

St. Dominic labored for ten years with untiring zeal to convert the Albigenses. He preached to them, he prayed for them, he shed tears for them, he did penance for them, but all seemed to be of little avail. Finally, as he prayed one day with unusual fervor, and besought the Blessed Mother of God, the refuge of sinners, to intercede with her divine Son for this benighted people, our Lady herself appeared to the saint and consoled him. It was in the forest of Bouconne that St. Dominic, wrapped in ecstasy, saw the Immaculate Mother of God coming towards him in dazzling brightness. Holding a Rosary in her hands, she addressed him in these words: "Be of good courage, Dominic. The fruits of your labors will be abundant. You know how much the salvation of this people has cost my Son. He does not wish that the work of salvation should become useless. Remember, then, that the redemption of the world was begun by the salutation of the angel, that it was completed by the bitter passion and death of my divine Son, and that it was established and secured by his glorious resurrection. The remedy, therefore, of so many evils shall be meditation on the mysteries of the life, death, and glory of my Son, uniting thereto the Angelic Salutation, by which the great mystery of redemption was announced to the world." She then explained to St. Dominic how this devotion was to be practiced and continued by means of the Rosary. "The earth," she added, "shall remain barren till watered by the heavenly dew of this devotion. You are to preach this devotion as a practice of piety most dear to my Son and to me; as a most powerful means of dissipating heresy, extinguishing vice, spreading virtue, imploring the divine mercy and obtaining my protection. I desire that this manner of prayer shall be perpetually promoted and practiced. The faithful shall obtain by it numberless benefits, and shall always find me ready to aid them in all their wants. This is the precious gift which, through you, I bequeath to the world." ("Annals of Ord. Prud." Naples, 1629).

Encouraged by this heavenly vision, St. Dominic went straightway to the neighboring city of Toulouse, and repaired to the cathedral. No sooner had he entered than the bells of the city began to ring of their own accord. The people flocked together from all quarters, crying: "The good angels are ringing the bells; let us hasten to church; something extraordinary must have happened." In a short time the large church was crowded with heretics as well as Catholics. St. Dominic ascended the pulpit and spoke as one inspired. He spoke of the rigor of God's judgments, of God's overflowing mercy and goodness, and then he related what had befallen him and the commission he had received from the Blessed Mother of God herself.

He began thereupon to explain the devotion of the Rosary, and he called on all present to recite it with him. But scarcely had he begun to pray when the proud heretics, excited by the evil one, began to cry out: "What! are we then little children that he wishes to teach us our prayers?" and they immediately rushed out of the church. No sooner, however, had they left the church than there suddenly arose a terrific storm of rain and hail. The vivid flashes of lightning and the deafening peals of thunder struck such a terror into the hearts of the heretics that they fled back trembling to the church. They there fell on their knees, and joined in prayer with the saint. They prayed with a fervor which their cold hearts had never before felt and their prayers had the due effect, for thousands were converted on the spot.

This was the first victory of the Rosary. Within a short time St. Dominic saw his labors crowned with complete success. Historians tell us that he received more than one hundred thousand heretics into the Catholic Church, in which alone true life and salvation are found. The devotion of the Rosary, the wonderful gift of the Blessed Virgin, spread rapidly through France and Spain and over the rest of Europe. It took hold of the Church, destined never to leave her.

CHAPTER 3

WHAT THE ROSARY IS

The Rosary, or beads, as it is often called, is a devotion consisting of a certain number of Our Fathers and Hail Marys, during the recitation of which the principal mysteries of the life of our Lord and the Blessed Virgin are meditated upon. We find the first traces of the use of beads among the pious solitaries of Egypt, who lived in the very first ages of Christianity. Those among them who were unable to say the Breviary or Psalter, recited instead as many Our Fathers as there are psalms in the psalter. Those good monks made use of little pebbles or beads in order to count more easily the required number of prayers. In the course of time these beads were attached to a string, and thus originated the present form of the Rosary. But the manner of reciting fifteen decades or tens of the Angelical Salutation, with one Our Father before each decade, in honor of the principal mysteries of the life of our Lord and of the Blessed Virgin, is ascribed to St. Dominic, who instituted the recitation of one hundred and fifty Angelical Salutations in imitation of the one hundred and fifty psalms; and on this account the Rosary has often been called the Psalter of the Blessed Virgin.

The Rosary, then, is made up of one hundred and fifty Hail Marys, to correspond to the number of psalms in the Psalter. These one hundred and fifty Hail Marys are divided into three parts called Mysteries, because they are recited in honor of the three principal parts of the mysterious life of our Blessed Lord and his Holy Mother; and hence we call them the Joyful, the Sorrowful, and the Glorious Mysteries. These mysteries are subdivided into tens or decades, each of which begins with an Our Father and ends with a Glory be to the Father. At the beginning of the Rosary we usually make the sign of the Cross, and then say the Creed, in order to make a profession of our faith and to enliven our confidence in God. We also add to the creed an Our Father and three Hail Marys, for an increase of faith, hope and charity. It is hardly necessary to remark that the entire Rosary of fifteen decades is generally said by religious and by devout persons in the world; the common form of the Rosary on the beads has only five decades.

If we briefly examine the component parts of the Rosary, we shall see that it is not a human invention, not the work of some pious monk or hermit, but that it really came from heaven.

1. "The Sign of the Cross." Our Lord himself has been pleased to refer, on more than one occasion, to the cross, the instrument of his passion. For he says: "He that taketh not up his cross and followeth me is not worthy of me" (Mt. 10:38); and he observes to his disciples: "If any man will come after me, let him deny himself, and take up his cross and follow me" (Mt. 6:24); and the Evangelist, in his enumeration of those terrible prognostics which are to herald the coming of the day of final judgment, mentions the appearance of the cross amid the heavens, where the sun shall then be darkened and the moon shall not give her light, and whence the stars shall have fallen: "And then shall appear the sign of the Son of Man in heaven, and then shall all the tribes of the earth mourn, and they shall see the Son of Man coming in the clouds of heaven with much power and majesty" (Mt. 24:30). All the most learned and ancient fathers, as St. John Chrysostom, St. Jerome, St. Hilarius, Theophylactus, and the Venerable Bede, are unanimous in interpreting "the sign of the Son of Man" to signify the cross, and the ablest among our Biblical scholars have applauded such an interpretation.

This instrument of our redemption through the blood of Jesus was perpetually before the eyes of the eloquent St. Paul, who so often makes beautiful and appropriate allusions to it in almost every one of his Epistles, but more emphatically in the concluding part of his letter to the Galatians, where he exclaims: "God forbid that I should glory save in the cross of our Lord Jesus Christ."

This reverence for the cross was imparted by the Apostles to the new believers, who, from considering it with horror as the instrument of ignominy, after their initiation in the Christian faith regarded it as the most glorious of trophies and the emblem of their victorious

Easter. They oftentimes impressed their foreheads with this mystic sign, to manifest their own Christianity or to recognize that of an unknown brother in the faith. Tertullian, who flourished in the year 194, observes: "At every step and movement, whenever we come in or go out, when we dress ourselves, or prepare to go abroad, at the bath, at table, when lights are brought in, or lying or sitting down – whatever we be doing, we make the sign of the cross upon our foreheads." St. John Chrysostom, who was Archbishop of Constantinople about the year 397, thus addresses his auditors: "Everywhere is the symbol of the cross present to us. On this account we paint and sculpture it on our brows, and we studiously imprint it on our souls and minds." The sign of the cross, then, is a divine sign.

2.   Next comes "The Apostles' Creed." It also is the work of God. It comes, as its name indicates, from the Apostles, and was composed by them before their dispersion over the world. Now, every one that has any pretensions to faith knows and believes that the Apostles were inspired by God.

3.   The "Our Father." This prayer was taught us by our Blessed Savior himself, who is the second person of the adorable Trinity. One day his disciples came to him and said: "Lord, John the Baptist teaches his disciples how to pray, do thou also teach us" (Lk.11:1); and then our Savior said to them, "When you pray, pray in this manner: 'Our Father who art in heaven,'" etc., and so he taught them that most simple and most sublime prayer which is, on this account, called the Lord's Prayer.

4.   The next prayer which is so often repeated in the Rosary is the "Hail Mary." This little prayer is certainly one of the shortest, sweetest, yet most powerful that human lips can utter.

But whence have we the Hail Mary? Who is its author? The Hail Mary is nothing less than the work of the three Divine persons of the ever blessed Trinity. It was the archangel Gabriel who brought to earth the first words of this prayer; and he came not in his own name, but as the ambassador of the Blessed Trinity, and as a faithful ambassador spoke those words which the Blessed Trinity had dictated to him. The angel entered the modest room of the Blessed Virgin Mary as she knelt in prayer in her humble cottage at Nazareth, and saluted her reverently, saying, "Hail Mary, full of grace, the Lord is with thee." He saluted the Blessed Virgin thus in the name of God the Father, who wished to confide to her his Divine Son; in the name of God the Son, who wished to choose her for his Mother; in the name of the Holy Ghost, who wished to work in her chaste womb the unutterable mystery of the Incarnation.

The first part, then, of the "Hail Mary" has God himself for its author. The second is also the work of God, for it was inspired by the Holy Ghost. As the Blessed Virgin, some time after the conception of her Divine Son, went to visit her cousin, St. Elizabeth, at the very sound of her heavenly voice the Saint was, according to Holy Writ, immediately filled with the Holy Ghost, and, inspired by his Divine Presence, she cried aloud, "O blessed art thou amongst women, and blessed is the fruit of thy womb!"

Finally, the last part of the Hail Mary was also composed by the Holy Ghost. In the year 431 the great Council of Ephesus, which represented the entire Catholic Church, condemned the infamous Nestorius, who dared attack at the same time the divinity of our Blessed Savior Jesus Christ and the divine maternity of his immaculate Mother. After the Council had condemned the heresiarch, they expressed their heartfelt, their unwavering devotion to the Blessed Mother of God by the short and fervent prayer, "Holy Mary, Mother of God, pray for us sinners, now and at the hour of our death." It was the Church then that composed the last part of the Hail Mary; and the Church, as all Catholics know, is inspired and directed by the Holy Ghost. We can justly say that as the Holy Ghost spoke by the mouth of the prophets and Apostles, so also does he speak by the mouth of the holy Church; and, consequently, God is also the author of the last part of the Hail Mary.

5.   It is hardly necessary to add that the "Glory be to the Father" with which each decade concludes was composed by the Church in the very first ages of Christianity, and, consequently, that it is also an inspired prayer.

Besides the Our Father and Hail Mary the Rosary contains also fifteen subjects of meditation. These meditations are called mysteries. They are taken from the life of our Lord and of his Blessed Mother, and are divided into three distinct parts, called the Joyful, the Sorrowful, and the Glorious Mysteries. The five Joyful Mysteries represent the Birth and Infancy of our Blessed Redeemer; the Sorrowful represent our Lord's Passion and Death; the Glorious represent the Risen Life of our Lord and his triumphant Ascension into heaven.

The string of beads is simply intended to assist the memory. The touch of beads quietly reminds us that it is time to pass from one prayer or from one point of meditation to another. Thus the Rosary may, in truth, be called the Gospel abridged, and a most holy and divine prayer. It has proved to be the great propagator of Christianity, the sweet nurse and sure preserver of faith, hope, and charity, the indomitable expeller of unbelief, the quick extinguisher of heresies, the infallible remedy for sadness and despair, the universal appeaser of the anger of God, the fruitful mother of tears, the entertaining companion on journeys, the irresistible destroyer of vice, the easy bridge over the high waters of temptation, the impregnable bulwark against all assaults of afflictions, the glorious standard and trophy in war, the substantial food of souls, the fertile source of all virtues, the wide and deep channel of all blessings spiritual and temporal, the powerful lever of the spiritual life, the patent medicine of the sick, the bright light of the understanding, the best riches of the poor, the inexhaustible treasure of all Christians, the never failing support of widows, the reliable protection of the just, the unsupportable torment of the devil, a most acceptable homage to God and the ever blessed Mother of God, the safe seal of virginity, the strong safeguard of nuptial fidelity, the safe harbor in the storms of this life, the city of refuge for sinners, the faithful friend and physician of the dying, the wonder working rod of Moses, a pillar of cloud by day and a pillar of fire by night, showing the way to heaven, the Piscina Probatita – that is, the pond of healing water wherein whosoever descends is healed of whatsoever spiritual infirmity he may lie under – the sweet milk of little children, the beautiful crosier of bishops, the unconquerable strength, courage, and persuasive power of priests, the golden key to heaven, the mother of good counsel, the celebrated school of eloquence, the unshaken constancy of the martyrs, a pious, gentle tyranny towards God, the impenetrable armor of all the faithful, who, when shielded by this heavenly armor, courageously fight and gloriously overcome all their enemies – the impious maxims of the world, the deceitful allurements of the flesh, and the subtle suggestions and snares of the devil – and thus obtain in the world to come that heavenly glory and endless happiness which the Lord has prepared for his faithful servants.

CHAPTER 4

THE ROSARY: THE MEMORIAL OF
THE DIVINE BENEFITS

Men are accustomed to erect monuments to commemorate extraordinary events, achievements, victories, and the like. The works of God, however, infinitely surpass those of men in greatness, power, and wisdom. What, then, more natural than to read in the Holy Scripture that God instituted the Sabbath day and solemn feasts to recall to the Jews the remembrance of his benefits; that for this same purpose he also had placed in the ark of the covenant the Tables of the Law and a vase of manna; that he left imprinted on the shore traces of the chariots of the Egyptians whom he had drowned in the Red Sea; that he commanded Joshua to take twelve stones from the bed of the Jordan, over which he and his army had passed, in order that these things might be, as it were, monuments of what he had done for them. But what are all the wondrous works which God performed in favor of the Jews in comparison with the stupendous prodigies which the Son of God performed on earth for thirty-three years and a half? What more natural than that he should have left to his followers a perpetual memorial of all his prodigies?

Boleslaus, King of Poland, used to wear around his neck a golden medal with the features of his father stamped upon it. When about to undertake an important work, he would take the medal in his hand, gaze at it with tearful eyes, and say: "O dearly beloved father, may I never do anything unworthy of thy royal name!" Thus, by means of a medal, did this king try to remember the blessings and example of his father. But our Lord Jesus Christ did not wish to be borne in memory by a medal or anything of such a nature. He wished to stay with us himself in person, in order that his own Presence might constantly recall to our mind all that he had done for us. He instituted the holy sacrifice of the Mass, not only to apply to our souls more effectually the all-sufficient merits of the sacrifice

29

of the Cross, but to be a perpetual memorial of all that he has done and suffered for us, and a sure pledge of his undying love for our souls.

It is now over eighteen hundred years since our Blessed Savior died for us upon the cross. Our Lord knew well that men are apt to forget favors, especially those which are long past. What a contrast between "Hosanna to the Son of David: blessed is he that cometh in the name of the Lord! Hosanna in the highest" and "Away with this man. Crucify him!" What a contrast between spreading their garments in the way before him and stripping him of his garments, casting lots for them, and putting on him the scarlet cloak of mockery! What a contrast between cutting branches of palm trees and strewing them where he passed, and plaiting a crown of thorns and putting it upon his head and a reed in his right and, bending the knee before him in mockery, and saying, "Hail, King of the Jews!" What a contrast between "King of Israel" and "We have no king but Cæsar!"

Our dear Savior knew this fickleness and instability of the human mind and heart, so he instituted the holy sacrifice of the Mass, wherein the sacrifice of the cross is daily renewed, in order thus to remind us continually of his sufferings and death. "Do this," said he to the Apostles, "in remembrance of me." Just as if he had said: "I am about to accomplish the work of your redemption; I then will return to my Father, who is in heaven. Now, I wish you never to forget me and all that I have done for you. To make sure of this, I have instituted the sacrifice of the Mass as the only sacrifice of the New Testament, as the sacrifice in which are contained all the mysteries of my life and passion and death." St. Thomas of Aquin says: "In this sacrifice we leave an abridgment of all his wonders, and a standing monument of all his prodigies."

But many Catholics do not understand what the Mass is to them, because they were never properly instructed on this all important mystery of our holy religion. Others neglect hearing Mass, or have no opportunity of hearing it. It may also be said, without exaggeration, that the greater part of Catholics neglect reading edifying books. Thus they become forgetful of God, ungrateful for his benefits, and neglectful of their most important duties. The duty of gratefully remembering

God's benefits seems to be forgotten by most men, even by the good and pious. It would not be easy to exaggerate the common neglect of this duty. There is little enough of prayer; but there is still less of thanksgiving. For every million of *Paters and Aves* which rise up from the earth to avert evils or to ask graces, how many follow after in thanksgiving for the evils averted or the graces given?

Men are grateful to their fellow-men, grateful even to animals. But to be thankful towards God, their greatest benefactor, seems unaccountably to have fallen out of most men's practical religion altogether. If we have reason to pity God, if we may dare so to speak with St. Alphonsus, because men sin against his loving majesty, still more reason have we to do so when we see how scanty and how cold are the thanksgivings offered up to him.

"This sin of ingratitude," says St. Bernard "is an enemy of the soul that entertains it in every way, depriving it of the good it has acquired, and preventing the acquisition of more; it is a scorching wind that dries up the sources of piety, the streams of mercy, and the torrents of grace. I have an extreme hatred of ingratitude, because it is a murderer which directly attacks the soul's salvation, and in my opinion there is nothing in religious, and in persons who practice piety, so displeasing to God as ingratitude for his benefits. Why is it that often God does not grant what we ask of him with the greatest earnestness? Is his power weakened? Are his riches exhausted? Has his affection for us waned? Alas, no! The true cause is that we do not thank God for his benefits. There are few who thank him as they ought for his favors."

Indeed, there is nothing more odious, even among men, than ingratitude. "The ungrateful man," says St. Irenæus, "is a vessel of ignominy into which God pours the gall of his anger." Need we wonder if we see so many fall away from the faith and lead immoral lives, since forgetfulness of God, ingratitude towards him, and ignorance of the truths of our religion, have at all times been the fruitful source of all moral evils?

To stop these evils in their source, to apply a remedy to them, God, through his Blessed Mother, gave to the children of his Church the Devotion of the Rosary, as a memorial of his great benefits and as a prayer of thanksgiving for the same. The fifteen mysteries of the Rosary are a short commemoration of the life, sufferings, and triumphant victory of Jesus Christ; and the Creed, recited at the beginning of the Rosary, is a short catechism containing the principal truths which he taught us; and the prayer, "Glory be to the Father," etc., is one of the best acts of thanksgiving that can be offered to the Blessed Trinity for the divine benefits. Thus the Rosary teaches us every day to think of Jesus and Mary, and be grateful to them; and to think of them and be grateful to them is to love them; and to love God and show gratitude towards him is the end of all religion, the very essence of Christianity.

The spirit of thanksgiving has been in all ages the characteristic of the saints. Thanksgiving has always been their favorite prayer. They learned this spirit from Our Lord Jesus Christ, who always thanked his Father in the beginning of his prayers and when about to work any miracle.

From the Epistles of St. Paul we learn that this great Apostle constantly exhorted the Christians "always to give thanks for all things, in the name of our Lord Jesus Christ, to God and the Father."

When the Archangel Raphael was about to make himself known to Tobias and his family, he said to them: "It is time that I return to him that sent me; but bless God, and publish all his wonderful works." Probably, as he parted from them, he showed them a glimpse of his angelic beauty, as they went immediately into an ecstasy of three hours, which filled them with a spirit of thanksgiving. "Then they, lying prostrate for three hours upon their face, blessed God, and rising up they told all his wonderful works."

The ancient Christians saluted each other with these words: "Thanks be to God." Those very words were always in the mouth and heart of the Blessed Virgin Mary. And in heaven, as St. John assures us, the blessed prostrate themselves before the throne of God to thank him continually for all his benefits. St. Cyprian, on hearing the sentence of his death, said: "Thanks be to God"; and gave twenty-five gold crowns to the man who was to cut off his head. St. Lawrence thanked God on his gridiron. St. Boniface, in the midst of horrible torments, exclaimed: "Jesus Christ, Son of God, I thank thee." St. Dulas, while he was being cruelly scourged, repeated: "I thank thee, my Lord Jesus, for having deemed me worthy to suffer this for love of thee." There is nothing more holy than a tongue which thanks God in adversity. To say but once "Thanks be to God" in adversity or illness, is better than to say it several thousand times in prosperity. Father Didacus Martinez the Jesuit who was called the Apostle of Peru because of his zeal for souls and his indefatigable labors in that province, used to say daily four hundred times, and often six hundred times, *"Deo gratias"* – "Thanks be to God," telling the ejaculations off on beads on purpose to be accurate. He tried to induce others to practice the same devotion, and declared that he knew there was no short prayer more acceptable to God, if only it be uttered with a devout intention.

These illustrious examples teach us how grateful we ought to be for the benefits of Almighty God. Now, to accomplish well our duty of gratitude towards Jesus Christ and his ever blessed Mother, next to offering the holy sacrifice of Mass, we can do nothing better than recite the Rosary. In this devotion we not only gratefully remember the benefits of creation, of redemption and sanctification, but we also offer up repeatedly acts of thanksgiving for the same; for to say, "Glory be to the Father, and to the Son, and to the Holy Ghost" is as much as to say, Glory be to the Father for having created me, to the Son for having redeemed me, and to the Holy Ghost for having sanctified me.

Surely, this is a very sweet and consoling reflection, which cannot fail to warm our hearts with love for the Rosary and inspire us with profound veneration for it. "Perform this devotion in commemoration of my Son and me," says the Blessed Virgin to every one of us. "My Son having lived and died out of love for you, I ask but one thing: that you should fondly cherish the memory of this ineffable benefit, particularly by saying the Rosary with devotion."

How pleasing this grateful remembrance of the divine benefits is to our Lord we learn from what he one day said to Blessed Angela of Foligno. This holy virgin heard from our Lord that the blessings which he would multiply upon those who were devoted to his Passion, and upon those who imitate it, and upon those who compassionate it, were as follows:

"Blessed are you of my Father who compassionate me, and who are sorrowing with me, and who, walking my road, have merited to wash your stoles in my blood. Blessed are you who compassionate me crucified for you, and afflicted with immense griefs, that I might satisfy for you, and redeem you from immense and eternal pains; for, compassionating me in my poverty, sorrow, and contempt borne for yourselves, you have been found worthy. Blessed are you who shall be mindfully and devoutly compassionate toward my Passion, which is the miracle of all ages, the salvation and life of the lost, and the sole refuge of sinners; for you shall be truly partakers with me of the kingdom and glory and resurrection which I have acquired by it, and co-heirs with me for ever and ever. Blessed are you of my Father and of the Holy Ghost, and truly blessed with the benediction which I shall give in the last judgment, because, when I came unto my own, you have not repulsed me, as my persecutors did; but, by your compassion, have received me, a desolate stranger, into the home and hospitality of your heart. You have compassionated me, stretched naked on the cross, hungering, thirsting, weak, nailed, and dying. You have willed to be my companions, and in this you have truly fulfilled the works of mercy. Therefore shall you hear in that terrible hour, 'Come, you blessed of my Father, receive the kingdom which was prepared for you before the foundation of the world.' For I was hungry on the cross, and, at least by compassion, you gave me to eat. Oh! happy you, truly happy, and blessed altogether; for if upon the cross I prayed to my Father with tears and weeping for my crucifiers and torturers, and excused them saying, 'Father, forgive them, for they know not what they do,' what shall I say for you who have compassionated me, and been devout partners, when, not upon the cross, but all blissful in my glory, I shall judge the world?"

CHAPTER 5

THE ROSARY:
THE DEVOTION OF THE CLERGY

We live in a most anti-Christian age. Infidel and immoral principles prevail everywhere. Iniquity is held in veneration: we see nothing but confusion in religion, in government, in the family circle. Sects spring up and swarm like locusts, destroying not only revealed religion, but rejecting even the law of nature. Fraud, theft, and robbery are practiced almost as a common trade. The press justifies rebellion, secret societies, and plots for the overthrow of established governments. The civil law, by granting divorce, has broken the family tie. Children are allowed to grow up in ignorance of true religious principles. Their fathers being without religion, or given up to the most detestable vices, or their mothers destitute of virtue, and infected in the highest degree with the spirit of vanity, the natural consequence is that these children are regardless of their parents. The number of apostates is on the increase, at least in the younger generation; immoral books and tracts circulate freely; daily journals, weekly magazines, the great organs of public opinion, become more unchristian every day – so much so that no one who has at heart the morality of his fellowmen, especially of youth, can with propriety recommend them for perusal; and yet how eagerly are they sought for and devoured by every class of men!

Many are of opinion that, to counteract and heal such diseases of the mind and heart, great learning is required. Learning can do much good, it is true; but, however much it may accomplish, experience teaches us, in the present as in the past, that moral evils never yield to any other force than the grace of God. A learned man may enlighten the minds of his fellow-men, and expel their darkness and errors, but unless the grace of God touch their hearts they will not embrace the truth. This truth was felt most keenly by St. Bernard whilst at Paris, 1123. He had scarcely arrived in the capital when he was pressed to deliver a discourse at the Academy of Philosophy and Theology. He yielded to this invitation, and, having to speak before a numerous assembly, he prepared himself with care, and pronounced a learned dissertation on the most sublime questions of philosophy; but when he had finished his discourse the audience remained cold and unmoved.

Alas! there are but too many who imitate St. Bernard in this point. Like him, they too know how to prepare very learned discourses; they use the most eloquent language. They may indeed enlighten the mind, but they do not reach the heart. The only fruits their sermons produce are a few unmeaning flatteries, which serve only to nourish their pride and self-love. "What a magnificent sermon!" the people will say; "what an eloquent speaker! what profound knowledge! what a clear mind! what a fascinating preacher! what a pleasure it is to listen to such a man! I never had such a treat in my life!" Would to God these preachers would imitate St. Bernard in his preparation for his second discourse! How different would be the fruit of their labors! When this saint had finished his first discourse, and saw that his audience remained cold and unmoved, he withdrew in sadness and confusion; he shut himself up in an oratory, where he sighed and wept abundantly before God. On the morrow, St. Bernard presented himself again in the same school: "but this time," says the author of the "Exordium" of Citeaux "the Holy Ghost spoke by his mouth, and guided his lips; and the admirable discourse which he pronounced made such an impression that many ecclesiastics, being deeply moved by it, placed themselves under his direction and followed him to Clairvaux, there to serve God under his guidance." It is related in the life of this saint that mothers used to keep their children, wives their husbands, and friends their friends, from listening to him, because the Holy Ghost gave so great a power to his words that no one could resist him; every one felt inspired to follow him, or at least to lead a better life.

After John Tauler had shone in the pulpit for many years, and won applause in Cologne and all Germany, he suddenly retreated to his cell, leaving the people astonished at his disappearance. The fact was, an unknown man accosted him after one of his discourses, and asked permission to speak his mind regarding him. Tauler having given this permission, the unknown replied: "There lives in your heart a secret pride; you rely on your great learning, and your title of doctor. In the study of letters, you do not seek God or his glory with a pure intention – you seek only yourself in the passing applause of creatures. Therefore the wine of heavenly doctrine and of Divine Word, though pure and excellent in themselves, lose their strength when passing through your heart, and drop without savor or grace into the breast that loves God" (Tauler's Life, by Darius, B.D.)

Tauler listened to these words, and was silent. The vanity of his present life was apparent to him. He withdrew from all commerce with the world, and abstained for two years from preaching or hearing confessions, night and day an assiduous attendant at every conventual exercise, and passing the remainder of his time in his cell, where he deplored his sins and studied and meditated upon the life, sufferings, and death of Jesus Christ. After two years of recollection and prayer he began again to preach. But now he preached Jesus crucified. He was filled with love for his divine Savior. Every word he spoke was a dart of love of God, and did more good than one of his former eloquent discourses.

What an important lesson! – a lesson which the Blessed Virgin wished to teach St. Dominic, and through him to all priests, when she revealed the Devotion of the Rosary. "Remember," said she to this saint, "remember that the redemption of the world was begun by the salutation of the angel, that it was completed by the bitter passion and death of my divine Son, and that it was established and secured by his glorious resurrection. The remedy, therefore, of so many evils shall be meditation on the mysteries of the life, death, and glory of my Son, uniting thereto the angelic salutation, by which the great mystery of redemption was announced to the world." Indeed, the frequent remembrance of Christ incarnate for us, born for us, dead for our salvation, risen for our justification, ascended to heaven as our eternal hope, cannot but produce most admirable effects, piercing into the inmost mind, heart, and will of man far below the deepest roots of evil, so that sin in its germ should be plucked from the will, and the sincere soul be unable to refuse consecrating her whole life to God. When we remember how our dear Savior manifested, in every step and action of his life, his love, his benevolence, his devotedness to us, we cannot help rejoicing greatly in the excess of his condescending compassion, and express in hymns of praise and thanksgiving our pious emotions, as far as the divinely enraptured soul of man can express them. He, therefore, who can explain, with love and affection, the mysteries of the life of our Lord and the Blessed Virgin, possesses the key to the grace of the conversion of the people. Should any one try another to open the treasure of graces acquired by the life and death of Jesus Christ, he will not be able to unlock it.

The Blessed Alain de la Roche relates that a bishop in Spain, notwithstanding all his endeavors, being unable to succeed in reforming his people, resolved, after the example of St. Dominic, to preach the holy Rosary, taking care to explain the mysteries and to teach them how to meditate. The faithful embraced this devotion with ardor, and, in a short time, numberless conversions were wrought; ignorance, impiety, immorality, and other vices were replaced by prayer, penance, the frequenting of the holy sacraments, and the practice of all Christian virtues. This zealous prelate could not sufficiently praise God for the change which had taken place in his cathedral town; he commanded the clergy of his diocese to employ the same means, which were followed with the same success; so that in a short time the whole face of his diocese was entirely changed.

The same Blessed Alain has also preserved for us the testimony of a virtuous priest, of which the following are the words: "I have exercised the office of pastor during several years; I have preached on all sorts of subjects as well as I was able; I have neglected nothing which could instruct, touch, and convert the souls entrusted to me; but seeing that I worked in vain, and reaped no fruit from my labor, I resolved to sacrifice the studied discourses which I had been accustomed to make, and try if I should succeed better by simply preaching the devotion of the holy Rosary, explaining the prayers which compose it and the mysteries on which it is grounded. I had neglected this excellent custom, notwithstanding the reproaches of my conscience, through human respect, fearing lest the world should ridicule me, and consider the subject unworthy of the pulpit. But I declare that, in less than a year, more conversions were made in my parish than during the thirty preceding years, when I had only delivered studied discourses."

A celebrated Spanish Dominican, Father Gonsalvo Lucero, went to carry the light of the Gospel to the West Indies. He was indefatigable in his zeal for the salvation of souls, and employed his whole life and strength to effect their conversion. He entered upon his mission with great courage, and no labor, sorrow, or danger could in the least deter him from duty, and a thousand times was he exposed to death. He penetrated even into the depths of the forest in search of the Indians, crossed mountains, inured himself to every hardship, adopted their mode of life, called himself their brother – all this and still more did he do, in order to enlighten their darkened minds. But the vices of the Europeans retarded the conversion of these poor savages, and the hatred they bore the Spaniards withheld them from embracing their religion. Seeing the little success of his labors, Father Lucero resolved to have recourse to the Rosary, with the hope that through its means he might obtain their speedy conversion. He had a picture painted of Our Lady of the Rosary, surrounded by the Fifteen Mysteries. He exposed it to view in the hut which served him as a chapel, and convoked the Indians to a great ceremony. When they had assembled around him he uncovered the painting, recited before it the Rosary, and sang a canticle composed for the occasion. Then rising, he explained in clear and distinct terms the meaning of the picture and the Fifteen Mysteries of the Holy Rosary. Nothing more was required to touch these simple souls. They then asked to be instructed in the doctrines of Christianity, and soon they brought their idols to the missionary that he might burn them, and earnestly solicited baptism at his hands. The Rosary had been to these poor darkened savages an eloquent and irresistible discourse ("Month of the Rosary").

Casimir II, King of Poland, was, then, right when he wrote to the Father-General of the Dominican Fathers in Rome: "I beg you to send me such fathers as can preach well the Devotion of the Rosary for they are the best reformers of the manners of the people."

Wherever the Devotion of the Rosary was introduced by St. Dominic a true amendment of life could be noticed in the people;

so much so, that if one was seen to live on in sin the people pointed at him with their fingers, saying: "Behold, one who does not say the Rosary!" Even many of the heretics were converted partly by the explanation of the mysteries of our religion as contained in the Rosary, partly by the recital of the prayers of which the Rosary is composed. Almighty God also showed repeatedly by miracles what pleasure he takes in this devotion. The heretics and Catholics put together in writing the strongest arguments in defense of their cause; those of the Catholics were the work of St. Dominic. It was proposed that both writings should be committed to the flames, in order that God might declare by his own interposition which cause he favored. Accordingly a great fire was made, and the two writings were cast into it; that of the heretics was immediately consumed to ashes, whilst the other remained unhurt after it had been cast into the fire three times and taken out again.

This public miracle happened at Fanjaux; the fruit of it was the conversion of great numbers of heretics of both sexes. The same kind of miracle happened at Montreal. St. Dominic drew up in writing a short exposition of the Catholic faith, with proof of each article from the New Testament. This writing he gave to the heretics to examine. Their ministers and chiefs, after much altercation about it, agreed to throw it into the fire, saying that if it burned they would regard the doctrine which it contained as false. Being cast thrice into the flames, it was not damaged by them.

No doubt the salvation of the people depends on devotion to Mary and confidence in her intercession. St. Bernardine of Sienna sanctified Italy by preaching this devotion. St. Louis Bertrand, in all his sermons, never failed to exhort his hearers to practice devotion towards Mary. Father Paul Segneri the younger, a celebrated missionary, in every mission preached a sermon on devotion to Mary, and this he called his favorite sermon "We can attest, in all truth," says St. Alphonsus, "that in our missions, where we have an invariable rule not to omit the sermon on Our Lady, no discourse is so profitable to the people, or excites more compunction in them, than that on the power and mercy of Mary." In the year 1835, the communions in a certain parish in the city of Paris, containing a population of

27,000, did not exceed 700 in the whole year. The good parish priest set to work to remedy this deplorable state of things; he formally placed the charge committed to him under the protection of Mary, and instituted her Confraternity among the people. In the year 1837, the communions amounted to 9,500, and every succeeding year they became more numerous.

To try to make the people good without inspiring them with love for the Blessed Virgin is to labor in vain. The better the people are made to understand what God has given us in Mary, the sooner they will do away with their evil habits and practice virtue. That priest, then, who understands best to promote love to Mary among the people by introducing the devotion of the Rosary, will meet with most success in his apostolic labors.

"The earth" that is, souls – said the Blessed Virgin to St. Dominic, "shall remain barren till watered by the dew of this devotion. You are to preach this devotion as a practice of piety most dear to my Son and to me – as a most powerful means of dissipating heresy, extinguishing vice, spreading virtue, imploring the divine mercy, and obtaining my protection. I desire that this manner of prayer shall be perpetually promoted and practiced. The faithful shall obtain by it numberless benefits, and shall always find me ready to aid them in their wants." This promise of the Blessed Virgin has always come true; for experience shows that no sooner do the people commence to practice this devotion than they open their hearts to the largest channel of grace, so as to be flooded with heavenly gifts.

CHAPTER 6

THE ROSARY: THE DEVOTION OF THE FAITHFUL – IT INCREASES AND PRESERVES THEIR FAITH

In our day and country it has become fashionable for a large number of men to have no religion, and even to boast of having none. To have no religion is a great crime, but to boast of having none is the height of folly. The man without religion is a kind of monster with the intelligence of a man and the cruelty and instincts of a beast. His religion is to disregard good principles; to do away, not only with all revealed religion, but even with the law of nature; to hold iniquity in veneration; to practice fraud, theft, and robbery almost as a common trade; to be regardless of parents and of all divinely constituted authority; to create confusion, not only in religion, but also in government and in the family circle; to contribute towards the increase of the number of apostates, and make of these apostates members of such secret societies as aim at the overthrow of governments, of all order, and of the Christian religion itself.

Now, the defect of faith in sinners does not arise from the obscurity of faith. The mysteries of faith, it is true, are to us obscure, and God wishes them to be obscure to us: first, because he wishes us to honor him by our faith in all the truths which he has revealed to his Church; and, secondly, because he wishes us to merit an eternal reward by believing what we do not see and comprehend. What merit to a man for believing what he sees and comprehends?

Still, even though what faith teaches be obscure and incomprehensible, the truth of faith itself is evident. That our faith is true is rendered clear by so many evident proofs, so that he who does not embrace it must be regarded as a fool. The first proof of the truth of faith is found in the prophecies contained in the Holy Bible, which were written so many ages before the events, and afterwards punctually fulfilled. Long before it happened, the death of our Redeemer was foretold by several prophets – by David, by Daniel, by Aggaeus, and by Malachias. The circumstances of his death were also foretold. It was foretold that, in punishment of the slaying of Jesus Christ, the Jews should lose their temple and their country; that they would remain blinded in their sin, and be scattered over the earth. We know that all this has been fulfilled.

The conversion of the world, after the death of the Messiah, was also foretold. This conversion was brought about by the holy Apostles, who, unaided by learning, worldly rank, riches, or the protection of the great, and even in spite of the opposition of the monarchs of the earth, converted the world, inducing men to forsake their gods and their inveterate, vicious habits, in order to embrace a faith which taught them to believe so many mysteries which they could not comprehend, and imposed on them so many precepts hard to be reduced to practice because of their repugnance to our bad passions. Such precepts were to love enemies, to abstain from pleasure, to bear insults, and to place all our affections, not on the goods which we see, but on the goods of a future life, which we do not see.

We have evident proofs of the truth of our faith in so many miracles wrought by Jesus Christ, through the apostles and other saints, in the presence of their very enemies, who, when they could not deny them, said that these prodigies were performed by diabolical agency. But true miracles which surpass the power of nature, such as the raising of the dead to life, giving sight to the blind and the like, cannot be wrought by the devils. God cannot permit a miracle except in confirmation of the true faith; were he to permit a miracle in confirmation of an error, he himself would deceive us, to say which would be blasphemy. True miracles, therefore, which are wrought in the Catholic Church, are infallible proofs of the truth of our faith.

The constancy of the martyrs is also a very strong argument in favor of our faith. In the first ages of the Church, in the reign of the tyrants, there were many millions, and among them many tender virgins and children, who, rather than deny the faith of Jesus Christ, embraced with joy torments and death itself. Sulpicius Severus writes

(Lib. 11 ch.47) that, in the time of Diocletian, the martyrs presented themselves to their judges with a greater desire of martyrdom than that with which men of the world embrace the dignities and riches of this earth. The martyrdom of St. Maurice and the whole Theban legion is famous in history. The Emperor Maximinian commanded all his soldiers to assist at an impious sacrifice which he one day offered to his false gods. St. Maurice and his soldiers, who were Christians, refused to obey. Having heard of their refusal, Maximinian, in punishment of their disobedience, ordered them to be decimated, or the head of every tenth man in the legion to be struck off. Each of them desired to die, and the soldiers who were left alive envied the happiness of those who were put to death for Jesus Christ. As soon as this was made known to Maximinian he ordered them to be decimated a second time, but this second decimation still increased their desire of martyrdom. Finally, the emperor ordered them all to be beheaded. With joy they laid down their arms, and, like so many meek lambs, gladly and without resistance submitted to death.

Prudentius relates (Lib. Peristeph.) that a child of seven years was tempted by Asclepiades to deny the faith of Christ; but when the boy refused to do so, and said that he had been taught by his mother, the tyrant sent for her, and in her presence caused the child to be scourged till his entire body was but one wound. All the bystanders shed tears of pity, but the mother exulted with joy at the sight of the courage of her son. The child, being thirsty, asked for some water.

"Son," said the mother, "have a little more patience; in a few moments you will be filled in heaven with eternal delight."

Enraged at the constancy of the mother and the son, the prefect commanded his head to be cut off without delay. After the execution of the order the mother took the dead child into her arms, and, full of joy at seeing him dead for Jesus Christ, she embraced him with maternal tenderness.

The learned John Picus, Prince of Mirandola, was, then, right to exclaim: "It is great folly not to believe the Gospel which the Apostles have proclaimed, which many saints and wise men have preached, which the blood of martyrs has cemented, which miracles have proved, which reason confirms, which the elements and insensible creatures have announced, which the demons themselves are constrained to acknowledge; yes, it is folly not to receive a doctrine glorious with so many victories, radiant with so many crowns, laden with the spoils of all its enemies."

It is not so much of the doctrines as of the morals of the Catholic Church that men are afraid. How often have I met men who told me that they would gladly become Catholics, but it is too hard to live up to the laws and maxims of the Church! They know very well that, if they become Catholics, they must lead honest and sober lives, they must be pure, they must respect the holy sacrament of marriage, they must check their sinful passions; and this they are unwilling to do. "Men love darkness rather than light," says Jesus Christ, "because their deeds are evil." Remember the well-known proverb: "There are none so deaf as those that will not hear."

They are kept back from embracing the faith because they know that the truths of our religion are at war with their sinful inclinations. It is not surprising that these inclinations should revolt against being immolated. The prudence of the flesh understands and feels that all is lost for it if the truths of faith are listened to and taken for the rule of conduct; that it must renounce the unlawful enjoyments of life, must die to the world and to itself, and bear the mortification of Jesus Christ in its body.

At the mere thought of this crucifixion of the flesh and its concupiscence, imposed on every one who would belong to the Savior, all is troubled in the imagination and in the senses. Self-love suggests a thousand reasons to delay at least the sacrifices that affright them. The prudence of the flesh being thus allowed, the ascendancy complicates the most simple truths, attracts and flatters the powers of the soul; and when afterwards faith endeavors to interpose its authority, it finds the understanding prejudiced, the will overcome or weakened, the heart all earthly-minded, and hard indeed is it for faith to reduce the soul to its dominion.

"Yes," says St. Alphonsus in his little book, *Love of Christ*, "the weakness or the utter want of faith is owing to a wicked life. He who despises God's friendship that he may not be deprived of forbidden pleasures would wish that there was no law to prohibit them, nor punishment to chastise them; he strives, therefore, to banish from his mind the thought of eternal truths, such as death, judgment, hell; these truths terrify him and embitter his pleasures. He endeavors to persuade himself that there is no soul, no God, no hell, that he may live and die like the brutes, which have no law nor reason."

"It was wicked lives that caused so many impious books and systems of materialists, indifferentists, deists, and naturalists to be published. O ingratitude and wickedness of men! God has created them in his mercy to make them eternally happy. He has given them an abundance of lights and graces, in order that they may obtain eternal life; has redeemed them through an infinite love by his painful sufferings; and those men force themselves to believe nothing, that, like a swine, they may wallow in the mire of sin. But, in spite of their wishes, these unhappy creatures can never deliver themselves from remorse or the fear of the divine vengeance. Would to God that they would renounce sin and love Jesus Christ! They would no longer have any doubts; they would firmly believe all the truths revealed by God to the Roman Catholic Church."

Our belief in a person's word is firm in proportion as we think that he is not deceived in his knowledge; that he knows well what he says, because he is wise and prudent; that he will not deceive us, because he loves the truth and fears God. Thus, in transacting business, we give more credit to a learned or able than to an ignorant man; to a learned man who is virtuous than to one who is not so.

Now, God is the first and essential Truth. His knowledge extends to all things and is infinitely perfect; he is essentially true in his words. He knows things only as they are, and can speak them only as he knows them. Therefore we must have the most respectful, submissive faith in all that he has revealed to us, and believe his mysteries with the utmost firmness and simplicity, with an unwavering conviction of their reality.

We must believe all the articles of faith more firmly than we believe the proposition, The whole is greater than a part; we should believe them more firmly than what we see with our eyes, hear with our ears, touch with our hands; we should be more certain of these articles of faith than we are of our own existence, because, though all these things are realities of which we cannot doubt, yet the things of faith are still more real, because they have been taught by God who cannot deceive us, while we know the others only through the senses, which often deceive us, and by the assurance of our mind, which, being enveloped in darkness, may easily be deceived; So that there is nothing true in the universe of which we ought to be so certain, of which our understanding should be so fully convinced, as of the mysteries of religion. "Faith," says St. Basil, "always powerful and victorious, exercises a greater ascendancy over minds than all the proofs which reason and human science can furnish, because faith obviates all difficulties, not by the light of manifest evidence, but by the weight of the infallible authority of God, which renders them incapable of admitting any doubt." It was thus that Abraham believed when, notwithstanding all the impediments of nature, he felt sure that he should see himself the father of a son, and through him of many nations. "He believed in hope against hope," says St. Paul, "that he might be made the father of many nations, according to what was said to him: "So shall thy seed be." And he was not weak in faith, for he considered neither his old age nor that of his wife Sarah. He distrusted not the promise of God, but was strong in faith, giving glory to God, being most fully convinced that whatsoever God has promised he is able to perform.

The faith of Moses was so great that St. Paul says of him that "he acted with the invisible God as though he were visible."

Similar was the faith of the famous and valiant Count de Montfort, who, being told that our Lord in the Host had appeared visibly in the hands of the priest, said to those who urged him to go and see the miracle: "Let those go and see it who doubt it; as for myself, I believe firmly the truth of the mystery of the Eucharist as our mother the holy Church teaches it. Hence, I hope to receive in heaven, a crown more brilliant than those of the angels; for they, being face to face with God, have not the power to doubt."

The noble Count St. Eliazer used to say that, with regard to matters of faith, he believed them so firmly that if all the theologians in the world strove to persuade him to the contrary, their logic would not have the slightest effect on him.

And, in effect, faith ought to take precedence of reason, demonstration, experience, and all other motives of certitude, with the true Christian and new man regenerated in Jesus Christ. "Consider," says St. Augustine, "that you are not called reasonable but faithful, since when anyone is baptized we say: He has become one of the faithful."

We must have this firm faith not only in some but in all the truths which God has made known, although they may be altogether incomprehensible to us. Faith will not allow of the rejection of even one; and he who should voluntarily entertain a doubt of one single article – one single point of faith – could not be said to have faith at all. We believe everything that God has revealed, precisely for this reason: that *God has said it.*

The word of God, who is infallible truth itself, and who cannot deceive nor be deceived, is the *why* and *wherefore* of our belief. To say or to think, I believe this article, this truth of faith, but I do not believe that, is as much as to say or think, I believe that God tells the truth in this point, but he tells it not in that other; it is as much as to say God is capable of telling a lie. This is blasphemy; it is even the denial of God's existence.

And also to say or to think, I cannot believe such an article or such a mystery of faith, because it is too obscure, too incomprehensible, and contrary to reason, is to exhibit a lamentable lack of reason. To be a man, it is necessary to have reason. Reason is the light of man. But reason tells us that it is necessary to submit to faith, and that there is no sense in him who wishes to submit to his reason the very essential principle of his reason, and that to wish to understand what is above his intelligence is to be without intelligence.

Reason tells us that our religion would not be divine if it were not above reason. For God would not be God if he were not incomprehensible, and my soul could not adore him if my mind could comprehend him. It is one thing to say that such a mystery is contrary to reason, and another to prove it. In order to prove that a doctrine is contrary to reason, we must have a clear, precise idea of what that doctrine is. We can say, for instance, that it is contrary to reason to assert that a square is a circle, for we have a clear, precise idea of what a square is, and what a circle is. But we cannot say with certainty that a doctrine or a mystery of our holy faith is contrary to reason, for we can never have a full, clear, precise idea of that doctrine or mystery. We cannot have this clear idea, simply because those doctrines are far above reason. We cannot say, for instance, that the doctrine of the Holy Trinity, the doctrine of three divine Persons in one divine Substance, is contrary to reason, because we can never have a clear, precise idea either of God's essence or of the nature of the three divine Persons. And what is true of the Trinity is true also of all the other doctrines and mysteries of our holy faith. They are not against reason, but they are above reason. Reason is above the senses, and faith is above reason.

"Certainly," says St. John Chrysostom, "since the works of God incomparably surpass the capacity of our minds, the thoughts whereby we seek to penetrate the abysses of faith are always accompanied with folly, and resemble labyrinths which it is very easy to enter, but from which it is almost impossible to come forth; these thoughts spring from pride, and as proud minds are ashamed to believe or to admit that which they cannot understand, they entangle themselves in difficulties from which they cannot easily issue. Is it true, then, proud man, that you can understand how the sun and stars were created; how the earth, with all its riches was called forth from chaos; how the magnet attracts iron; how a single grain of corn sown in the earth produce a thousand other grains? You are not ashamed to own that you cannot answer these things; and when there is question of things of a more sublime nature, of things that are above the comprehension of angels, you will not avow your ignorance – you make bold efforts to understand them. Fool! the shame is not the inability to comprehend them, but the daring to sound them."

Speaking of Rahab, who received the spies, and of whom St. Paul says that her faith saved her from the unhappy fate of her fellow-citizens, St. Chrysostom praises the simplicity of her faith, and adds: "This woman did not examine what the spies said, neither did she reason with herself thus: How can it be possible that the captives and fugitives now wandering in the desert will capture a city so strong and so well provided as ours? Had she argued thus, she would have been lost."

Those of the Israelites, on the contrary, who hearing of the prodigious strength and power of the countries they were to conquer, yielded to diffidence, notwithstanding the divine assurance that they should vanquish their enemies even without fighting them, were deprived by their infidelity of the happiness which God had promised to their faith.

What could be more strange or more opposed to reason than to command a father to sacrifice his only and most innocent son? And yet Abraham put himself in readiness to do so, without discussing the commandment or adducing arguments to prove its unreasonableness; he considered only the divinity and wisdom of him who commanded.

Another person, wishing to show himself more reasonable, refused to strike a prophet, as he had been ordered to do, because the thing seemed to him improper. But his disobedience was soon punished, for a lion rushed upon him and devoured him, not far from the place where the fault had been committed.

Saul, having been ordered by God to put the Amalekites to death with their flocks and herds, found it reasonable to spare the king, and to set aside the best and fattest of the flocks for sacrifice; in recompense for his fine reasoning on the subject he was overwhelmed with many evils, and finally lost his kingdom.

The child at the mother's breast takes what it sees not; sometimes he will even close his eyes when he might see, as though he confided entirely in his mother and in the love she bears him; in like manner the soul sucks the milk of faith from the bosom of the Church, which she sees not; she reposes on the infinite wisdom and goodness of Jesus Christ, who can teach her nothing but what is true, and give her nothing that is not good. It is on this juice of divine faith that the just man lives, as St. Paul tells us.

The faith of St. Teresa was so firm that it seemed to her she could convert all the heretics from their errors; and so simple that she said the less she comprehended a mystery, the more firmly she believed it and the more devotion it excited in her; she tasted a singular pleasure in not being able to comprehend it. She silenced all objections to a mystery by saying: "The Son of God, Jesus Christ, has revealed it to us, and we have no more questions to ask."

Such faith is absolutely necessary. It is necessary by necessity of precept. Our Blessed Lord says: "He that believeth and is baptized shall be saved. He that believeth not shall be condemned." This precept is affirmative in as far as it obliges us to believe all that God has revealed; it is negative in as far as it forbids us to hold any opinions contrary to the revealed truth.

Such faith is necessary by necessity of medium, for "without faith it is impossible to please God" (Heb. 11:6). "If you believe not, you shall die in your sins" (Jn. 5:38, 7:27).

It is therefore false, utterly false, to assert that all Christian religion consists merely in loving God with our whole heart and our neighbor as ourselves. If we love God and our neighbor, we indeed fulfill God's moral law; but we are also bound to believe God's sacred word. "The one we must do, and the other we must not omit."

The observance of God's laws is the worship of the heart; but the belief in his word is the worship of the mind. We must love God with our whole heart, but we must also love him with our whole mind.

Such should be our faith. Indeed, the fact that Jesus Christ has said it, has done it, has taught it to his Church and commanded her to teach it to all nations, must be for us the weightiest of all reasons to believe it. The famous word of the Pythagoreans, "The master has said it," was with them a foolish idolatry, believing as they did that no one could be deceived. Applied, however, to Jesus Christ, it must be a first principle, a sacred axiom for every Christian. The heavens and the earth shall pass away, but "the truths of the Lord remain for ever" (Ps. 116:2). He has said: "What is great before men is an abomination before God." He has said: "Sooner will a camel pass through the eye of a needle than the rich enter the kingdom of heaven." He has said: "Woe to you who now rejoice, for you shall weep"; "Blessed are those who weep." He has said: "He who renounces not all, and himself also, cannot be my disciple." He has said it. Reason, perhaps, might suggest that these oracles must be explained, softened, modified; that it cannot comprehend how we can find peace in war, glory in contempt, delights in crosses. But the good Christian listens only to his Master. "He has said it." He would not have said it were it not true.

It is thus that the true disciple of Jesus Christ becomes blind in order that he may see; renounces the prudence of the flesh to follow that of the Spirit; becomes a fool in order to be wise, for the wisdom of this world is folly before God.

As our modern pagans are far more guilty in the sight of God than those of old, and are living, as it were, in sworn hatred of Jesus Christ and his holy religion, it is easily to be foreseen that, a few years hence, they will persecute the Catholics and far exceed in cruelty their pagan brethren of old. Happy the Catholic who keeps himself ready to undergo any kind of trial for the love of Jesus Christ and in defense of his holy faith. To do this properly, next to receiving Holy Communion and assisting at Mass, we can do nothing better than say daily the Rosary. Our holy faith, and our love for the same, are so much strengthened and increased by the daily practice of the Rosary that this devotion might be called the Nurse of Faith, because it more than any other confirms us in the virtue of faith. As one – to go from the lower to the higher – who often commits the sin of drunkenness becomes a confirmed drunkard, so also one who often makes acts of faith becomes confirmed in faith. Now, every sign of the cross we make, every Our Father, every Hail Mary, every Glory be to the Father we say, every recital of the Apostles' Creed, is an act of faith. Each time, therefore, that we say the Rosary we make no less than one hundred and seventy acts of faith. Should we say but five decades of the Rosary, and begin by making the sign of the cross and saying the Apostles' Creed, we make no less than sixty acts of faith.

In making the sign of the cross we pronounce the words: "In the name of the Father, and of the Son, and of the Holy Ghost." We thus profess our faith in the existence of one God in three persons; we profess our faith in the truth that the Son of God, the second Person of the Blessed Trinity, became man for us, and died upon the cross for our salvation. By making the sign of the cross we proclaim to the world that we are not ashamed of the cross of Jesus, and of our belief in a crucified Redeemer.

The recital of the Apostles' Creed is still a greater act of faith; for in its recital we profess our faith in the principal truths which Jesus Christ came to teach us for our salvation.

Prayer, too, is a great act of faith; for by praying to God we acknowledge our dependence on his goodness. As the subjects of a king acknowledge their allegiance to their sovereign by paying the taxes he lays upon them, so also, by offering up to the Almighty the tribute of our prayer, we acknowledge ourselves to be constant mendicants before the gate of his divine mercy; we believe that he knows our wants, and is able and willing to grant us whatever we ask of him.

Faith, however, is increased and strengthened not only by making acts of faith, but particularly by praying for its increase and strength. Jesus Christ has promised every grace to prayer, and we give him the greatest pleasure when we ask of him the inestimable gift of a lively faith. We may rest assured that he will hear our prayer for the increase of faith, for he is more desirous to bestow this gift upon us than we are to receive it. After the Apostles' Creed, we say one Our Father and three Hail Marys for an increase of faith; need we wonder that those who daily say the Rosary are also daily so strengthened and confirmed in their holy faith as to be ready to die for it if necessary?

For over three hundred years the Irish people have suffered, struggled, and died for the faith. They suffered poverty with all its bitterness, they endured exile with all its sorrows, they suffered outrage, and even death itself, rather than lose their God. The minions of hell enacted the fiendish penal laws, and soon that country, so rich and fruitful in colleges and convents, became one vast, dreary wilderness.

In tracts of country thirty, forty, fifty miles in extent, the smoke from an inhabited house, as English chroniclers themselves declare, was nowhere to be seen. The people had disappeared and left only skeletons in the land. The living were to be met only in the glens and dark caves of the mountains. There they dragged out a wretched existence, feeding on the weeds and garbage of the earth. Like shadows they moved about, haggard and wan, starving and wounded, and they endured the cruel pangs of hunger, till God, in his mercy, took them to a better world. Again and again were these harrowing scenes repeated. Ireland became prosperous again in spite of the most galling oppression; and the people of Ireland were again starved and massacred for their faith, and those that survived were shipped off to the British West Indies, and sold there as slaves. The British fleet was ordered around the coast. Over eighty thousand of the most influential and most distinguished of the Irish Catholics were packed on board, and their bones have long since rotted in the soil of the English sugar plantations of Jamaica.

The last effort of tyranny is still fresh in the minds of all — I mean the late famine years. There are, no doubt, some of my readers who have witnessed the appalling scenes of that gloomy period, and, once witnessed, they can never, never be forgotten. Ah! no. Like living fire, these horrid scenes burn into the memory, and leave there a horrid scar — a mark that can never be effaced. There were thousands and thousands wasting away and dying of hunger. They were falling and dying as the leaves fall in autumn. The corn and food that was sent to the poor people from America was kept in the harbors until it rotted. And there, in the sight of the famishing people, the wealthy Protestant, the overfed wives and daughters of the sleek, oily Protestant persons, had plenty of food for their cattle, they had food in abundance for their pet birds or their lap-dogs, whilst the poor starving Catholics wished to eat even the husks of the swine, and it was not given them.

A few years before that gloomy reign of terror, there lived near a certain town in Ireland a poor, honest farmer with his wife and children. They were poor, indeed, but yet they were contented and happy. Never did the poor or the stranger pass their door without partaking of their hospitality; and what they had they gave with a willing heart. But the famine year came on. The good farmer was unable to pay the tithes. His little property was distrained. The police entered his farm; they seized his unreaped corn; they took away his crops; they drove his cattle to the pound. The poor unhappy man himself was expelled from that little spot of earth on which he was born, where he had lived so long, and where he had hoped to die. He was turned into the public road with his wife and children. No roof, no food, no clothing – he was cast in beggary and nakedness into the cold, heartless world. He sought for a shelter for his little ones. He sought for employment, but could find none. He was a Catholic. His neighbors around were bitter Protestants of the blackest dye. They offered him shelter, food, and clothing, but on one condition – that he would apostatize.

O God! who shall tell the agony of that poor, heart-broken father? No hope to cheer him save the hope of death; no eye to pity him save the all-merciful eye of God! He saw his poor wife dying before his eyes. He saw her wasting day by day – slowly pining away, while praying and weeping over her starving children; he heard his famished children crying for food, and their piteous cries rent his very soul. Oh! he could help them, he could provide them food, clothing, and a pleasant home – but then he must apostatize, he must renounce his holy faith! Oh! what a sore trial, what a cruel martyrdom! His loving wife died before his eyes – died of hunger. She died with words of patience, words of hope, upon her lips. The poor husband wrung his hands in anguish. He bent over the lifeless form of his wife. Dark night was thickening around him – thickening even within him; he felt the cruel pangs of hunger, gnawing at his very vitals. And were he not upheld by his holy faith he would have yielded to despair. But the cries of his children roused him. He forgot for a moment his own sufferings. He took his two weak, starving babes in his trembling arms, and hurried away with tottering steps. He begged from house to house, from door to door; he begged for a crumb of bread for his poor, starving little ones, but not one gave him a morsel of food. They offered him food and clothing and shelter if he would only apostatize, if he would give his children to be brought up in their false creed. "But," cried the heart-broken father, "Oh! how could

I give my children to be brought up in a false creed and deny their holy faith? Oh! how could I sell their souls to the evil one for a mess of pottage?" After some time the unhappy man felt a heavy load weighing like lead upon his trembling arm. He looked. One of his poor babes had ceased moaning. It was dead – cold and stiff in death. The heart-broken father sat down beneath a tree by the wayside and prayed, but he could not weep. Ah! no; his eyes were dry, his heart was withered. In wild, passionate tones he called on Heaven to witness his agony – he called God to witness that he did not wish the death of his children, that he would gladly lay down his life to save his family, but he could not – oh! no! no! – he could not deny his holy faith; he could not sell their souls to the devil. He tried once more to obtain some food for his remaining child, but in vain, and at last the poor, innocent sufferer gasped and died too in his arms.

Ah! whose heart can remain unmoved at the sufferings of the Irish Catholics? But what was the source of that grace which made men and women of Catholic Ireland triumph even over the arts and ingenuity and most cruel outrages of Protestantism? A venerable priest, who lately died at Rome in the odor of sanctity, declared that the faith had been preserved in Ireland solely by the devotion of that ancient people to the Rosary.

The same may be said of many towns and hamlets in Germany, which have preserved the faith in its full freshness and vigor. One who travels through Protestant Germany meets here and there a little town or hamlet which is entirely Catholic. Like the oasis in the desert, it remains green and smiling amidst the dreary waste of heresy which surrounds it. These little towns have always preserved the faith; and when all around them was withered and burned by the poisonous breath of heresy, they kept the faith in its full freshness and vigor. The cause of this miraculous preservation was their perseverance in the devotion to the Blessed Mother of God. Every Sunday the good parish priest assembled his flock, and recited with them the holy Rosary. And when the priest was banished or had died, the good people assembled of their own accord and continued to recite the Rosary. Whilst reciting the beads, they prayed to God and to his holy Mother. They called to mind the holy lives, the sufferings and death of Jesus Christ and his blessed Mother. Thus thinking of God, and praying to him, they could not but help knowing and loving God. Now, those who know and love God do not go astray, they live up to the truths of faith, and remain faithful in God's service. The venerable Curé of Ars declared emphatically that in this century it was the Rosary which restored religion in France, and we know by the testimony of saints and of our Blessed Lady herself, it was the preaching of the Rosary which, at two terrible epochs, reanimated and saved the faith of Southern Europe.

There is a certain curious instrument which marks with great accuracy the different degrees of temperature. It contains a fluid which rises when the weather is warm, and falls again as the weather grows cold. You have seen, no doubt, the instrument of which I speak: it is called a thermometer. Now, there is another kind of thermometer, which marks very accurately the different states of temperature, not indeed of the natural, but of the supernatural life – a thermometer which indicates very correctly the warmth of faith in a Catholic, in a family, in a community; and this instrument is the Rosary. It is a well-known fact that wherever the Devotion of the Rosary is practiced, there faith is warm and active. "Formerly," says Alanus de Rupe, "if any one had to begin a new state of life, or assume any high office, or offer himself to any trade, and did not appear with a Rosary of beads, he would have endangered his reputation as a good man"; and he adds that "the beads in his time were regarded as the distinguishing sign of a good Catholic."

One day some of the companions of St.Ignatius traveled through Germany on their way to Venice. As they passed through those places which had fallen off from the faith, those good religious wore the Rosary publicly around their necks, to show that they gloried in being children of the Catholic Church, and that they prided themselves on being servants of Mary. As they came near the apostate city of Constance, they saw an old woman coming towards them. As soon as she saw the Rosaries she expressed the most lively joy. She raised her eyes and hands to heaven, and made repeatedly the sign of the cross. She was a good Catholic. Neither the promises nor the threats of her apostate townsmen could make her deny her holy faith. On account of this heroic fidelity to the dictates of her conscience, she was driven out of the city by the bigoted Lutherans. She was overjoyed at seeing Catholics once more. She kissed their Rosaries again and again, and then, requesting them by signs to wait for a moment, she ran in haste to the hospital in which she lived, and brought with her all the Protestants she could meet. Then pointing to the strangers, she said to her apostate townsmen: "See here, ye wretched apostates! Look at these men, and see what lies you have been telling me. You said that the whole world believes in your Luther, and that nobody believes any more in the Catholic religion. Now, where do these men come from? See their Rosaries. Are they not Catholics? And are they not of this world?" This good woman loved her faith; she lived up to it; she even defended it, because she practiced the Devotion of the Rosary. One who is faithful in the daily practice of this devotion often reflects upon the sacred truths of our holy religion. Everywhere he carries with him their wholesome impression. The truths of faith animate him in all the details of life. He has for his principle of action the Holy Ghost – the spirit of Jesus Christ. It is no more he who lives; it is Jesus Christ who lives in him. Accordingly, he judges of the things of this world in the knowledge which Jesus Christ has given us in their regard – that is, he judges of them even as Jesus Christ himself judges of them. Hence it is that he fears only that which faith teaches him to fear. He desires only those things which faith tells him to wish for; he hopes only for that which faith teaches him to hope for. He loves, or he hates, or he despises all that faith teaches him to love, or to hate, or to despise. What does he say of the riches of this world? He says with Jesus Christ: "Blessed are the poor in spirit, for theirs is the kingdom of heaven" (Mt. 5:3); and, "Woe to you that are rich, for you have your consolation" (Lk. 6:24).

What does he say of the honors of this world? He says with Jesus Christ: "Woe to you when men shall bless you" (Lk. 6:26).

What does he say of the wisdom of this world? He says with St. Paul: "The wisdom of this world is foolishness with God" (1 Cor.3:19). And with Jesus Christ he says: "Unless you become as little children, you shall not enter the kingdom of heaven."

What judgment does he pass upon the pleasures of this world? He says with Jesus Christ: "Woe to you that now laugh, for you shall mourn and weep" (Lk.6:25). " Watch ye, therefore, because you know not at what hour the Lord will come" (Mt. 24: 25).

What judgment does he pass upon old age? With the Holy Ghost, he says: "Venerable old age is not that of long time, nor counted by the number of years, but a spotless life is old age" (Wis. 4:8).

What does he say of the trials, persecutions, and injustices of this world? He says with Jesus Christ: "Blessed shall ye be when men shall hate you, and when they shall separate you, and shall reproach you, and cast out your name as evil, for the Son of Man's sake. Be glad in that day and rejoice, for behold your reward is great in heaven" (Lk. 6:22).

Thus he thinks, judges, and acts according to the truths of the Gospel, or the principles of Jesus Christ, and it is thus that he lives by faith, as St. Paul says. Faith is the life of the just man. It is the life of his intellect, by the truths which enlighten him; it is the life of his heart, by the sentiments of justice and holiness which it imparts; it is the life of his works, which it renders meritorious for all eternity; and this happy life is obtained by the Devotion of the Rosary.

CHAPTER 7

THE ROSARY: THE DEVOTION OF THE FAITHFUL
IT INCREASES THEIR HOPE

Many years ago a strange sight, a singular contrast, might have been witnessed in the rich Eastern city of Babylon. Throughout the streets and public places of that populous city, the inhabitants might be seen feasting, singing, and rejoicing. Everywhere, whithersoever you turned, you could behold signs of triumph and gladness. But see! in the midst of this rejoicing there is one spot in which sadness reigns. Upon the banks of Babylon's streams s vast multitude is assembled. There you see strong men borne down by sorrow. There you see feeble women pining away with grief. There are old men whose hoary heads are bowed down with sadness; you see little children languishing in pain. The faces of all are pallid; their eyes are filled with tears. They rest their wearied limbs beneath the shade of the mournful cypress. Their harps, their musical instruments, hang sadly upon the branches of the willow. No hand is raised to touch them, no finger evokes sweet music from their chords. They are silent; they are neglected. There nought is heard save the sighs, the moans, the sobs of the multitude, as they blend confusedly with the murmur, the dash of the stream. Nought is seen save the tears that trickle down from their eyelids and blend with the flood. Ah! let us draw near those poor unhappy creatures! Let us ask them the cause of their tears. Perhaps their feet are loaded with chains, or their hands bound by cruel manacles? No! they are not chained – this is not the cause of their grief.

Are they, perhaps, needy, suffering from the bitter pangs of hunger? or are they crushed and down-trodden – condemned to hard labor, to degrading servitude? Are these, perhaps, the cause of their grief? Ah! no; these are not the cause of their tears. They weep, they are heart-broken, because they are exiles; because they are far, far away from their home, their native land. This, this alone is the cause of their tears.

How mournful are the days of exile! How sweet it is to breathe once more the air of our native land! The bread of the stranger, like the bread of the wicked, is bitter to the heart. The streams of a foreign land may murmur in soothing tones, but,Oh! they speak an unknown tongue. The birds in foreign lands may sing sweetly, but they want one melodious note – they do not sing to us of home. The scenes in other lands may be wildly fair, but, Oh! they have not that sweet, that soothing charm which endears every object in our native land. We are poor exiles here below, far away from heaven, our true home; we, therefore, constantly suffer the pain of exile. We are never satisfied in this world. We always crave for something more, something higher, something better? Whence is this continual restlessness which haunts us through life and ever pursues us to the grave? It is the homesickness of the soul. It is the soul's craving after God.

It is God who made our heart, and he made it for himself. When man first came forth from the hand of God, his heart turned to God naturally, and he loved creatures only as loving keepsakes of God. But sin and death came into the world. The heart of man was defiled and degraded. He turned away from the pure and holy love of God, and sought for love and happiness amid creatures. But our heart seeks in vain among creatures. Our heart is small indeed, but its love is infinite. It can find rest only in God. Whatever we love out of God brings only pain and bitter disappointment.

There is a man whose heart thirsts for praise and honor. He labors through sleepless nights and weary days. Year after year he watches and toils, till at last he obtains what his heart has craved so long. Praises and honors are showered upon him. His name is on every lip. But is he happy? Is his weary heart at rest? Ah! No. Every new honor brings new cares; envy and jealousy pursue him. His heart ever thirsts for more honors. He yearns to climb still higher and higher. His heart is never at rest.

There is another. His dream, his waking thought, day and night, is to grow rich, to live in splendor and luxury. His life is spent in planning and thinking and toiling. Ah! his desires consume him. But give him all the kingdoms of the earth; give him all the gold of the mountains, all the pearls of the ocean; give him the desire of his heart. Will he be happy? Will his heart be at rest? Ah! no. You cannot cure a sick man by clothing him in a robe of silk and gold. The gorgeous palaces of the rich are but the gilded prisons of weary, restless hearts. There is another. His heart, his imagination, is fascinated by sensuous pleasures. He loves the false, fleeting beauty of earthly forms. He loves the wild, fitful gratification of sinful passions. Ah! he is fearfully deceived. The cup of sensual pleasure is mingled with bitter poison. It defiles and degrades the noble soul. The guilty, feverish joy of the moment is followed by the scalding tears of remorse, and often by the fearful death of the suicide, and the long endless night of black despair in hell! Ah! ask those who have drunk deep of all false joys of earth, and they will tell you in heart-broken accents that they were bitterly deceived.

Strange and inexplicable indeed is the human heart! We are often a burden to others, and oftener a burden even to ourselves. Our heart is always restless, because we are always in want of something; our heart is always yearning for pleasure, and yet all the pleasures of this life bring us only disappointment and bitterness. We have a natural horror of pain and sadness, and yet we live in a world where pain and sorrow accompany us at every step. At times our desires are so vast, so noble, that we can be contented only with God himself, and this earth, with all its wealth and beauty, seems but a dreary prison – a place of banishment – a valley of tears; and again at times our heart is so degraded by sin, so much inclined to evil, that we have to watch over it unceasingly, and repress all its inordinate affections if we wish to enjoy true peace. Our heart is at the mercy of every passion, the plaything of joy and sorrow. We rejoice at times, and we know not why, and again we are sad and heart-sick, and we know not wherefore. Our heart is filled with hatred and dislike, and the object of our hatred is not removed; our heart is filled with love, and the object of our love is torn away from us. How often has not our heart, with its hopes and sorrows and fears, been a weary burden to us!

Ah! we are poor exiles here below. God created us, and he created us for himself, and until we can enjoy God, and see him face to face, we can never find true rest. There is always an aching void in our heart – a void which cannot be filled by father or mother, by brother or sister or our dearest friend – it can be filled by God alone; and he will fill it in heaven to the fullest extent of our desires, for there we shall possess him, the source of all happiness. There, he says: "Well done, good and faithful servant; because thou hast been faithful over a few things, I will place thee over many things: enter thou into the joy of thy Lord" (Mt.25:23). Our Lord does not say that his joy and happiness is to enter into his servant, but that his faithful servant is to enter into his joy. Were we told to receive into ourselves all the water of the sea, we should say: "How can this be done? It is utterly impossible." But were we bade to plunge into the water of the sea, we should see no impossibility in this. Now, our Lord is an infinite ocean of joy and happiness. Impossible for the soul to receive this happiness all into herself, but most easy for her to enter into this ocean of happiness when our Lord tells her: "Well done, good and faithful servant: enter into the joy of the Lord." In the very instant that the soul hears these words, she sees, by the light of glory, the infinite beauty of God face to face; she is at once filled, and as it were all consumed, with love; she is lost and immersed in that boundless ocean of the goodness of God; she forgets herself, passing over into God and dissolving into him; the Lord communicates himself substantially to her, giving himself up to her in a manner most sweet and intimate. On this account St. John says: "Behold the tabernacle of God with men; and he will dwell with them: and they shall be his people, and God himself, with them, shall be their God" (Apoc. 21:3); "He that shall overcome shall possess these things: and I will be his God, and he shall be my son" (Apoc. 21:7).

As a king is always with his people, a father with his children, a teacher with his pupils, so God will always be with the elect in heaven, recreating and feeding them, and filling them with numberless delights and unspeakable happiness. They will constantly enjoy his presence, which was hidden from them here below; they will see God, and speak to him face to face, and he will penetrate them with ineffable sweetness and consolation; for "he shall be their God," their Father, their Protector, their Glorifier, their All.

"He will be their God"; that is, he will be all their joy, all their honor, all their wisdom, all their riches, all their good; so that the blessed exclaim, with the Psalmist, "For what have I in heaven, and besides thee what do I desire upon earth?" (Ps. 72:25), and with St. Francis, "My God, my love, and my all." Each one will possess God whole and entire; for God will give himself up to each one as much as he will give himself to all together, so that every one will enjoy and possess God as completely as if God belonged to him alone. "I shall be thy exceedingly great reward," said God to Abraham. "Thou, my Lord, art my portion in the land of the living." If a king sits on an elevated throne, he is seen equally well by all; he is present to all at the same time, and each one enjoys his presence as much as the whole assembly does; so God is seen by the blessed as an immense sun, as it were, and enjoyed and possessed by each one in particular as well as by all together; and just as fine music fills the ear of every individual with as much delight as it does a large assembly, so God communicates himself, and all he has and is, to every one just as much as he does to all. Thus all and each one will, like a fish in the water, swim in this ocean of God's happiness and delight; being made partakers of the divine nature, they enjoy true, solid, immense, and incomprehensible happiness. They will retain, it is true, their own nature, but they shall assume a certain admirable and almost divine form, so as to seem to be gods rather than men.

As a sponge thrown into water becomes quite penetrated and saturated with it, so do the blessed become penetrated with the divine essence when entering into the joy of the Lord. If an iron be placed in the fire, it soon looks like fire; it becomes fire itself, yet without losing its nature. In like manner, the soul, transformed into God by the light of glory, though it retains its being, is like unto God.

In virtue of this union they become pure like God, holy like God, powerful, wise, and happy like God. He will transform them into himself, not by the destruction of their being, but by uniting it to his. He will communicate to them his own nature, his greatness, his strength, his knowledge, his sanctity, his riches and felicity. In the plenitude of their joy, the blessed will exclaim: "Oh! it is good for us to be here."

God, then, will fill the souls of the blessed with the plenitude of his light; he will fill their will with the abundance of his peace; he will fill their memory with the extent of his eternity; he will fill their essence with the purity of his being; and he will fill all their senses and the powers of their soul with the immensity of his benefits and the infinity of his riches. They see him as he is; they love him without defect; they behold him, the source of all beauty, and this sight ravishes their mind; they see him, the source of all goodness, and the contemplation thereof satiates their souls with enjoyment. O sweet occupation! O inestimable happiness!

This unspeakable happiness, the everlasting enjoyment of God, is the principal object of Christian hope. What more sweet, more agreeable, or better calculated to fill the heart with the purest consolation than the divine virtue of hope? It is the best sweetener of the bitterness of this life, the greatest comfort in our pains, the most healing balm which can be applied to the wounds of our hearts. The poor, the miserable, the unhappy are sustained under their miseries by the sweet hope of a happy eternity. What renders hell the most intolerable of all evils is that hope is banished from it and will never enter it. Hope is given us as a domestic consolation in all our adversities; it inclines our will to expect with firm confidence that God, through the merits of Jesus Christ, will supply all our wants here below, and grant us eternal happiness hereafter, if our life is in conformity to the doctrine of the holy Roman Catholic Church.

But, according to the Apostle, this our hope of salvation must be firm and immovable. In the Devotion of the Rosary we have a most powerful means to render our hope unshaken in God. How much is not our hope nourished and strengthened by the sign of the cross alone, by which we begin the Rosary; for this holy sign continually reminds us of the Passion and of the sacred Blood of Christ, in which we place all our hope for grace at present and for mercy and happiness hereafter.

In saying the Rosary, we make profession of our faith in God the Father. We repeat this sweet name at least thirty-three times. And shall it be possible for one to repeat that word "Father" so many times without remembering its meaning, without thinking of the reason why Jesus Christ has taught us to pray "Our Father who art in heaven," etc.? What is more peculiar to a father than the great yearning of communicating to his children himself and all his goods as far as possible? In our "Heavenly Father" that yearning is infinite; it us quite essential to his nature. Hence he made the heavens to give us light and rain, the fire to give us warmth, the air to preserve our lives, the earth to produce various kinds of fruit, the sea to give us fish, the animals to give us food and clothing: he gives his divine nature to his well beloved Son; he gave us his own Son in the manger of Bethlehem, he gave him to us upon the cross, and he gives him to us every day at each Holy Mass, at each Holy Communion. O God! thou art almighty, but thy omnipotence is not able to give us anything greater in proof of thy unspeakable love and liberality towards us. I find no better words to express my wonder than those of the saints: "Lord, thou hast become foolish from love towards us! Thou hast given heaven, thou hast given earth, thou hast given thy kingdom, thou hast given thyself – what more hast thou to give? Allow me to say it: How prodigal art thou of thyself!"

The name "Father" is the most pleasing to God. By calling him Father, we give him more honor than by any other title, for it is something far greater in God to be Father than to be Lord. As Father, he generates his Son from all eternity, who is equal to himself; whilst as Lord he has created the universe, which is infinitely less than himself. "Abba, Father." This sweet word touches his heart. The prodigal son knew how guilty he was in the sight of his father, yet, remembering the affectionate love of his father's heart, he felt quite consoled and full of hope and confidence, and said to himself: "I will arise, and will go to my father, and say to him: Father, I have sinned against heaven and before thee" (Lk 15:18). He knew very well that he had not behaved like a good son, yet, in spite of his bad conduct, he felt confident that his father's love for him was not yet dead. He knew that his father's heart would speak for him more powerfully than he himself could do; he knew that by calling him by the endearing name of father his heart would be moved with compassion.

What increase of hope must we not experience whenever we think of our Heavenly Father, whom no one can equal in kindness and liberality! He says of himself: "Can a woman forget her infant so as not to have pity on the son of her womb? And if she should forget, yet will I not forget thee. Behold, I have graven thee in my hands" (Is. 49:15). Jesus Christ assures us of the same thing when he says: "And I say not to you that I will ask the Father for you, for the Father himself loveth you" (Jn. 16:26).

But if God is our Father, we are his children, and the laws of all nations, in accordance with those of nature grant to children a holy right to their father's goods, especially so if these were given him to be transmitted by him to his children. To illustrate: One day a poor man called Peter went to his friend Paul, and spoke to him of his great poverty. "My dear friend," said Peter, "do you not know any one who could help me?" "Yes, I do," replied Paul; "go to Mr. Bonus, a rich nobleman; he will help you." "I am afraid," said Peter, "he will not receive me." "You need not be afraid," said Paul, "because this nobleman is goodness, liberality, and charity itself; he receives every one that comes to him with the greatest affability. Some time ago he issued a proclamation, in which he declared that he was the father of the poor, inviting all to come and tell him their wants. He never feels happier than when he bestows alms upon the poor. He is exceedingly rich. He had a dearly beloved son, to whom he bequeathed all his possessions; but his son died a short time after, and on his death-bed willed all his property to the poor, and made his father the executor of his will. Now, this good father considers himself bound in conscience to distribute this property to the poor. There is no reason, then, why you should fear to call on him; you will certainly receive as much as you need." These words filled the heart of Peter with great hope and confidence; he went to see the rich nobleman, and received what he asked of him.

Now, we are all like this poor man. We are in want of many things; we need especially the grace of God; we need the gift of perseverance in the friendship of Almighty God in order to obtain heaven. The grace of God and perseverance in it are the objects of our hope. How much are we not strengthened in this hope by the

67

remembrance that in all our wants we can have recourse to a Lord who is far more compassionate and infinitely richer than the kind hearted nobleman of whom I have spoken. This good Lord is our Heavenly Father. He has issued a proclamation, recorded in Holy Scripture: "Every one who asks receiveth" (Lk. 13:10), and "All things whatsoever you shall ask in prayer, believing, you shall receive" (Mt. 21:22). God the Father also gave everything to his Divine Son Jesus: "All things are delivered up to me by my Father" (Mt. 21:27). His Son Jesus died, and made us heirs to all his graces and merits. His Heavenly Father considers us as his dear children, who may, in justice, lay claim to the merits and graces of his Divine Son, who called our special attention to this right of ours when he said: "If you ask the Father anything in *my Name,* he will give it to you" (Jn. 16:23). He means to say: You must represent to your Heavenly Father that he is your Father, and that you are his children, and have as such, according to all divine and human laws, a claim upon all his goods. This claim of yours is so much the stronger as I have acquired it by my Passion and Death.

Now, this is precisely what we do in saying the Rosary. In the Five Joyful Mysteries of the Rosary we represent to our Heavenly Father the merits of the Incarnation, of the Birth, and of the Infancy of his Divine Son, our Lord Jesus Christ; in the Sorrowful Mysteries we represent to him the merits of the Passion and Death of our Divine Redeemer; and in the Glorious Mysteries we represent to him the merits of the Risen Life of our Savior and his triumphant Ascension, asking of our Heavenly Father, through these merits of his Son, that his name may be hallowed, his kingdom come to us, his will be done by us; that all we need for soul and body may be granted us; especially the forgiveness of our sins, preservation from temptations, and delivery from all evil; and in the Hail Mary, which we add to the Our Father, we ask the Mother of God to receive our prayers and present them with the merits of her Divine Son to the Heavenly Father, that he may hear them for the sake of his Son and her own powerful intercession.

Who does not see that our hope in God is nourished and strengthened more and more whenever we say the Rosary?

God's faithfulness to his promise, to grant us whatever we ask of him in the name of Jesus Christ, is an impregnable bulwark of our hope. The power and mercy of God are indeed strong motives for hope, but the strongest of all motives is God's fidelity to his promise, because, though we believe that God is infinite in power and mercy, nevertheless we could not have the unwavering certainty that God will save us unless he himself had given us the certain promise to do so, provided we ask him to save us. As God gives the grace of prayer to every one, no one can reasonably fear to be lost if he perseveres in prayer. Hence St. Alphonsus says: "As for myself, I never feel greater consolation, nor greater assurance of my salvation, than when I am praying to God and recommending myself to him. And I think the same must happen to every other Christian. There are several signs by which we can become certain of our salvation, but there is none so certain as prayer, for we know with infallible certainty that God will hear him who prays with confidence and perseverance." Now if, by prayer, the anchor of hope is cast very deep, it is evident that by the best of prayers – the holy Rosary- this anchor of hope is cast into the very depths of the immense ocean of God's goodness and mercy. So that the Devotion of the Rosary may be called, in truth, the nurse of hope. It is for this reason that St. Alphonsus, that most zealous doctor of the Church, made a vow to say the Rosary every day. The Rosary was always his special devotion. In his old age he used to say it several times a day with his servant or with Brother Francis Anthony. He was seen with the Rosary in his hands from morning to night. He never omitted to meditate on the Mysteries. It was beautiful to hear the disputes which he daily had with the servant or the brother, either because he thought he had not made the intention properly, or because he thought he had not carefully distinguished the Mysteries, and then he would begin anew.

One day, when his dinner was ready, he fancied he had not finished his Rosary. So he refused to go to dinner, saying: "One Hail Mary is worth all the dinners in the world." Once he was found in a state of profound lethargy. To raise him from it the brother said to him: "My lord, we have still to say the Rosary." At the word

Rosary, his lordship moved, opened his eyes, and began. "In the name of the Father," etc.

Another time he doubted whether he had said the Rosary. So he asked his servant whether he had seen him say the Rosary. "Yes," said he, "I saw your lordship say it; it seems to me you are too scrupulous on this point." "When I have a doubt as to whether I have said the Rosary," replied the bishop, "you must not cause me any displeasure; for you ought to know that the salvation of my soul depends on saying the Rosary." He performed this devotion up to the time of his last illness. ("Life of St. Alphonsus," Vol. 5, ch. 38.)

Let us embrace the sentiments of this holy bishop and great doctor of the Church concerning the Rosary, let us adopt his practice of saying it daily, and, like him, we shall die with great confidence in the mercy and goodness of our heavenly Father.

CHAPTER 8

THE ROSARY:
THE DEVOTION OF THE FAITHFUL
IT INCREASES THEIR CHARITY

Our divine Savior has declared that his object in becoming man was to enkindle in all hearts the fire of his holy love. "I have come to cast fire upon earth, and what will I but that it be enkindled" (Lk. 12:49). What marvelous flames of love has he not lit up in a multitude of souls! Oh! how many hearts are blest in the wounds of Jesus, which, like glowing furnaces, are so penetrated with the fire of his love that they have not refused to consecrate to him their goods, their lives, their entire selves, surmounting with a generous courage all the obstacles they met in the observance of the divine law. But where did the saints find the courage and constancy to overcome themselves, to despise the world, renounce its pleasures and amusements, and endure heroically all the troubles and trials of this life? It was in the study of Jesus Christ crucified.

We read in the life of St. Catherine of Sienna that from her very childhood she experienced a great desire to love our Lord as much as possible. The older she grew, the better she understood that to love our Lord as much as possible was the duty of every Christian, and that she could not please our Lord perfectly unless she loved him with her whole heart and with all her strength. So she most fervently begged God to teach her the shortest way to become his own by love and lead a life most pleasing to him. Our Lord heard her prayer, and said to her: "Know, then, that the salvation of my servants and their perfection consists in this alone – that they do my will at all times. The more carefully they do my will, the more they advance in perfection; for then it is that they adhere and unite themselves more closely to me, who am supreme perfection itself. In order that you may understand this great truth, consider my Christ, in whom I am well pleased. He annihilated himself, taking the form of a servant, being made in the likeness of man, in order that by his example and word he might lead you back to the way of truth, from which you had gone so very far astray, walking in the greatest darkness of the intellect. He was obedient unto death, teaching you by his persevering obedience how your salvation depends altogether on your firm resolution to do nothing but my will. He who carefully reflects and meditates upon his life and doctrine will soon come to understand that the summit of perfection consists in nothing else than in the uninterrupted and persevering accomplishment of my will. This he has declared repeatedly: 'Not every one who says to me, Lord, Lord, shall enter into the kingdom of heaven, but he who obeys the will of my Father who is in heaven, shall enter into the kingdom of heaven.' He means to say that no one, whoever he may be, and whatsoever exterior good works he may perform for my name's sake, shall be admitted to the glory of life everlasting if he has not performed all according to my will".

It is indeed our duty to form ourselves upon the divine model which our Heavenly Father has given us in his well-beloved Son, Jesus Christ. We can, therefore, have no better intention in all our actions than to perform them after the example shown us by our Divine Savior. But to do this well we must often consider them with great attention and make our mind dwell upon them with delight; for a child who loves his father endeavors to acquire a conformity of disposition and inclinations with his, to imitate him in all his actions. Great indeed are the fruits and wonderful the effects produced in the soul by the frequent consideration of the mysteries of our Lord's life. This consideration is best calculated to produce in our hearts pious affections and fervent petitions for all the graces necessary for our salvation and sanctification, and to enable us to form firm resolutions to avoid some particular fault and to practice some particular virtue; and this leads infallibly to the reformation of life. Hence our Lord has declared, by several revelations, that no devotion is more pleasing to him than that which we have to the Mysteries of his Life, Passion, and Death.

He said to St. Mary Magdalene of Pazzi: "If every Friday you will pay attention to the hour on which I expired upon the cross, you will at once receive particular graces from my spirit, which I then returned to my Eternal Father; and although you do not feel this grace, it shall always rest upon you." Our Lord said to the Blessed Veronica, of the Order of St. Augustine: "I wish all men to do their utmost to sorrow in their hearts through veneration for my Passion, as if compassionating me. If they shed one little tear over it, they may be sure they have done a great thing; for the tongue of man cannot tell what joy and satisfaction that one little tear causes me." To St. Bridget he said: "I counsel you to have always two thoughts in your heart. First, the remembrance of what I have done for you in suffering and dying; this thought will excite love of God. Secondly, the consideration of my justice and the future judgment; this will strike fear into your soul." When the Blessed Angela Foligno asked God what she could do to please him more, he vouchsafed to appear to her several times, both sleeping and waking, always as crucified on the cross, and told her to look at his wounds, and then showed her, in a wonderful manner, how he had endured all those sufferings for her; and lastly, he said, "What then can you do for me which would be enough?" St. Mary Magdalene, that incomparable lover of Jesus Christ crucified, having retired into the famous solitude of St. Baume, and having begged of our Lord to make known to her in what exercise he desired she should chiefly be employed, that so she might become more agreeable to him and thereby daily testify her love to him, our Savior sent an angel to her with a cross in his hand, which he placed at the door of her cell, telling her that she should ever have that cross before her eyes, and that she ought to be continually taken up with the consideration of the mysteries that were wrought upon it. She followed this advice for the space of the thirty-two years she lived afterwards. We read of St. Bridget that, when she was very young, our Savior appeared to her nailed to the cross and quite covered with blood, which he seemed to have then newly shed and from that time she ceased not to meditate on the passion of the Son of God, and shed many tears during her meditations. We likewise read in the life of St. Francis that, having three times opened the Mass book, there to learn evangelical perfection, by a particular providence of God he always opened it at the Passion of Christ, as if God would have thereby said to him: "You seek the means of making yourself perfect. You will become perfect by giving yourself to the contemplation and imitation of my sufferings." To the same end the cross was shown to that holy man seven times, as the pattern which he ought to follow; and, to load him with favors, our Lord appeared to him in the form of a crucified seraph, and imprinted the marks of his five wounds upon him, filling his heart at the same time with the tenderest devotion to his sufferings. It was in the sweet school of the crucifix that St. Francis became a seraph on earth. Whenever he meditated on the sufferings of Jesus Christ, he wept so constantly that in the end he came near losing his sight. One day a person heard him utter the most plaintive cries, and asked him what was the matter. "What is the matter?" said he; "I am weeping over the sufferings and affronts of my Savior, and my grief is increased when I think of the ingratitude of men who do not love him, and who live without thinking of him." Every time he heard a lamb bleat he melted into tears at the remembrance of Jesus, the lamb without spot, who was immolated for the sins of the world. And being all inflamed with love, this holy man could recommend nothing so impressively to his brethren as the frequent remembrance of the Passion of Christ.

The great servant of God, Brother Bernard of Corlien, a Capuchin, did not know how to read, and his fellow-religious wished to teach him. He went to ask advice from the crucifix, and Jesus answered him from the cross: "What necessity for books or reading! I am your book − a book in which you can always read the love I have borne you."

The angels revealed to the Blessed Johanna of the Cross that the divine majesty took such complacency in sorrow for the Passion of Christ, and that such sorrow was so grateful a sacrifice, that it was reckoned equal to the shedding of our blood or the endurance of great afflictions.

St. Bernard declares that the mere thought of our Lord's Passion is a spiritual communion. Father Balthazar Alvarez said that ignorance of the treasures which we possess in Jesus was the cause of the ruin of Christians. Hence, the favorite and most ordinary subject of his meditations was the Passion of Jesus Christ. He dwelt particularly on these three great sufferings of our Lord – his poverty, his humiliations, his agonies. He recommended his penitents to meditate frequently on the Passion of our Savior, and said to them: "We must not think we have done anything until we have reached this point, that we never in our hearts forget Christ crucified." St. Theodore Studita cautions us that, though Easter is come, we must on no account let the memory of the Passion fade away, but keep the life-giving wounds, the cross, and burial always before our eyes.

The Blessed Albertus Magnus used to say that a single tear shed over our Lord's Passion was better than a year's fast on bread and water, with watchings and disciplines. St. Augustine says: "What enkindles, urges, inflames, and drives me to love more than anything else, is the most ignominious and bitter death which thou, O good Jesus, didst endure for the work of redemption. This alone, this altogether, easily claims for itself all our life, all our labor, all our devotion, and, finally, all our love. This, I say, best excites, most sweetly seeks, most amply multiplies our devotion." ("Conf." 2:16). St. Bonaventure says. "Whosoever wishes to increase always in virtue and grace, should meditate without ceasing on the Passion of Jesus; for nothing conduces more to sanctify a soul than the frequent remembrance of the sufferings of Christ." This, too, was the great devotion of our Blessed Lady, as she herself revealed to St. Bridget: "My thoughts and my heart were always in the sepulchre of my Son"; and she bade the saint to be always meditating on his Passion. So successfully did St. Bridget train her daughter Catherine in this devotion that we read in Catherine's life how every night, before going to bed, she spent four hours in succession making genuflections, and beating her breast, with many tears, because of the remembrance of Christ's Passion, offering herself all the while as a holocaust to God.

But what need have we to search for revelations to prove the excellency of the devotion to the Passion of Jesus crucified? Does not Holy Scripture teach us that our Savior thought continually on his Passion and Death? "My sorrow is continually before me" (Ps. 37:18). Do we not read in the Gospel that his Passion was the subject of his discourse to his apostles and disciples, even so far as to speak of it to Moses and Elias in the midst of the glory of his transfiguration on Mount Thabor? And did he not carry with him his five wounds to heaven, to bear before his eyes the marks of his Passion for all eternity?

What shall we say of the great St. Paul? Did he not profess that he knew nothing but Christ crucified? What did he preach but the Passion of Jesus Christ crucified? In what did he glory but in the cross of our dear Savior? What other devotion had he than to be crucified with our Lord Jesus Christ? Jesus crucified is the book which we should often read. From it we learn to fear sin and to love God, who, to cancel sin, suffered so cruel a death, and who, to show us the extent of his love, underwent so many incomprehensible sufferings.

But what method are we to adopt in order to remember easily, and meditate with profit upon, the life and sufferings of our dear Savior? We cannot find and adopt a better method than that which the Blessed Virgin has given us in the Devotion of the Rosary. In the contemplation of the Five Joyful Mysteries, the soul is brought to dwell upon the virtues of the holy infancy of the Savior and the marvelous qualities which drew the favor of heaven upon the Blessed Virgin. In the contemplation of the Sorrowful Mysteries, the soul is inspired with a true spirit of penance, which is one of the characteristics of a good Christian. In the contemplation of the Glorious Mysteries, the soul enters into a divine relation with our Lord Jesus Christ, and arrives at a great union with God. It is thus that the Rosary becomes for the soul a school of perfection, a true and constant nurse of divine charity, the means of her sanctity, and a source of her eternal happiness.

The daughter of a prince went to live with a certain family in which piety was greatly relaxed. There she advanced but little in virtue, although she was a person of pious dispositions. By the advice of a good confessor she began to say the Rosary with the Mysteries, and became so changed that she was an example of virtue and piety to all. The other members of the family, taking offence at her for withdrawing from them, attacked her on all sides to induce her to abandon her newly-begun way of life. One day, while she was saying the Rosary and praying to Mary to assist her in that persecution, she saw a letter fall from above. On the outside were written these words: "Mary, Mother of God, to her daughter Jane, greeting," and within: "My dear child, continue to say my Rosary, withdraw from intercourse with those who do not help you to live well, beware of idleness and vanity, take from thy room whatever is superfluous, and I will be thy protectress with God." A good priest soon after visited that family and tried to reform it, but he did not succeed. One day he saw a great number of demons entering the rooms, except that of Jane, for the divine Mother, before whose image he saw her praying, banished them from her room. When the priest heard from Jane of the Devotion of the Rosary which she practiced, and the letter she had received, he prevailed upon the family to practice the Devotion of the Rosary, and it is related that by means of this devotion all the members of the family became models of virtue. ("Glories of Mary," by St. Alphonsus.)

St. Alphonsus relates also that there was a wicked woman, named Ellen, who entered a church where she heard a sermon on the Rosary. On leaving the church she purchased a pair of beads, but wore them concealed, as she did not wish it to be known that she had them. She began to recite them, and though she said them without devotion she experienced such great sweetness and consolation in her soul that she could not cease repeating the Hail Marys. Not long after she began to feel an extreme horror of her wicked life. She could no longer find peace, and was obliged to go to confession. She confessed her sins with such unusual contrition that the priest was filled with astonishment. After confession she went to the foot of the altar of the Blessed Virgin, where she heard the good Mother address her in these words: "Ellen, you have offended God and me too long; from this moment amend your life, and I will be to you a mother of grace." The poor sinner, in deep confusion, replied: "Ah! most holy Virgin, it is true that hitherto I have been a wicked sinner; but you can do all; help me; I abandon myself to you; I will spend the remainder of my life in doing penance for my sins." With the assistance of Mary, she distributed all her goods to the poor, and began to lead a life of penance. She was tormented with dreadful temptations, but she recommended herself always to the Mother of

God, through whose assistance she always remained victorious. She was favored with many extraordinary graces, with visions, revelations, and even with the gift of prophecy. Finally, before her death, the hour of which was made known to her by Mary, the most Blessed Virgin came herself with her Divine Son to visit her, and when she had expired her soul was seen flying towards heaven in the form of a beautiful dove. ("Glories of Mary," part 1, ch. 2.)

Many are the evil tendencies from which the sacred waters of baptism do not free the soul, and many are the blemishes which still tarnish the soul even after the remission of grievous sins in the sacrament of penance. There remain, for the soul, temporal punishments to be cancelled; there remain, in the soul, a certain lassitude, inconstancy, and discouragement in combating the temptations of the devil, of the world, and of the flesh; there remain a certain proneness to and affection for the vanities of the world, a sovereign horror for suffering, for contempt, and the like. Now, the prayer of the Rosary removes these blemishes from the soul in proportion as she gives herself up to this holy devotion. Witness St. Margaret of Cortona. After her conversion from a very sinful life, she gave herself to the frequent recital of the prayers of the Rosary. Being poor, she was obliged to support herself and child at the washtub. Her work did not prevent her from praying, and her prayer was the Rosary. She repeated the holy Mysteries constantly, and meditated on them. God enlightened her, and showed how good he had always been to her, and how wickedly and ungratefully she had acted towards his goodness. In proportion as she realized this goodness of God and her own ingratitude towards him, she repented more sincerely. In the first instant of her conversion she repented from the imperfect motive of having deserved hell, but she soon began to repent rather for the love of God. She wept over her sins; she conceived a great hatred of the least fault; she even shuddered at the very name of sin; she felt penetrated with the spirit of penance, and was ready to accept any kind of trouble and hardship in order thereby to satisfy the justice of God.

Whilst reciting the prayers of the Rosary, she felt inspired with courage to combat all her enemies, and patiently to endure every cross and trial. From being weak, she became strong; from being indolent and slothful, she became fervent and bold; from being perplexed, she became enlightened; from being sad and cast down, she became joyful; from being effeminate, she became manful; from the tower of the prayers of the Rosary she came forth courageous to brave her disorderly affections, to face the wily attacks of Satan, to set the numerous allurements of the flesh at defiance, and to undertake fearlessly the crucifixion of her body, mind, will, and heart.

In the prayer of the Rosary, she was raised above herself, to her God in heaven, where she saw the vanity of all earthly things, and despised them as mere trifles. There she discovered that only in heaven true riches, honors and pleasures are to be found. She soon ceased to be mortal, not indeed by nature, but by her manner of thinking, speaking, and acting, which was divine, having, as it were, already passed to eternal life; for those who enter into familiarity with God must necessarily become raised above everything transitory and perishable.

By the prayers of the Rosary, she was united to the angelic choirs, who, lost in the contemplation of God, taught her how to forget herself, so that, being penetrated with seraphic happiness and reverential awe at the same time, she was lost to everything earthly, beholding herself standing, as it were, in the midst of the angels and offering with them the same sacrifice of praise. How great was the wisdom, how great the piety, how great the holiness, how great the temperance with which she was filled in the devotion of the Rosary!

In this devotion she was also enlightened as to how all the crosses and sufferings of this world, poverty, sickness, hunger and thirst, privations of all kinds, persecutions, contempt, mockeries, insults, and whatever may be repugnant to human nature, are to be counted as nothing, and are not worthy to be compared with the glory to come that shall be revealed in us.

In the prayers of the Rosary, she was united to God in a manner most wonderful. As one who frequently enjoys the company of a wise, prudent, and learned man, whom he truly loves and esteems, will gradually adopt his manners and his way of speaking, judging, and acting, so also St. Margaret of Cortona, who, by means of the Rosary, conversed often and long with God, received gradually more and more of his divine attributes. She felt so strongly united to God that she wished only what God wishes; nay, her will was so disposed that it could not wish except what God wishes; but to wish what God wishes is already to be like unto God. Hence she was often wrapped in ecstasy, and, regardless of earth and the love of created things, she would exclaim in a transport of delight, "My God and my all! my God and my all!" Her countenance was often seen shining with a heavenly light – a mark of her close union with God – a light whose beams radiated in the shape of horns, to signify that she was not only enlightened in her prayer and familiar intercourse with God, but had also become *cornuta*, – i.e., horned – namely, constant, firm, strong, intrepid, and capable of undergoing every suffering, and of enduring all kinds of hardships, for the glory of God and the salvation of souls.

It was by constantly saying the Rosary that she was introduced into this happy country of the interior life – a country overflowing with milk and honey. Here she learned more of God in one moment than by reading all the books in the world; she spoke to God and God spoke to her, in a manner inexplicable, enkindling in her that strong, ardent, and seraphic love for himself which made St. Paul exclaim: "Who, then, shall separate us from the love of Christ? Shall tribulations? or distress? or famine? or nakedness? Or danger? or persecution? or the sword? I am sure that neither death, nor life, nor angels, nor principalities, nor powers, nor things present, nor things to come, nor might, nor height, nor depth, nor any other creature shall be able to separate us from the love of God, which is in Christ Jesus our Lord" (Rom. 8:35-39). Who, after all this, will remain still cold, careless, and indifferent in the practice of the devotion of the holy Rosary? Most assuredly he only who is not of God and loves darkness more than light?

CHAPTER 9

THE ROSARY: THE DEVOTION OF CHILDREN

We read in Holy Scripture that Agar was wandering in the sandy deserts of Arabia with her little boy Ismael. She could find no water in the deserts. When the water in the bottle was finished, she placed the little boy under one of the trees and went a great way off from him, saying, I will not see the boy die of thirst. Then she sat down and lifted her voice, and began to cry for the poor dying boy. Whereupon an angel of God called to Agar from heaven, and said: "What art thou doing, Agar? Fear not, *for God hath heard the voice of the boy.* Arise, take up the boy!....And God opened her eyes, and she saw a well of water, and went and filled the bottle, and gave the boy to drink" (Gen. 21:17-19). So God heard the voice, *not of the mother, but of the child,* and he gave them water to drink. Thus does God hear the prayers of children.

There is a feeling, common to all people, that the prayer of children is all-powerful with God. We know this from the revelation of God himself: "Out of the mouths of infants thou has perfected praise" (Ps. 8.)

In a town called Bethulia the church was one day full of children. What was the cause? Soldiers were on their road to this town to kill the people. The people knew that God hears the prayers of children, for they had read in the Holy Scriptures "that out of the mouths of infants comes forth perfect praise of God." So they made all the children go into the church, and bow their heads down to the ground and pray for the people. God heard the prayers of the children. He made the cruel soldiers go away, and the people were saved by the children's prayers.

Dear little child, if you have parents who do not lead a good life, God looks to you for their conversion. But what can you do? The good example of a child speaks to the heart of a parent. Then there is prayer

– will God turn a deaf ear to the prayer of a child praying for the conversion of its father or mother? No; the Hail Mary which you say every day for their conversion, the prayer you say for them each time you hear Mass, the Holy Communions you offer for them, the sighs of your heart, all rise up, before God, and are not forgotten by him; and the day will come when God will send down from heaven the grace of conversion into the hearts of your parents.

During one of our missions, a certain child knelt down every night to say three Our Fathers and three Hail Marys for the conversion of his father. One night, towards the end of the mission, when the child was again kneeling down and praying, the father said: "Child, what are you doing there?" "Father," replied the child," "I am praying for your conversion." At that moment the father felt touched by the grace of God. Next day he went to church, made a good confession, and was reconciled with God. Thus it was by the prayer of this good child that God was moved to bestow the grace of conversion upon his father.

God often makes use of children to convert others. Louis Veuillot, editor of *L'Univers*, in Paris, gave the following account of his conversion: "I had been brought up," he said, "in ignorance of the truth, with no respect for religion, and hating the Catholic Church. I had a little child, which was wild, passionate, and stupid. I was cross and severe to this child. Sometimes my wife used to say to me: 'Wait a little; the child will be better when it makes its First Communion.' I did not believe it. However, the child began to go to catechism. From that time it became obedient, respectful, and affectionate. I thought I would go myself to hear the instructions on the catechism, which had made such a wonderful change in my child. I went, and I heard truths which I had never heard before. My feelings towards the child were changed. It was not so much love as respect I began to feel for the child. I was inferior to it. It was better and wiser than I was. The week for the First Communion was come. There were but five or six days remaining. One morning the child returned from Mass, and came into a room where I was alone. 'Father,' said the child, 'the day of my First Communion is coming. I cannot go to the altar without asking your blessing and forgiveness for all the faults I leave committed and the pain I have often given you. Think well of my faults, and scold me for them all, that I may commit them no more.' 'My child,' I answered, 'a father forgives everything.' The child looked at me with tears in its eyes, and threw its arms round my neck. 'Father,' said the child again, 'I have something else to ask you.' I knew well – my conscience told me – what the child was going to ask; I was afraid, and said: 'Go away now; you can ask me tomorrow.' The poor child did not know what to say, so it left me, and went sorrowfully into its own little room, where it had an altar with an image of the Blessed Virgin upon it. I felt sorry for what I had said; so I got up and walked softly on the tips of my feet to the room of my child. The door was a little open; I looked at the child; it was on its knees before the Blessed Virgin, *praising with all its heart for its father.* Truly, at that moment I knew what one must feel at the sight of an angel. I went back to my room, and leaned my head on my hands. I was ready to cry. I heard a slight sound, and raised my eyes – my child was standing before me; on its face there was fear, with firmness and love. 'Father,' said the child, 'I cannot put off till tomorrow what I have to ask you – I ask you, on the day of my First Communion, to come to the Holy Communion along with mamma and me.' I burst into tears, and threw my arms around the child's neck, and said: 'Yes, my child, yes, this very day you shall take me by the hand and lead me to your confessor, and say, Here is father.'" So this child also obtained, by its prayer, the grace of conversion for its father.

You may ask why is it that the prayer of little children is so powerful with God? It is because they are innocent, and God willingly hears the prayer of an innocent heart. When our dear Savior lived on earth, he embraced the little children; he laid his hands upon them, and he blessed them. He rebuked those who tried to prevent them from being presented to him, that he might bless them. He said, "Suffer the little ones to come unto me, and forbid them not; for of such is the kingdom of God" (Mk.10:13-16). Now, children go to Jesus, if they pray to Jesus; and Jesus never lets them go away without having blessed them-that is to say, without having heard their prayers.

There is one prayer which is particularly pleasing to God if it is said by children; it is the prayer of the Rosary. God sent the Blessed Virgin eighteen times to a child who liked to say the beads.

Bernadette Soubirous, of Lourdes, was in 1858 a little girl of fourteen, humble amongst the humbler of this world. This child hid a treasure which God guarded; and the treasure was the innocence of her soul. Simple, childish, extremely docile, very affectionate, all was candor in her looks, speech, and face. She had a horror of sin, and faults committed in her presence pained her. She often scolded her sister for not caring to pray, for her abruptness and her rough ways. During prayer her posture was always very respectful; she never leaned against anything; she was inclined to recollection. Notwithstanding her ignorance, the simple child prayed much. She loved prayer, although as yet she only knew the Rosary. With her poor beads, she often spoke during the day to the Blessed Virgin Mary. The Virgin, Mother of God, loved Bernadette, let her grow humble and pious, and waited for her. One day the parish priest met her; the child's air of innocence and candor made a deep impression on him. He saluted her with a sort of respect; and going back to look at her again, he said to himself: "The children to whom the Blessed Virgin appeared on the mountain of La Salette must have been like this little one."

On the 11th of February, 1858, Bernadette accompanied her little sister and a neighbor, who were going to look for dead wood. Whilst sitting down before a grotto, she beheld a wonderful apparition at the end of the grotto. In the midst of a dazzling light, but sweet and peaceful like everything heavenly, a Lady admirably beautiful appeared to the eyes of the child. She was clad in a long white robe, which was fastened at the waste by a flaming azure girdle. A large, plain white veil, like the dress, covered her head and shoulders and whole body, reaching to the ground. Her hands were clasped on her breast as if in silent prayer; she held a long Rosary, as white as snow, whose beads seemed joined by a chain of glittering gold; a beautiful golden cross hung from the Rosary.

The countenance of the Apparition was of ineffable beauty. It breathed at once majesty, innocence, goodness, peace, and tenderness. From the midst of the light the beautiful Lady smiled most sweetly on Bernadette. She seemed to salute her with her hands, and kindly bent her head.

Bernadette instinctively sought in her pocket, took out her Rosary, and attempted to make the sign of the cross; but her hand felt powerless, a certain uneasiness took possession of her. At that moment the Lady took, with her right hand, the cross of the Rosary, made the sign of the cross, and by a smile of ineffable kindness seemed to say to the child: Do as I do. The Lady clasped her hands and passed the beads of her Rosary between her fingers. Bernadette said the beads.

The Sunday following, Bernadette and some other children went again to the grotto. "Let us kneel down," said Bernadette, "and say our beads." The holy prayer had no sooner begun than the radiant Lady was there before the child as on the first time, surrounded with splendor, with smiling face, and the beautiful white and gold Rosary passing silently through her fingers. "Look!" said Bernadette, "look! there she is! Oh! see, she smiles, and she salutes me." Bernadette knelt down, made the sign of the cross, and began to say the Rosary. The Blessed Virgin received the child's prayer and showed herself to her, continuing to pass through her sacred hands the beads of her Rosary. The heavenly Apparition disappeared almost always at the instant when the favored little one had finished her Rosary. So appeared the Immaculate Virgin to Bernadette the eighteen times that she deigned to appear in the favored grotto of Lourdes.

In appearing thus continually to little Bernadette, the Blessed Virgin daily took more powerful possession of the innocent child, prepared her for her mission, and disposed the people, by the oft-repeated miracle of this quiet ecstasy, to receive her as the messenger of her will. The Blessed Mother of God repeatedly told the child to pray for the conversion of sinners, and request others to pray for their conversion; to kiss the ground for the conversion of sinners. "Penance!" she said, "penance! penance!"

The heart of Mary was revealed. It was sinners whom she called by Bernadette's prayer and humiliation. It was sinners she also sought by the many miracles which were to be performed in that favored grotto.

In one of the apparitions the Blessed Virgin told Bernadette "to drink and wash herself at the spring." She looked round her in astonishment. There was no spring in the grotto; there never had been one. Not finding it, and wishing to obey, she told her embarrassment to the heavenly Lady by a glance. In obedience to another sign, the child bent down, and, scraping the earth with her little hands, began to make a hollow in the ground. All at once a mysterious water came out beneath the hand of the child of Mary, and soon filled the little hollow. Mingling with the earth, it was quite muddy, and poor Bernadette drank the muddy water and bathed her face with it. Next day the Blessed Virgin's fountain, visibly increasing, flowed already a finger's breadth. At the end of a few days it gushed out of the earth, pure and limpid, about as broad as a child's arm.

With her feeble hand Bernadette had unconsciously opened the source of cures and of miracles. The attention of the public was drawn to these heavenly apparitions and to the water that miraculously issued from the grotto of Lourdes. All kinds of diseases have been cured by the use of that miraculous water.

Those repeated apparitions of the Blessed Virgin are very significant in their circumstances. She appears to an innocent child to show that we must endeavor to become more and more innocent every day. She appears to a child saying her beads, and her apparition vanishes at the end of the Rosary, to teach us how pleasing this devotion is to God and to her, especially when practiced by children. She always appears with the beautiful white and gold Rosary in her hands joined in prayer, to teach us all to love and practice this devotion. She asks of the child to pray for poor sinners and do penance for them, and ask others to do the same, to give us to understand that God's anger, so justly enkindled against sinners, will be appeased if the just as well as sinners practice the devotion of the Rosary and join good works with their prayer. The Blessed Virgin appears in a grotto, in a retired place, to show us the necessity of withdrawing from the wicked world and its pleasures and amusements, and attending principally to prayer as the great means of salvation. She causes water to flow from the grotto, by which all kinds of diseases of the body have been cured, to teach us anew what she taught St. Dominic – viz., that the devotion of the Rosary is a fountain of healing water for all kinds of diseases, especially for those of the soul. At first the water was muddy, and after a while it became quite limpid, to show that from a soul quite muddy with sin, soon after it has begun the practice of the Rosary, the muddy water, as it were, of imperfect contrition, comes forth by degrees, continuing to flow more and more purified and in greater abundance in proportion as the sinner perseveres in the devout recital of the Rosary. All, especially parents, who reflect on the meaning of those apparitions of the Blessed Virgin, cannot help saying to themselves: "God and his blessed Mother wish us to practice the Rosary as a family devotion, and teach it to our children as soon as they are able to learn the Our Father and the Hail Mary; for then the Mother of God will love them and us, and preserve us from harm in body and soul."

There is a Catholic mother whose child is yet young and innocent. In the holy sacrament of baptism it has become a living temple of the Holy Ghost – a child of God and heir of heaven. It is now an angel, but will it always remain an angel? It is now the joy of her soul, but will it always be to her a source of joy and happiness? Now she loves to press her child to her heart; but the day may come when this very child will cause her heart to bleed, will cause her poor heart to break for very grief and pain. Her eyes now beam with joy as she looks on her child. She seems never to weary of gazing on it; but perhaps the day will come when those very eyes of hers will be filled with tears, bitter, burning tears, and she will weep tears of blood over her wayward child!

She now loves to press her lips again and again to the cheek of her innocent child, but the day may yet come when her lips will tremble with rage and pain, and she will curse the day on which that child was born!

She now loves to sing to her child, and to lull it to sleep, but the day may come when her song of gladness will be changed into sad wailing, and she will only know how to make bitter complaints against her profligate child.

She now loves to carry her child in her arms; her hands seem never to grow weary of serving it; but perhaps the day will come when those very hands of hers will be condemned to hard labor, and even to the beggar's staff, and this child of hers will be her cruel taskmaster.

Now she fondles and caresses her child; she loves to see it reposing on her bosom; but the day may come when she will bless God a thousand times that she can at length lay it in the bosom of the earth, in the cold, dark grave.

Often, and in the lone, silent hours of night, she fondly fancies to herself that she sees her child already grown up; she fondly hopes that he will be her comfort in her old age, that he will grow rich and learned, and be an honor to her name; but perhaps this very child whom she now nourishes with such tender care will become a disgrace to his fellowmen; perhaps he will die a death of shame and find a dishonored grave!

She nourishes and watches over him now with all the tender anxiety of a mother's love, but perhaps she only nourishes him to become one day the food of the birds of prey, and to be mangled and trodden to death beneath the hoofs of maddened horses on the blood stained battlefield. "O God!" she says, "is this possible? Can this really happen to my child?" And why not? Has it not happened to hundreds of others in our day and country? Was there ever a mother that nursed her child and thought that he would one day hang upon the gallows? And what has happened to so many others, may it not also happen to you and to your child?

Oh! were God to lift the veil of futurity, could you behold the eyes of lurking demons lying in wait to ruin your children by means of secret societies, godless education, bad example, and a thousand other means, you would see the necessity of placing them daily under the special protection of the Blessed Mother of God; you would see that in our day and country it is more than ever necessary to teach them to love Mary, to be devout to Mary, to pray to Mary, and to call on her in every danger; you would see the necessity of teaching them especially, by word and example, to love and practice the holy devotion of the Rosary. To bequeath this devotion to them is to make them rich enough, for then Mary will watch over them as a mother, and guard and guide them until you see them one day united to you again in heaven.

A priest was called one night to administer the sacraments to a young man who had led a very dissolute life. He had received a stroke of apoplexy, and was quite unconscious when the priest arrived. As it was after midnight, the priest went in haste to say Mass for him. After Mass, a messenger arrived, stating that the young man had come to himself again. The priest hastened back to him, found him filled with most hearty contrition, and generously offering up his life in atonement for his sins. The young man made his confession and received the sacraments with unusual devotion. The priest, astonished and touched at such an evident grace, asked the young man how he had merited so signal a favor after such a sinful life. "Ah! father," replied the young man, with a voice broken by sobs, "it is purely the effect of God's mercy. I can only attribute it to your prayers and to those of my good mother. When my mother was about to die, she called me to her bedside and expressed her fears at the dangers I would have to encounter in the world. She then said to me '1 leave you under the protection of the Blessed Virgin Mary. I have a slight favor to ask of you; it is a pledge of the love that you bear to your dying mother. Promise me that you will recite the Rosary daily.' I promised it on my knees. I have kept my promise, and I confess that for these ten years it is the only religion I have performed." The priest saw clearly that it was this persevering devotion to Mary, this perseverance in reciting the holy Rosary, that had obtained for him that most desirable grace – the grace of a happy death, the grace of being joined to his dear mother in heaven.

In the bright land of fair Provence
A lowly orphan dwelt,
And day by day at Mary's shrine
The little maiden knelt.

No watchful mother's tender care
The child had ever known;
And so, the simple peasant folk
Had called her Mary's own.

And as among the woods and fields
The little orphan grew,
The old church-windows' storied panes
Were all the books she knew.

And surely, for Our Lady's child,
No better books could be;
For of her Mother's life they showed
Each wondrous mystery.

And never passed a day, whate'er
The orphan's task might be,
But at Our Lady's feet she knelt
To say the Rosary.

But once it chanced that, wearied out,
She sought her humble bed,
Forgetting quite that she had left
Her Rosary unsaid.

When, lo! within her little room
She saw a wondrous light;
And by her bed Our Lady stood
In robes most fair and bright.

She knew her by the twelve bright stars
The radiant brow that crowned,
And by the mantle, azure blue,
With fairest roses bound.

The child knelt down, while love and awe
Her wondering spirit fill;
When, lo! upon Our Lady's robe
A rose is wanting still.

And softly, sweetly Mary spoke:
"My child, these roses see,
The fragrant wreath that love hath twined
From day to day for me.

"But wherefore hast thou left undone
The work of love to-day?"
How comes it that thou hast forgot
My Rosary to say?

"So many on the great, wide earth
Forget their Lord and me,
And bring no flowers; but surely thou
Wilt not unfaithful be?"

The little child bowed down her head
In shame upon her breast,
And, ere Our Blessed Lady left,
With tears her fault confessed,

And, kneeling, said the Rosary;
But ever from that day
The child drooped slowly, like a flower
That fades from earth away,

As though she could not linger here –
To whom it had been given
To see Our Lady, and to have
That moment's glimpse of heaven.

And pilgrims to Our Lady's shrine
Would often go to see
Her grave whom Mary's self had taught
To say the Rosary.

From the Ave Maria.

CHAPTER 10

THE ROSARY: THE DEVOTION OF SINNERS

One day our dear Savior went to a city called Naim; and when he came nigh to the city, behold, a dead man was carried out, the only son of his mother, and she was a widow; and many people of the city were with her. And when our Lord saw her he had compassion on her, and said to her: "Weep not." And he went near the bier and said: "Young man, I say to thee, Arise." And the young man sat up and began to speak. And Jesus took him to his mother (Lk. 7:12-15). The good widow, overjoyed, thanked and glorified God for his goodness.

Our dear Savior goes about still in the persons of good priests, good Brothers, devoted Sisters, pious Christians. They meet with many who are dead to the grace and friendship of God, who have been living in the dark night of sin almost from the moment that they were first capable of sinning. Their passions are their rule of life. The devil, who is their master, drags them down from one abyss of sin into another. Like a child who has lost its parents and protectors, the sinner feels helpless and abandoned. Oh! would to God, he cries, that I were free from this accursed habit of drinking, of swearing, of sinning against the holy virtue of purity. What am I to do? Ah! there is no hope of salvation for me. At last he gives himself up to despair, he grows hardened in sin, he becomes like an incarnate devil. He sins, although he sees hell open before him. All the powers on earth are not able to touch his heart or to induce him to do penance. There is but one power that can soften that hard heart and fill those eyes with tears of repentance; and that power is the power of Almighty God. This power is at our disposal. God does not wish the sinner's death, but that he be converted and live. The conversion of sinners is, undoubtedly, one of the most praiseworthy objects for which we can pray. Our Lord Jesus Christ taught us in the "Our Father" to pray not only for ourselves but also for all our fellow-men. By his example he taught us also to pray for others. Indeed, we may say that his whole life was a continual prayer, for the just as well as for sinners. "And not for them only (the Apostles) do I pray, but for them also who, through their word, shall believe in me, that they all may be one, as thou, Father, in me and I in thee, that they also may be one in us, that the world may believe that thou hast sent me" (Jn. 17:20-21). While hanging on the cross and suffering the most excruciating pains our dear Lord prayed for the greatest sinners and his most bitter enemies."Father, forgive them, for they know not what they do" (Lk. 23:34). To imitate this example of our Savior, we should also often recommend to God all poor sinners, schismatics, heretics, and infidels.

Remarkable instances of sinners leaving their evil ways and returning to God occur every day. No doubt their conversion is owing to the prayers of the just; "for God willingly hears the prayer of a Christian," says St. John Chrysostom, "not only when he prays for himself, but also when he prays for sinners. Necessity obliges us to pray for ourselves, but charity must induce us to pray for others. The prayer of fraternal charity is more acceptable to God than that of necessity" (Chrysost. Hom. XIV., Oper. Imper. in Matt.) "The prayer for sinners," says St. Alphonsus, "is not only beneficial to them, but is, moreover, most pleasing to God; and the Lord himself complains of his servants who do not recommend sinners to him." He said one day to St. Mary Magdalen of Pazzi: "See my daughter, how the Christians are in the devil's hands; if my elect did not deliver them by their prayers, they would be devoured."

Inflamed with holy zeal by these words, this saint used to offer to God the Blood of the Redeemer fifty times a day in behalf of sinners. "Ah!" she used to exclaim, "how great a pain it is, O Lord! to see how one could help thy creatures by dying for them, and not be able to do so!" In every one of her spiritual exercises she recommended sinners to God, and it is related in her life that she scarcely spent an hour in the day without praying for them; she even frequently arose in the middle of the night to go before the Blessed Sacrament to offer prayers for them. She went so far as to desire to endure even the pains of hell for their conversion, provided she could still love God in that place, and God responded to her wish by inflicting on her most violent pains and infirmities for the salvation of sinners;

and yet after all this she shed bitter tears, thinking she did nothing for their conversion. "Ah! Lord, make me die," she often exclaimed, "and return to life again as many times as is necessary to satisfy thy justice for them." God, as is related in her life, did not fail to give the grace of conversion to many sinners on account of her fervent prayers. "Souls," says St. Alphonsus, "that really love God will never neglect to pray for poor sinners."

How could it be possible for a person who really loves and knows his ardent love for our souls, and how much he wishes us to pray for sinners, and how much Jesus Christ has done and suffered for their salvation – how could it be possible for such a one, I say, to behold with indifference so many poor souls deprived of God's grace without feeling moved frequently to ask God to give light and strength to these wretched beings, in order that they may come out of the miserable state of spiritual death in which they are slumbering? It is true God has not promised to grant our petitions in behalf of those who put a positive obstacle in the way of their conversion; yet God, in his goodness, has often deigned, through the prayers of his servants, to bring back the most blind and obstinate sinners to the way of salvation by means of extraordinary graces. Therefore we should never fail to recommend poor sinners to God in all our spiritual exercises; moreover, he who prays for others will experience that his prayers for himself will be heard much sooner. In the life of St. Margaret of Cortona we read that she prayed more than a hundred times a day for the conversion of sinners; and, indeed, so numerous were their conversions that the Franciscan Fathers complained to her of not being able to hear the confessions of all those who were converted by her prayers.

The Curé of Ars, who died in the odor of sanctity, relates the following in one of his catechetical instructions: "A great lady, of one of the first families in France, was here, and she went away this morning. She is rich, very rich, and scarcely twenty-three. She has offered herself to God for the conversion of sinners and the expiation of sin. She mortifies herself in a thousand ways, wears a girdle all armed with iron points; her parents know nothing of it; she is as white as a sheet of paper" ("Spirit of the Curé of Ars").

The same saintly pastor said one day to a priest who complained of not being able to change the hearts of his parishioners for the better: "You prayed, you wept, you sighed; but did you fast also? Did you deprive yourself of sleep? Did you sleep on the bare ground? Did you scourge yourself? Do not think you have done all if you have not yet done these penances."

If we do not love poor sinners that much, if we think it above our strength to perform similar penitential works for their conversion, let us at least do something; let us often say the Rosary for them, and thus offer to God the merits, the prayers, the tears, and blood of Jesus Christ for their conversion.

We read in Exodus (Ex. 32:20) that the Jews, notwithstanding the astounding miracles which God wrought in their behalf when freeing them from the galling yoke of Egyptian tyranny, fell into the most heinous crime of idolatry. Angered by so great an offense, the Lord resolved to blot out this ungrateful people from the face of the earth. He was on the point of pouring out his wrath upon them, when Moses, the faithful servant of God, interceded for them. "Why, O Lord!" said he to God, "why is thy indignation aroused against thy people whom thou hast brought out of the land of Egypt with great power and a mighty hand? Let not the Egyptians boast, I beseech thee: He craftily brought them out that he might kill them in the mountains and efface them from the face of the earth; let thy anger cease, and be appeased upon the waywardness of thy people." And "the Lord was appeased" by the prayer of Moses, "and did not the evil which he had spoken against his people." If God was appeased by the prayer of Moses, let us rest assured that by the prayer of the Rosary his wrath against sinners will also be appeased on account of the Life and Death which, in this devotion, we offer him for the conversion of sinners. Lancisius tells us "that the offering of the Blood of Christ, or of his Passion and Death, to the Eternal Father, or to Christ himself, in order to appease him for the sins of the world, is of boundless efficacy." This practice was taught by God to St. Mary Magdalen of Pazzi, when he vouchsafed to complain to her that there were so few in the world who made any effort to appease his anger against sinners.

Once, in a rapture, she cried out: "As often as the creature offers this Blood, by which it is redeemed, it offers a gift which has no price that can be paid back for it. Nay, the gift is so great that the Eternal Father reckons himself under obligation to his creatures; for he sees it in its misery, which his infinite goodness desires to compassionate, compassionating to communicate himself to it; and thus this offering is the cause of his communicating now, and for ever continuing to communicate, his goodness to his creature."

"This devotion," says Lancisius, "glorifies and recreates God with the most excellent and noble of all offerings. It asks, or rather in a certain sense exacts, for our past sins remission, preservation from sin in time to come, the conversion of sinners and heretics, and freedom from the temporal pain due to sin."

St. Vincent de Paul was once told that a dying man despaired of his salvation on account of his many grievous sins. He went immediately to see him and encourage him to hope in God's mercy. "My dear brother," said he, "you know that Jesus Christ died to save your soul. How can you, then, despair of his mercy? This sin is more displeasing to him than the sins of your whole life." In reply to this, the unhappy man said: "I wish to die a reprobate to displease Christ still more." "And I wish," answered the compassionate pries – " I wish to save you from hell, in order to give pleasure to Jesus Christ." St. Vincent invited all the standers-by to say the Rosary with him to obtain the grace of repentance for the dying man. Their prayer was heard. The heart of the sinner was changed, he repented of his sins and confessed them with deep sorrow, and soon after died in peace and with great confidence in the mercy of God (Schmid's "Hist. Catech.," Vol 1, p 342).

Ah! how powerful is the prayer of the Rosary for the conversion of sinners! This power, however, is still greater and perceived much sooner if the sinner himself begins to practice this devotion. Hardly has he begun it than he experiences that secret influence which the Blessed Virgin exerts hourly over the hearts of men, over human passions and motives of action, over the invisible enemies of our salvation. Gradually the devil loses his power over him, his temptations grow weaker, confidence in God's mercy is restored, tears of repentance flow, an irresistible desire takes him to confession, the absolution of the priest restores him to the grace of God, and the kiss of peace is given him in Holy Communion. Yes, all this will come true, even in the worst of sinners, soon after he has begun to practice the devotion of the Rosary. This prayer gives free access to the spiritual treasures of God; it causes them to flow streams upon sinners, and to work wonderful changes in their souls. By this prayer sinners are changed from enemies into friends of God, from reprobates into chosen vessels of election, from children of the devil into children of God, from heirs of hell into heirs of heaven.

In Saragossa there lived a nobleman named Peter, a relative of St. Dominic, but a most wicked man. One day whilst the saint was preaching he saw Peter enter the church. He begged our Lord to show to the congregation the miserable state of his relative's soul. In an instant Peter appeared as a monster from hell, surrounded and dragged about by many devils. Every one, even his wife, who was in the church, and the servants who accompanied him, began to fly. St. Dominic then sent him word by a companion that he should recommend himself to Mary and begin to recite the Rosary. Upon receiving the message Peter humbled himself, and then saw, to his great horror, the devils who surrounded him. Without delay he went to confess his sins with many tears to the saint, from whom he received the assurance that God had forgiven him. He persevered in saying the Rosary, and ever afterwards led a most edifying life (Cartag. "De Area Deip." c. 19, 114).

In 1858 there lived in Philadelphia a young lady who had gone so far in her wickedness as to commit the most heinous crimes, no longer through weakness, but out of pure hatred of God. Her accomplice had died suddenly in the very act of a most shameful sin, and afterwards appeared to her enveloped in flames of fire. From that time forward she felt in herself as it were an inward burning so intense that she imagined herself in hell, and uttered most frightful cries. This punishment, far from making her repent of her sinful life, served only to increase her hatred of God. For three months she did nothing but pour forth the most execrable blasphemies against God, the blessed

Mother of God, and the saints. The sins which she committed during that time are so enormous that the mere recital of them would make one shudder with horror. So impious a wretch, it may be thought, could never be converted. But, O the wonderful power of the Rosary! The sinner of our story had a lady friend who had heard an instruction on the Rosary, and, full of confidence in the intercession of the Blessed Virgin, she gave her own Rosary to her friend, begging her to recite it. She took it and put it in her pocket. Two days afterwards she began to recite it, and her conversion was accomplished. At that time some of our Fathers gave a mission in Philadelphia. She went to one of them to make her confession. Her sorrow for her sins was so great that she could hardly speak in the confessional. She requested her confessor to make known the great mercy which God had shown her after having said the beads a few times.

It may he asked, Why is it that a sinner receives the grace of conversion soon after he has begun to practice the devotion of the Rosary? I answer: When saying the Rosary, the sinner naturally thinks of the life of his Savior; he remembers and reflects on his sufferings. Now, to remember the Passion of his Savior, to meditate on it whilst praying, is to present one's self before the Heavenly Father, with all the merits of his well beloved Son; he thus appeases the wrath of the Heavenly Father and regains his favor; for though God the Father be angry with the sinner, casting his eyes upon Jesus Christ crucified, he sees a Son, infinitely worthy of being heard – a Son equal to himself in power, wisdom, and holiness; a Son infinitely amiable, who offers to him his divine Life in sacrifice, who shed all his blood for the reparation of his honor; and the Heavenly Father sees himself thus infinitely more honored by this magnificent reparation than he had been dishonored by the sins of the world. Hence God the Father never beholds a sinner devoted to the sufferings of Jesus Christ without the utmost complacency; he is moved with compassion towards him, and feels himself forced, as it were, to love him and grant him the grace of true repentance.

In Rome there was a woman known by the name of "Catherine the Fair," whose life was very unedifying. One day she went to hear a sermon of St. Dominic. The subject of the sermon was the Rosary.

Deeply impressed by the words of the saint, she had her name enrolled in the Confraternity of the Rosary, and began to practice the devotion, but without changing her life. One evening she was visited by a young man of noble mien. She received him very courteously. Whilst they were at supper she remarked that, as he was cutting bread, drops of blood trickled from his hands, and that there was blood on all the food he took. She asked him what was the meaning of this. The young man replied that "the food of a Christian should be tinged with the blood of Jesus Christ, and seasoned with the remembrance of his Passion." Astonished at this answer, Catherine asked him who he was. "Later," he said, "I will tell you." Then, going into an adjoining room, the appearance of the young man changed: he was crowned with thorns, his flesh mangled and torn; and he said: "Do you wish to know who I am? Do you not recognize me? I am your Redeemer. O Catherine! when will you cease offending me? See what I have endured for you. You have grieved me long enough; change your life." Catherine burst into sobs and tears. Jesus encouraged her, saying: "Love me now as much as you have offended me. Know that I have granted you this grace on account of the Rosary by which you have honored me and my Mother." Jesus then disappeared. Next morning Catherine went to confession to St. Dominic, gave all she had to the poor, and ever afterward led a holy life. Our Blessed Lady often appeared to her, and our dear Savior revealed to St. Dominic that this penitent had become very dear to him (Diotall. tom. 3. Domen. Quinquag.)

In the neighborhood of Caposelle, a town of Italy, there lived in 1718 a wretched sinner who had for three years been confined to bed by a most painful illness. Every night he saw the devil, under the form of a goat, place himself on his breast, and press his throat and his sides until he was almost choked. One morning when he awoke he saw the Blessed Virgin appear in his chamber, radiant with glory, and accompanied by two angels. "My son," she said to him, "how hast thou still the boldness to continue to live in sin? Quick! change your life; tomorrow thou shalt see my children of the house of *Mater Domini*. Repent of thy sins and confess them, and Jesus will pardon thee." The vision disappeared, and the sinner felt encouraged to hope for pardon, but without knowing what to think of the vision.

Next day he heard the bells ringing, and, on asking what it was, he was told that the Missionaries of Alphonsus de Liguori had arrived. Full of joy, he said he must see one of them without delay. Father Matthew Criscuolo went to see him, and heard his confession amid torrents of tears. The father, on hearing of the vision, asked him if he had been in the habit of practicing some devotion in honor of the Blessed Virgin. "I have made a vow," replied the sinner, "to recite the Rosary daily, and I have never omitted this devotion." He died during the mission, giving evident signs of true repentance ("Life of St. Alphonsus," Vol. 1 Ch. 25).

But there is no necessity of going back to the times of St. Dominic or St. Alphonsus to find examples of the power of the Rosary for the conversion of sinners. Such examples are of daily occurrence among ourselves. The Very Rev. Father Parke, of Parkersburg, VA., sent me the following account of the conversion of Joseph Eisele, alias Shofer, who was arrested in the act of murdering his fourth man: "I attended the murderer Joseph Eisele, who was hanged here for the murder of three men. At first he sulked and was reticent. I sent him a mission book and a pair of beads. When I next called, he burst out into tears, avowed his crimes, and resolved to confess all publicly. His remaining days were consistent with this beginning. What divine grace and the mission book began, the Rosary fortified and brought to maturity. The Rosary beads from the fourth day of his prison life were his armor and his constant solace. Except when writing his confessions or taking a brief repose, he was ever found saying the beads. His cell was an iron cage in the center of a large room -- itself a prison. In this room, around his cage, stalked harlots, drunkards, and other hardened creatures. A week before his execution, Satan put it into the hearts of some of those abandoned women to strike up a sympathy with him. The man of sorrow (for such he now was) was at his Rosary when this assault was made on him. 'Begone! poor creature,' said he, 'begone! I am a most unhappy man, and deserve the wrath of God; but, sad as my fate is, yours is worse, unless, like me, you repent and turn yourselves to God.

"Another lure of Satan was equally upset by Mary's power. Who would believe that, amidst dispositions so brave and so holy,

Satan had still a lien on this his lifelong victim. Yet so it was. To my horror, a short time before his death, one morning the prisoner, with a face brighter than usual, advanced to meet me. 'I have good news for you, father,' said he, 'very good news today.' 'What is it?' replied I. 'Do you see' (pointing to a piece of strong bed cord on the floor), 'do you see that rope there?' 'What of it? how came it there?' Can it be, said I in my own mind, that despair and Satan have again been at work on this wretched soul? 'I will tell you all,' said the convict. 'Not till last night did I see it was a sin for me to carry stealthily that rope in my pocket. When first immured here, I found it in the cell, rejoiced at my good luck, and have preserved it till now, for I know not what use it be put to, in case I should feel pushed to extremity.' In plain words, to hang himself with, under Satan's dictation.

"Another proof of the depth of the contrition of this great sinner was his desire to suffer death, even on the gallows, and the joy he thence derived, as thereby he would no longer in future be in a position to offend so good a God. How sincere he was in this was seen in his refusal to cooperate for his own escape, when help was tendered him by some of his fellow prisoners who effected their escape. Eisele, who had been consistent in crime, was now consistent also in his conversion, because he persevered to the last in saying the beads."

What encouragement must not all poor sinners draw from these examples to return to God with confidence! I repeat what I have said above. Let the life of a sinner have been ever so wicked, ever so full of crimes, if he begins to say the beads, he will soon be delivered from the chains of his sins and endowed with the liberty of the children of God.

The pious Queen Blanche, mother of St. Louis, King of France, was one day passing by a prison: one of the prisoners besought her for his liberty in most pitiable accents. "It is not in my power," said the queen, "to release you from your prison, but I will intercede with the king for you that he may grant you this favor." Thereupon she went to her son, begging him to accompany her to an unhappy prisoner. "My son," said the queen, upon arriving at the prisoner's cell, "my son, pardon this unhappy man for my sake, and release him from his imprisonment." "I pardon you," said the holy king to the captive; "but I assure you were it not for my mother you would not have lived to see another day. Be always grateful to her."

Jesus Christ says the same to us all: "Thousands of sinners would never have been released from the captivity of sin, from the slavery of the passions, from the bondage of the evil spirits, had it not been for the prayers of my Mother; but because they began to practice the devotion of the Rosary, from being enemies of mine they became my dearest friends and most beloved children."

Isaias had prophesied that God would prepare his throne in mercy. But what throne has God established in mercy? St. Bonaventure replies that the throne of the divine mercy is Mary, the Mother of Mercy, in whom all men find the relief of mercy. As a fond mother who sees her child weeping or suffering from a wound, so the tender Mother Mary never desists from her supplications to her Son in favor of the sinner, until the wounds made in his soul by sin are bound up and healed. Who ever invoked Mary without being heard? Who ever craved her patronage and received a refusal? It appears to be an established law of Providence that mercy shall be shown to all those for whom Mary intercedes. The law of clemency is on her tongue. St. Bernard, inquiring of himself why the Church invokes Mary by the sublime title of Queen of Mercy, replies that this is done in order that we may firmly believe that Mary throws open the treasury of the divine mercy to whom she pleases, when she pleases, and as she pleases. So that the sinner can never be lost if Mary protects him. The repentant sinner is never rejected by Mary. However numerous may be his crimes, however frightful their deformity, if he breathes with confidence at the feet of Mary one heartfelt sigh of sorrow, she instantly extends her merciful hand, withdraws him from the precipice of despair, and never abandons him until she beholds him reconciled with God, especially if he perseveres in saying the Rosary.

Father Crasset relates that a military commander told him that once, after a battle, he found a soldier in the camp who, holding a Rosary in his hand, asked for a confessor. His forehead was pierced by a musket ball, which had come out at the back of the head, so that the brain was visible and came out through each opening; – so much so, indeed, that naturally he could not live. He raised himself up, made his confession to the chaplain with great compunction, and expired after he had received absolution (Crasset, tom. 2, tr. 6, pr. 14).

St. Vincent Ferrer said to a man who was dying in despair, "why are you determined to lose your soul when Jesus Christ wishes to save you?" The man answered that, in spite of Jesus Christ, he was determined to go to hell. The saint replied, "And you, in spite of yourself, shall be saved." He began with the persons in the house to recite the Rosary, when, behold! the sick man asked to make his confession, and, having done so with many tears, he expired (Cantiprat. lib. 2., cap. 29, n. 6).

Not in vain have the holy and devout servants of the Mother of the Rosary called her the gate of heaven, the glory of the human race, the support of the elect, the fountain of graces, the harbor of the shipwrecked, the shield of combatants, the mother of orphans, the protection of widows, the advocate of penitents, the prototype of the just, the hope and glory of Christians, the title of honor of Catholics, the refuge of abandoned sinners, and the consolation of the desolate.

It is only a few years ago that a priest was called one evening to administer the sacraments to a dying woman. He was engaged at the moment; so he took down the address of the sick person, and promised to be there as soon as possible. No sooner was he at liberty than he set out on his errand of charity. It was a cold winter evening, and the rain poured down in torrents. But what cared he for the cold and the rain? There was a soul to save; he was to assist a poor soul in her last struggle, and that was enough to make him forget everything else. After many turnings and windings through dark alleys and narrow streets, the priest came at last to the house of the sick person. "No.18," thought he to himself; "this is the house to which I was told to come." The house was poor, very poor. There was no latch on the door, so the priest entered without difficulty. He had then to grope his way up narrow, rickety stairs, till he came at length to a door. He knocked. The door was opened by a sour looking individual, who, on perceiving a priest, immediately flew into a passion. He loaded the priest with insults, and slammed the door in his face. The good priest thought of the example of his heavenly Master, and offered up a prayer for the unfriendly churl. He knocked at the next door, but met with no better reception. He then ascended a second flight of stairs. He then met a child, and inquired of him where the sick woman lived. The boy told him that there was a sick woman in one of the neighboring rooms. "She is very ill," said the boy. "I heard she cannot live until morning; but I think that her name is not as you said." "No matter," said the priest, "the name is not of much importance; come and show me the room." The boy led him to the door; the priest opened it and entered the sick woman's room. There was a man sitting beside the sick bed, who started up immediately and seemed quite bewildered at seeing a priest in the room. The good father saluted him kindly, and inquired how his wife was. "For I suppose she is your wife, and you are Mr. N____." "I?" said the man gruffly. "No, sir, that is not my name. Who told you to come here and meddle in our family affairs?" "Why," said the priest, astonished, "it is scarcely an hour ago since a messenger requested me to come to Mrs. N-, who was dangerously ill. It may be that I have been mistaken in the street or in the number of the house, but anyhow I think the poor woman here seems to be very ill. It is certainly the all merciful hand of God that has led me to assist this poor soul in her last struggle." "No, sir," said the man, flying into a passion, "you shall not hear her; she is my wife. These ten years no priest has ever entered my house. Go about your business, I say." "My good man, you are mistaken," answered the priest in a calm and manly tone of voice." She is your wife, but she belongs also to God; she has an immortal soul, and over that you have no power. If your wife wishes to confess, I shall hear her confession; it is my duty as a priest of God. I will assist her in her last struggle unless she herself refuses to accept my assistance." The priest then approached the sick person and asked her: "My good woman, do you wish to be reconciled to God? Do you wish to receive the sacraments?" The poor woman raised her hands and eyes to heaven, and began to weep from sheer joy. "Oh!" cried she, "it is the all merciful God that has brought you here. This whole week I have been begging of my husband to send for a priest, but he always refused. Oh! I wish to be reconciled to God; I wish to make a good confession." The priest then turned to the husband, and requested him to leave the room for a few moments till he had heard her confession, and he spoke in such a firm and resolute tone that the husband was compelled to retire. The poor woman could scarcely speak for joy. "See," said she, pointing to a Rosary that hung near her – "see, it is this blessed Rosary that has saved me. I have been so unfortunate as to fear my husband more than God. To please him I have neglected my religious duties these ten or eleven years. But I never forgot to recommend myself to the Blessed Mother of God. Scarce a day passed in which I did not say some part of my Rosary, and so I have always preserved in my heart a love for the Blessed Virgin Mary. I am sure it is this good Mother that brought you here; reverend father, it is she that has saved my soul."

You may imagine the joy of the good priest at finding this poor sinner so well disposed. He saw clearly that it was an effect of the unutterable mercy of the ever Blessed Virgin Mary. He thought to himself, How good it is to be devout to Our Lady of the Rosary! He heard the poor woman's confession, gave her absolution, and told her to prepare for the Holy Viaticum and the Extreme Unction. Going in haste to the neighboring church to take with him the Blessed Sacrament and the holy oils, he returned quickly to the sick person. On entering the room he found her dead! She had received the absolution at the last moment! It was the Blessed Virgin Mary, Our Lady of the Rosary, who had obtained for her this crowning grace. The good priest now looked at his memorandum book, and found that he had really made a mistake. He had been called to No. 28, and had, by mistake, come to No.18, just in time to save a poor soul! Going to No. 28, he found the sick person who had sent for him, and administered to her the last sacraments.

How great is the power and mercy of the Blessed Virgin for those who are faithful in the practice of the Rosary! If you wish, then, to save your soul, practice the devotion of the Rosary with fervor and perseverance. If you wish to save the souls of those who are near and dear to you, try to introduce this devotion without delay into your family.

CHAPTER 11

THE ROSARY:
THE SOURCE OF TEMPORAL BLESSINGS

Some years ago there was a poor widow who had an only son. She loved this son dearly, and spared no pains to instill into his heart the principles of virtue. In spite, however, of all her care, the young man went off with wicked companions, and became the scandal of the whole neighborhood. He often abused and struck his mother, and even threatened to kill her. This unhappy young man gave himself up to every crime. At last he was arrested and cast into prison. One day a stranger knocked at the prison door. The jailer came out to see who it was, and learned to his surprise that it was the mother of this wicked man. "Ah!" she said, weeping, "I wish to see my son." "What," cried the jailer in astonishment, "you wish to see that wretch! Have you forgotten all that he has done to you?" "Ah! I know it well," replied the widow, "but he is my son." "Why," cried the jailer, "he has robbed you of every cent." "I know it," she replied, "but he is still my son." "But he has struck you, abused you, and even threatened to kill you," said the jailer." "It is true," was the answer. "I am still his mother – he is still my son." "But," cried the jailer, "he has not only abused and robbed you, he has shamefully abandoned you. Such an unnatural son is not worthy to live." "Ah! but he is my son; I am his mother." And the poor widow sobbed and wept, till at last the jailer was touched and permitted her to enter the prison; and the fond mother threw her arms around the neck of that unnatural, ungrateful son, and pressed him again and again to her breaking heart.

Now, we do not wonder at the love of this mother for her offspring. God has made the love of mothers for their children a necessary love. It is proverbial. Indeed, there is no love so pure and so thoroughly disinterested as the love of a good mother for her child. The patriot expects fame, the friend sympathy, and the lover pleasure.

Even religion, while she waters her faith with tears, looks forward to the best fruit of her labors and her love. But motherly affection springs from the breast, uninvoked by the wand of hope, unadulterated by the touch of interest. Its objects are the weak and woeful. It haunts the cradle of infantile pain, or hovers near the faint and forsaken. Its sweetest smiles break through the clouds of misfortune, and its gentlest tones rise amid the sighs of suffering and of sorrow. It is a limpid and lovely flow of feeling, which gushes from the fountainhead of purity, and courses the heart, through selfish designs and sordid passions, unmingling and unsullied.

A mother's love knows no change. Time and misfortune, penury and persecution, hatred and infamy, may roll their dark waves successively over it, and still it smiles unchanged; or the more potent allurements of fortune, opulence and pride, power and splendor, may woo her, and yet she is unmoved; a mother loves and loves for ever. Brothers and sisters have forgotten each other; fathers have proved unforgiving to their children; husbands have been false to their wives, wives to their husbands; children, too, often forget their parents; but you rarely hear of a mother forgetting even her ungrateful, disobedient children, whose actions have lacerated her heart, and caused dark shadows to cross her life and enter her very soul. Still there are moments when her faithful heart yearns towards them; when the reminiscences of the happy past obliterate the present sorrow, and the poor wounded spirit is cheered for a while, because there is still one of the fibers of the root of hope left in her forlorn breast, and a languid smile will flit over her wan and faded face. Yes; she forgives, though there is nothing for her to drink from in this life, showing that her love is the purest and most lasting in this world, and the nearest approach to the love that God has so graciously bestowed upon her. Who can measure the depth of the wonderful love of a mother's heart?

I know a Mother, the best of mothers, whose equal is not to be found. I love to call her my Mother, she is so good, so merciful, and withal so powerful. I never doubt of her power or of her good will to assist me; she is my hope, my consolation in this weary life. This Mother, whom I love to call my Mother, is the Blessed Mother of God, the immaculate Virgin Mary.

God alone knows the inmost yearnings of the human heart. God alone can fully understand and compassionate our weakness. At our birth to this natural life God gave each of us a father and a mother to be our guide and support, our refuge and consolation; and when, in the holy sacrament of baptism, we were brought again to the true life of grace, God gave us also a father and a mother. He taught us to call him "Our Father who art in heaven." He gave us his own Blessed Virgin Mother to be our true and loving Mother. That Mary is our Mother we were told by Jesus himself when hanging on the Cross: "Behold thy Mother" (Jn. 19:27). By his all powerful word God created the heavens and the earth; by his word he changed water into wine at the wedding feast; by his word he gave life to the dead; by his word he changed bread and wine into his Body and Blood; and by the same word he made his own beloved Mother to be truly and really our Mother also. He kept this gift to the last, because it is his desire that we should ever remember it; because it is so precious in his sight, so dear to his heart, so necessary for all those who will believe in him; and because it is to be the means of preserving all the other divine gifts, or of recovering them when lost. Mary, then, is our Mother, as Jesus willed and declared; and Mary, our Mother, is an all powerful Mother. God alone is all powerful by nature but Mary is all powerful by her prayers. What is more natural than this?

Mary is made *Mater Dei,* the Mother of God. Behold two words, the full meaning of which can never be comprehended either by men or angels. To be Mother of God is, as it were, an infinite dignity; for the dignity of that Mother is derived from the dignity of her Son. As there can be no son of greater excellence than the Son of God, so there can be no mother greater than the Mother of God. Hence St. Thomas asks whether God could make creatures nearer perfection than those already created, and he answers yes, he can, except three: i.e., 1, The Incarnation of the Son of God; 2, The maternity of the Blessed Virgin Mary; and, 3, The everlasting beatitude; in other words, God can create numberless worlds, all different from one another in beauty, but he cannot make anything greater than the Incarnation of Christ, the Mother of God, and the happiness of the blessed in heaven. And why can he not? Because God himself is involved in and most intimately united to each of these works, and is their object. *("Haec tria Deum involvunt et pro objecto habent.")* As there can be no man as perfect as Christ, because he is a Man-God, and as there can be no greater happiness than the beatific vision and enjoyment and possession of God in heaven, where the soul is, as it were, transformed into God and most inseparably united to his nature, so also no mother can be made as perfect as the Mother of God. These three works are of a certain infinite dignity on account of their intimate union with God, the infinite Good. There can, then, be nothing better, greater than, or as perfect as, these three works because there can be nothing better than God himself. The Blessed Virgin gave birth to Christ, who is the natural Son of God the Father, both as God and as man. Christ, then, as man, is the natural Son both of the Blessed Virgin and of God the Father. Behold in what intimate relation she stands with the Blessed Trinity, she having brought forth the same Son whom God the Father has generated from all eternity.

Moreover, the Blessed Virgin is the Mother of God, who had no earthly father; she was both mother and father to Jesus Christ. Hence she is the Mother of God far more than others are the mothers of men; for Christ received of the Blessed Virgin alone his whole human nature, and is indebted to his mother for all that he is as man. Hence Christ, by being conceived and born of the Blessed Virgin, became in a certain sense her debtor, and is under more obligations to her for being to him both mother and father than other children are to their parents.

If Mary is the Mother of God, what wonder, then, that God has glorified and will glorify, through all ages, her power of intercession with him for all men? The Eternal Father has chosen Mary to be the mother of his only Son; the Holy Spirit chose her as his spouse. The Son, who has promised a throne in heaven to the apostles who preached his word, is bound in justice to do more for the Mother who bore him, the eternal Word. If we believe in honoring our mother, surely he believes in honoring and glorifying his. Now, what honors, what prerogatives, should God bestow on her whom he has so favored, and who served him so devotedly! How should she be honored whom the King of Heaven deigns to honor!

A king was once in great danger of being assassinated, but a faithful subject discovered the plot, revealed it, and thus saved the monarch's life. The king was moved with gratitude, and asked his ministers, "How could he be honored whom the king desires to honor?" One of his ministers replied: "He whom the king desires to honor should be clad in kingly robes; he should be crowned with a kingly diadem, and the first of the royal princes should go before him and cry aloud, 'Thus shall he be honored whom the king desires to honor.'" In this manner did an earthly king reward him who saved his life. And how should the King of heaven and earth reward her who gave him his human life? How should Jesus reward the loving Mother who bore him, nursed him, saved him in his infancy from a most cruel death? Is there any honor too high for her whom God himself has so honored? Is there any glory too dazzling for her whom the God of glory has chosen for his dwelling place? No; it is God's own decree: Let her be clad in royal robes. Let the fullness of the Godhead so invest her, so possess her, that she shall be a spotless image of the sanctity, the beauty, the glory of God himself. Let her be crowned with a kingly diadem. Let her reign for ever as the peerless Queen of heaven, of earth, and of hell. Let her reign as the Mother of mercy, the Consoler of the afflicted, the Refuge of sinners. Let the first of the royal princes walk before her. Let the angels, the prophets, the apostles, the martyrs, let all the saints kiss the hem of her garment and rejoice in the honor of being the servants of the Mother of God.

No wonder, then, if we rarely hear of Mary but in connection with a miraculous demonstration of the power of God. She was conceived as no other human being ever was conceived. She again conceived her Son and God in a miraculous manner; miracles attended her visit to her cousin St. Elizabeth; the birth of her divine Child was accompanied by many striking prodigies. When she carried him in her arms to present him in the temple, behold new miracles followed her steps. The first miracle of her divine Son was wrought at her request. She took part in the awful mystery of the Passion. She shared in the sevenfold gifts of the Holy Spirit of Pentecost. In a word, miracles seem to have been the order in her life, the absence of miracles the exception; so that we are as little surprised to find them attend her everywhere as we should be astonished to hear of them in connection with ourselves.

Mary was a living miracle. All that we know of her miraculous power now is but little when compared with the prodigies which were effected through her agency during her earthly career. She saluted her cousin Elizabeth; and when that holy woman "heard her salutation she was filled with the Holy Ghost." She addressed her divine Son at the marriage feast, and said, "They have no more wine"; and immediately the filial charity which had bound him to her for thirty years constrained him to comply with her request. He whose meat and drink it was to do the will of his heavenly Father seemed to make the will of Mary the law of his action rather than his own. Again, there was a moment when the mystery of the Incarnation hung upon the word of her lips; the destiny of the world depended upon an act of her will. When God wished to create the world, "He spoke and it was done"; when he wished to redeem the world, he left it to the consent of his creature, and that creature was Mary. She said, "Be it done to me according to thy word," and the miracle of all miracles, the mystery of all mysteries, was consummated. "God was made flesh and dwelt amongst us."

It cannot surprise us, then, that she should continue to be a center of miraculous action. Her whole previous history prepares us for this. It seems to be the law of her being; she represents to us the most stupendous miracle that the world ever witnessed. It seems, therefore, almost natural that she should be able to suspend here and there the course of natural events by the power of her intercession. All that we know of her miraculous power now is as nothing when compared with the prodigies which were effected through her agency during her earthly career, and which we must believe, unless we would forfeit the very name of Christian. The apostles did not enter upon their office of intercession till the coming of the Holy Spirit at Pentecost; after that, whatever they should ask the Father in Christ's name they were certain to receive. Mary began her office of intercession at Cana. Its commencement was inaugurated by Christ's first miracle. It is true that his answer, in words at least, seemed at first unfavorable. But only observe how every circumstance of that event strengthens the Catholic view of our Lord's conduct. Mary's faith in her Son's power, and in his willingness to grant her request, never wavered, even when he seemed to make a difficulty. Whether his words had a meaning wholly different from that ordinarily attached to them now, or whether she, whose heart was as his own, read his consent in the tone of his voice or in the glance of his eye, her only answer was the words addressed to the servants. "Whatever he shall say to you, do it," evidently proving that she never for an instant doubted the favorable issue of her request. Now, if what appeared to be an unseasonable exercise of Mary's influence resulted in a miracle, and the first of the public miracles of our Lord; and if he predicted the coming of an hour when the exercise of her influence should no longer be unseasonable, as his words clearly imply, what prodigies must not her intercession effect at the present time! If she could thus prevail with God in her lowliness, what can she not obtain now in her exalted state! Now, how can we avail ourselves of her great power of intercession with God? By the practice of the devotion of the Rosary. When the Blessed Virgin revealed this devotion to St. Dominic, she said to him: "By this devotion the faithful shall obtain numberless benefits and shall always find me ready to help them in their wants." The Blessed Virgin has never failed to keep her promise.

In 1571 the haughty Sultan Selim II, puffed up by his many victories, resolved to bring all Europe under his iron sway. With a large fleet he sailed for Italy, and threatened to lay waste her sunny fields and blooming vineyards. The holy Pontiff Pius V called upon the princes of Europe, and Catholic Spain and Genoa and Venice united their forces to repel the Moslem invader. But the Holy Father did not place his trust in human aid alone. With sighs and tears he besought the assistance of the God of Armies. He prayed especially to Mary, the help and hope of Christians. He called upon all the faithful to unite with him in imploring the special protection of the immaculate Mother of God, and in every city and hamlet the faithful united in the touching devotion of the Rosary. Everywhere the voices of thousands ascended to heaven, saluting the Blessed Mother of God and her divine Son, imploring them to crush once more the might and pride of their enemies. The prayer of so many thousands united in the holy Rosary could not but be granted.

The Admiral John of Austria attached a rosary to the royal ensign, and let it float above the smoke and roar of the battle. He thus placed the entire fleet under the special protection of the Queen of the Rosary. The Christians saw that their fleet was far outnumbered by the Turks, and they felt that only the aid of Heaven could give them victory over such fearful foes. At first the wind was unfavorable to the Christians, and the dazzling sun prevented them from watching the movements of the enemy. But on a sudden the wind turned as if by a miracle, and a dark cloud arose and intercepted the blinding rays of the sun. The Christians could now watch the enemy closely, and they perceived that the Turkish fleet had made a move to surround them. The signal was given. The battle began. The fiery tempest lasted with unabated fury for several hours. The Turks as well as the Christians fought with desperate valor. At length the Christians succeeded in boarding the flag-ship of the Turkish admiral, and soon the head of Ali Pasha appeared upon a Christian spear.

At the sight of this bloody trophy, the air resounded with shouts of joy and songs of triumph; for it was considered a triumph, not merely of arms, but of Christianity. The hearts of their enemies quailed with terror. The Christians gained a complete victory. They captured and sank 200 Turkish vessels, killed 50,000 of the enemy, and struck off the chains of 20,000 Christian captives. The Turkish pride and power were broken for ever, and found a grave in the blood-stained waves of Lepanto.

While the battle was raging, the holy Pope Pius V was sitting with some of his cardinals many hundred miles from the scene of the battle; he suddenly rose, walked to the window, and looked out at the sky for some time; then returning to his seat, he said: "Let us return thanks to God for the great victory which the Christian army has won."

To perpetuate the remembrance of this signal victory, which was clearly owing to the miraculous interposition of Our Lady of the Rosary, several popes decreed that the Feast of the Rosary should be celebrated yearly by all the faithful on the first Sunday of October. By this public manifestation of her power with God, the Blessed Virgin gave a convincing proof to all Christians that the blessings promised to the devotion of the Rosary will be obtained by those who are faithful in its practice.

One of the most awful punishments with which God can afflict a nation is to strike it with pestilence. When the destructive angel of pestilence passes through the streets of a large city, it is a sight that fills the beholder with horror beyond description. God visited with this scourge the city of Bologna in 1630. Within a short time the city was but one large field strewn with dead bodies, which remained in the fiery spots where they had been stricken by the plague. More than a third of the inhabitants fell victims to the scourge of God. All commerce was stopped, all communications were cut off, all stores were closed up, whole families died out. The city with its suburbs – a terrestrial paradise – was changed into a graveyard. The living were too few to bury the dead. The atmosphere was poisoned by the pestiferous odor that came forth from the dead bodies, which lay unburied and in a state of decomposition. Sobs and sighs, moans and groans, cries of distress, were heard in every street, in every house. At last those who had been spared by the hand of the destructive angel had recourse to the Blessed Mother of God. They began to say the Rosary in common. Wonderful to relate, scarcely had they begun to send up the prayer of the Rosary to the throne of mercy than the shadows of death began to disappear, the mortality ceased, and the inhabitants of that city and its suburbs were delivered from the pestilence. God visited with the same plague the city of Naples in 1656, Lisbon in 1564, Tortosa in 1510, Vienna in 1713, Paris in 1748; and it was by the prayer of the Rosary that they were delivered.

Blessed Alan relates that there was a lady named Dominica, who for a time said the Rosary, but, having afterwards given up this devotion, she fell into such great poverty that one day in despair she gave herself three stabs with a knife. When she was on the point of expiring, and the devils were already preparing to take her to hell, the most Blessed Virgin appeared to her and said: "Daughter, although you have forgotten me, I would not forget you on account of the Rosary, which at one time you used to recite in my honor. But now, if you will continue to recite it, I will not only restore you to life, but will also restore to you the property which you have lost." Dominica recovered her health, and, persevering in the recitation of the Rosary, regained her property, and on her death-bed was again visited by Mary, who praised her for her faithfulness (De Psalt. p. 5, c. 67).

Thomas Cantipratensis relates that a certain woman lived in sin, fancying it was the only means by which she could gain her livelihood. She was advised to recommend herself to Mary by saying the Rosary. She followed the advice, and, behold, one night the divine Mother appeared to her and said: "Give up sin; and as to thy support, trust in me – I will provide for that." In the morning she went to confession, changed her life, and never suffered from want again.

A poor widow, whose chief support rested upon the favorable result of a lawsuit, knowing that the judge was averse to her claim, made a vow to Our Lady of the Rosary. Three different times the judge was about to pronounce sentence against her, but an unknown power dictated a judgment altogether conformable to the interests of the woman. The most clement Mother of God had interceded with her divine Son, and he who is blessed by excellence, and who is the blessed Judge among all, had put words of justice into the mouth of this man, and had forced him to bless when he would have condemned.

Students whose minds are dull and incapable of understanding human sciences should frequently recite the Rosary, and the Mother of divine Wisdom will obtain wisdom for them as she did for Alfred the Great, who, through this good Mother, obtained such marvelous learning that he merited a place among the princes of science.

A woman desires to be blessed with a child. Let her remember that Our Lady of the Rosary can obtain this blessing for her. The birth of St. Louis, king of France, was the fruit of devotion to the Mother of God and the holy Rosary. The pious queen, Blanche of Castile, desired ardently to give an heir to the throne who might be according to God's own heart. St. Dominic, who lived at that time, advised her to have recourse to the Blessed Virgin and to the devotion of the Rosary, to recite it often, and to engage the most devout persons of the kingdom to offer frequently in her name the same homage; and he encouraged her to hope that the blessing she desired would be the fruit of her prayers. Queen Blanche faithfully followed this advice. The virtue of the holy Rosary, and the piety of the religious princess, soon obtained the desired effect. She had a son, and in her son a king who made sanctity to reign on the throne; who consecrated his crown by all Christian virtues; who illustrated his life by the most heroic actions; in a word, who carried his baptismal robe unsullied to the tomb, enriched with all the merits which make saints.

This holy king never forgot that he was the fruit of the Rosary, and out of gratitude he obliged his chaplains and soldiers to say the Rosary, even amid the bustle of camp life.

Number those, if you can, who, through the devotion of the Rosary, have recovered from sickness; how many captives have been set at liberty; how many have been delivered by Mary who were in danger of perishing by fire, in danger of shipwreck, in danger of war and pestilence. Go to the sanctuaries of Our Blessed Lady, and see there the many votive offerings, ornaments of gold and silver and precious stones, in commemoration of miraculous cures or other extraordinary favors obtained through the devotion of the Rosary; for in these sanctuaries of the Blessed Virgin the blind are restored to sight, the lame walk, the demons are expelled from the bodies of men. These are authentic facts, attested not only by persons of note who have heard them from others, but by thousands of eyewitnesses whose sincerity we cannot doubt; facts so numerous that, if they were all written, it would take years to read them. What favor and blessing is there that cannot be obtained by the devotion of the Rosary?

Thomas Cantipratensis relates that, in an earthquake, a poor woman was buried under the ruins of a house which had been overthrown. A priest had the stones and rubbish removed, and under them found the mother, with her children in her arms, alive and uninjured. On being asked what devotion she had practiced, she replied that she had always said the Rosary.

A Carthusian monastery, situated in Spain, was devastated by war; even its grounds and revenues were confiscated by the conquerors. The religious were reduced to the utmost extremity of distress; hunger and every species of misery were their daily lot. The prior, being touched with compassion for the great sufferings of his brethren much more than for his own, was inspired to have recourse to the most holy Mother of God, whom he invoked with great fervor. He persevered during fifteen days in prayer, when one evening, while performing his devotions, he saw our Lord Jesus Christ in the glory of his Passion holding in his hand fifteen weapons of great beauty; these were five arrows, five swords, and five lances. These arms glistened with the blood of our Savior, and they seemed as resplendent as so many brilliant stars. The good prior, frightened, prostrated himself on the earth. The most sweet Son of Mary then said to him: "Peter, fear not, for with these arms thou wilt have power over thy enemies." "Lord," replied the humble monk "what are these glorious arms?" The Savior then said: "They are the fifteen excellences of the Lord's Prayer and Angelic Salutation; they contain a virtue that will deliver thee in thy necessities. Go and preach the Rosary of my Mother pray with thy brethren, and thou shalt soon feel the efficacy of these prayers." The Carthusian, confiding in these words, practiced with fervor the devotion of the Rosary, and very soon the face of affairs changed. Those who were the authors of the spoliation freely made restitution of their grounds, and delivered over all the goods of the monastery. The monks, now in possession of their patrimony, were happy; peace and security once more returned; and, like exiles, they rejoiced at being again within the walls of their cloister. (Month of the Rosary.)

Let us never forget these words of our Lord: "The Rosary contains a virtue that will deliver thee in thy necessities. Say it, and thou shalt soon feel the efficacy of these prayers."

CHAPTER 12

THE ROSARY: THE GREAT DEVOTION
FOR THE SOULS IN PURGATORY

A short time ago, a fervent young priest of this country had the following conversation with a holy bishop on his way to Rome. The bishop said to him: "You make mementos, now and then, for friends of yours that are dead, do you not?" The young priest answered: "Certainly, I do so very often." The bishop rejoined: "So did I when I was a young priest. But at one time I was grievously ill and given up as about to die. I received Extreme Unction and the Viaticum. It was then that my whole past life, with all its failings and all its sins, came before me with startling vividness. I saw *how much* I had to atone for; and I reflected on how few Masses would be said for me, and how few prayers! Ever since my recovery I have most fervently offered the Holy Sacrifice for the repose of the pious and patient souls in Purgatory; and I am always glad when I can, as my own offering, make the 'intention' of my Masses for the relief of their pains" (*Freeman's Journal*, November, 1869).

Indeed, no one is more deserving of Christian charity and sympathy than the poor souls in Purgatory. They are *really poor souls*. No one is sooner forgotten than they.

How soon their friends persuade themselves that the souls departed are in perfect peace! How little they do for their relief when their bodies are buried. There is a lavish expense for the funeral. A hundred dollars are spent where the means of the family hardly justify the half of it. Where there is more wealth, sometimes five hundred or a thousand and even more dollars are expended on the poor dead body. But what is done for the *poor living soul?* Perhaps it is suffering the most frightful tortures in Purgatory, whilst the lifeless body is laid out in state and borne pompously to the graveyard. It is right and fitting to show all due respect even to the body of a deceased friend, for that body was once the dwelling place of his soul. But, after all, what joy has the departed, and perhaps suffering, soul in the fine music of the choir, even though the choir be composed of the best singers in the country? What consolation does it feel in the superb coffin, in the splendid funeral? What pleasure in the costly marble monument, in all the honors that are so freely lavished on the body? All this may satisfy, or at least seem to satisfy, the living, but it is of no avail whatever to the dead.

Poor, unhappy souls! how the diminution of true Catholic faith is visited upon them. Those that loved them in life might help them, and do not, for want of knowledge or of faith!

Poor, unhappy souls! your friends go to their business, to their eating and drinking, with the foolish assurance that the case cannot be hard with one they know to be so good! Oh! how much and how long this *false charity* of your friends causes you to suffer!

The venerable Sister Catherine Paluzzi offered up for a long time and with the utmost fervor prayers and pious works for the soul of her deceased father. At last she thought she had good reason to believe that he was already enjoying the bliss of Paradise. But how great was her consternation and grief when our Lord, in company with St. Catherine, her patroness, led her one day in spirit to Purgatory. There she beheld her father in an abyss of torments, imploring her assistance. At the sight of the pitiful state his soul was in, she melted into tears, cast herself down at the feet of her heavenly Spouse, and begged him, through his precious Blood, to free her father from his excruciating sufferings. She also begged St. Catherine to intercede for him, and then, turning to our Lord, said: " Charge me, O Lord! with my father's indebtedness to thy justice. In expiation of it, I am ready to take upon myself all the afflictions thou art pleased to impose upon me." Our Lord graciously accepted this act of heroic charity, and released at once her father's soul from Purgatory. But heavy indeed were the crosses which she, from that time forth, had to suffer!

This pious sister seemed to have good reason to believe that her father's soul was in Paradise. Yet she was mistaken. Alas! how many are there who resemble her in this. How many are there whose hope as to the condition of their deceased friends is far vainer and more false than that of this sister, because they pray less for the souls of their departed friends than she did for her father.

"No defiled thing," says St. John, "shall enter the heavenly city of Jerusalem." How easy was it for the departed soul to defile itself in this life, where it was surrounded by all kinds of snares and dangers.

St. Severinus, Archbishop of Cologne, was a prelate of such great sanctity that God wrought many remarkable miracles through him. One day after his death he was seen by a canon of the cathedral to suffer the most excruciating pains. Upon being asked why he suffered so much, he who, on account of his holiness of life, ought to be reigning gloriously in heaven, replied: "I suffer this torment merely for having recited the canonical hours hurriedly and with willful distraction" (St. Peter Dom. Epist.14, Edit. Desid. c. vii.)

It is related in the life of St. Mary Magdalene of Pazzi that one day she saw the soul of one of her deceased sisters kneeling in adoration before the Blessed Sacrament in the Church, all wrapped up in a mantle of fire, and suffering great pains in expiation of her neglecting to go to Holy Communion, on a day when she had her confessor's permission to communicate.

If St. Severinus, so holy a prelate of the Church, if a holy nun who spent her life in the convent, had to suffer most excruciating pains in purgatory in expiation of small faults, what reason have we to imagine so readily that the souls of our departed friends are already enjoying the beatific vision of God – who perhaps were never very much in earnest about leading a holy life; who perhaps made light of venial faults; who perhaps often spoke uncharitably of their neighbors; who perhaps neglected so many Holy Communions and other means of grace and sanctification; who in their youth may have committed hundreds of secret mortal sins of the most heinous kinds, and may never have conceived any other than imperfect sorrow or contrition on account of them; who perhaps spent their whole lives in the state of mortal sin, and were converted only on their death-bed?

Ah! how much combustible matter, how many imperfections, venial sins, and temporal punishments due to mortal and venial sins, may they not have fallen with them to be burned out in the flames of purgatory!

The Venerable Bede relates that it was revealed to Drithelm, a great servant of God, that the souls of those who spend their whole lives in the state of mortal sin and are converted only on their death-bed are doomed to suffer the pains of purgatory to the day of the last judgment (Hist. Angelic. 55. c. 13).

In the life and revelations of St. Gertrude, we read that those who have committed many grievous sins, and who die without having done due penance, are not assisted by the ordinary suffrages of the Church until they are partly purified by divine justice in purgatory.

After St. Vincent Ferrer had learned of the death of his sister Frances, he at once began to offer up many fervent prayers and works of penance for the repose of her soul. He also said thirty Masses for her, at the last of which it was revealed to him that, had it not been for his prayers and good works, the soul of his sister would have suffered in purgatory to the end of the world (Marches. Diar. Dom. 5 Apr.)

From these examples we may draw our own conclusions as to the state of our deceased friends and relatives. The judgments of God are very different from the judgments of men. "My thoughts are not your thoughts," says the Lord "nor your ways my ways. For as the heavens are exalted above the earth, so are my ways exalted above your ways, and my thoughts above your thoughts" (Is. 4:8).

We know that souls of great perfection have been deprived of the beatific vision of God for having committed little faults. This we learn from many apparitions of the souls of the faithful departed, who have been saved and who praised the mercy of God, declaring at the same time that the judgments of the Lord are strict and terrible beyond description, and that mortals could never reflect too deeply upon this truth. The true reason of this great rigor of the judgments of God is found in his infinite sanctity, justice, and love.

God's sanctity requires an adequate expiatory punishment, because everything that is not good and perfect is essentially opposed to his divine nature; hence he cannot admit into heaven, to the contemplation of his divine Essence, a soul that is still spotted with the least stain of sin.

God's justice requires no less severity than his sanctity, because every sin is an offence and outrage against his divine Majesty; for which reason he cannot help defending his divine right and absolute dominion over all creatures by requiring full satisfaction from every soul that has offended against this divine Majesty.

Neither can God's infinite love be less severe, because He wishes to see the souls of His elect pure, beautiful, perfect in every way; for which reason he purifies them from every stain, as gold is refined in a furnace, until they become his true image and likeness, according to which he created the first man in sanctity and righteousness. He takes no pleasure in seeing these souls suffer, but, wishing to render them capable and worthy of being united to him as to their supreme happiness, he makes them pass through a state of the most frightful sufferings, a state of the greatest poverty imaginable – the privation of the beatific vision of God.

No sooner has the soul departed this life than it beholds God, and from this sight it receives at once so deep and vivid a knowledge of God and all his infinite perfections that thenceforth it is utterly incapable of being occupied with anything else than the divine beauty and goodness; it feels so violently drawn towards God, the supreme Lord of all things visible and invisible, that it finds it altogether impossible to wish, to seek, and to love anything but God. It experiences at once an insatiable hunger and thirst after God; it pants for its supreme good with a most ardent desire. "God! God! I must be with God!" is its constant cry. But at the very moment when the soul is endeavoring to unite itself to God, it is repulsed by him and sent to purgatory to cleanse itself from the sins not cancelled in this life. In this banishment from the sight of God the soul finds the bitterness of its torments. As it is the height of happiness to see a God infinitely amiable, so it is the greatest of all pains to be rejected from his presence. It

122

is true that, during this life, the soul experiences but a feeble desire to see God, and, as it does not know the greatness of this heavenly benefit, it does not comprehend how great a pain and misfortune it is to be deprived of it. But once the soul has quitted the body, it conceives so high an esteem for the possession of the supreme good, it burns with so ardent a desire to obtain it, it tends with so much force to enjoy it, that the greatest of all its torments in purgatory is to be repulsed, if only for an instant, from the presence of its Creator. In a word, the soul suffers more from the privation of the beatific vision of God than from all the other torments of purgatory. For such is the infinite beauty of God that to have seen him for a single instant, and in that same moment to be rejected from his presence, is to experience at once the torment of hell. In heaven love for God is the happiness of the elect; but in purgatory it is the source of the most excruciating pains. It is principally for this reason that the souls in purgatory are called "poor souls," they being, as they are, in the most dreadful state of poverty – that of the privation of the beatific vision of God.

After Anthony Corso, a Capuchin brother, a man of great piety and perfection, had departed this life, he appeared to one of his brethren in religion, asking him to recommend him to the charitable prayers of the community, in order that he might receive relief in his pains; "for I do not know," said he, "how I can bear any longer the pain of being deprived of the sight of my God. I shall be the most unhappy of creatures as long as I must live in this state. Would to God all men could understand well what it is to be without God, in order that they might firmly resolve to suffer anything during their life on earth rather than expose themselves to the danger of being damned and deprived for ever of the sight of God" (Annal. PP. Capuc. ad 1548).

The souls in purgatory are poor souls, because they suffer the greatest pain of the senses, which is that of *fire*. Who can be in a poorer and more pitiful condition than those who are buried in fire? Yet such is the condition of these souls. They are buried under waves of fire. The smallest spark of this purgatorial fire causes them to suffer more intense pains than all the fires of this world. In it they suffer more than all the pains of distempers and the most violent diseases, more than all the most cruel torments undergone by male-factors or invented by barbarous tyrants; more than all the tortures of the martyrs summed up together. Could these poor souls leave the fire of purgatory for the most frightful earthly fire, they would, as it were, take it for a pleasure garden; they would find a fifty years' stay in the hottest earthly fire more endurable than an hour's stay in the fire of purgatory. Our terrestrial fire was not created by God to torment men, but rather to benefit them; but the fire in purgatory was created by God for no other purpose than to be an instrument of his justice, and for this reason it is possessed of a burning quality so intense and penetrating that it is impossible for us to conceive even the faintest idea of it.

A religious of the Order of St. Dominic, when about to depart this life, most earnestly begged a priest to say Mass for the repose of his soul immediately after his death. The good religious had scarcely expired when the priest went to say Mass for him with great fervor and devotion. Hardly had he taken off the sacred vestments after Mass than the soul of his deceased friend appeared, rebuking him severely for the hardness of his heart in leaving him in the torments of purgatory for thirty years. Quite astonished, the good priest exclaimed: "What, thirty years! An hour ago you were still alive!" "Learn, then, from this," said the deceased, "how excruciating are the pains of the fire of purgatory, since one hour's stay therein appears as long as thirty years" (Da Fusian, tom. 4.)

Another reason why these holy prisoners and debtors to the divine justice are really poor is because they are not able to assist themselves in the least. A sick man afflicted in all his limbs, and a beggar in the most painful and destitute condition, has still a tongue left to ask relief. At least they can implore Heaven – it is never deaf to their prayer. But the souls in purgatory are so poor that they cannot even do this. The cases in which some of them were permitted to appear to their friends and ask assistance are but exceptions. To whom should they have recourse? Perhaps to the mercy of God! Alas! they send forth their sighs plaintively: "As the hart panteth after the fountains of water, so my soul panteth after thee, O God.

When shall I come and appear before the face of God? My tears have been my bread day and night, whilst it is said to me daily: Where is thy God" (Ps. 41:1). "Lord, where are thy ancient mercies" (Ps. 88:50). "I cry to thee, and thou hearest me not; I stand up, and thou dost not regard me. Thou art changed to be cruel toward me" (Job 30:20-21). But the Lord does not regard their tears, nor heed their moans and cries, but answers them that his justice must be satisfied to the last farthing.

Are they to endeavor to acquire new merits, and thereby purify themselves more and more? Alas! they know that their time for meriting is passed away, that their earthly pilgrimage is over, and that upon them is come that fatal *"night in which no one can work"* (Jn. 9:4). They know that by all their sufferings they can gain no new merit, no higher glory and happiness in heaven; they know that it is through their own fault they are condemned to this state of suffering; they see clearly how many admonitions, exhortations, inspirations, and divine lights they have rejected; how many prayers, opportunities of receiving the sacraments, and profiting by the means of grace within their reach they have neglected through mere caprice, carelessness and indolence. They see their ingratitude towards God, and the deep wounds they have made in the Sacred Heart of Jesus; and their extreme grief and sorrow for all this is a worm never ceasing to gnaw at them, a heartrending pain, a killing torment – that of knowing that they have placed themselves willfully and wantonly in this state of the most cruel banishment. "O cruel comforts! O accursed ease!" they cry out, "it is on your account that we are deprived of the enjoyment of God, our only happiness for all eternity!"

Shall they console themselves by the thought that their sufferings will soon be over? They are ignorant of their duration unless it be revealed to them by God. Hence they sigh day and night, hence they weep constantly, and cry unceasingly: "Woe unto us, that our sojourn is prolonged!"

Shall these poor, helpless souls seek relief from their fellow-sufferers, all utterly incapable of procuring mutual relief? Lamenting, sobbing, and sighing, shedding torrents of tears, and crying aloud, they stretch out their hands for one to help, console, and relieve them. We alone have it in our power to assist them in their sufferings.

After the Emperor Henry had besieged a certain city for a considerable time, and found the inhabitants still unwilling to surrender, he notified them that he would give orders to his soldiers to take the city by assault, and massacre all its inhabitants, even the little children. Alarmed at this proclamation, and seeing no hope left of saving themselves except by moving the emperor to compassion, the inhabitants of the city had recourse to the following expedient: They collected all the little children from six to ten years of age, and, after arraying them in procession, made them march before the emperor and throw themselves on their knees, striking their breasts and crying aloud in pitiful accents: "Have pity on us, O Emperor! O Emperor, have pity on us!" This heartrending scene affected the emperor so much that he himself could not help weeping. He pardoned the inhabitants of the city, and raised the siege immediately.

Could we only open the dungeons of Purgatory and see the immense procession of poor suffering souls coming forth, and crying aloud in the most lamentable and heartrending voice:

O God! O God! how weary, weary
    This lingering, waiting, suffering here
In these fierce flames, this dungeon dreary,
    Where each sad hour's a long, long year!
O friends beloved! Have you forgotten
    The hours we spent in bygone years?
These joyous hours have flown for ever,
    And left us naught but pain and tears!

Can you forget the love that bound us –
    The love you vowed should never die –
The love that cast a halo round us –
    Can you forget while here I lie?
When racked with pain and deathly anguish
    You kissed my cheek, my pale, cold brow;
Ah! now, 'mid torturing fires of anguish,
    Can you, loved friend, forsake me now?

Can you forget the loving mother
    That nursed and bore you in her pain,
Forget the hand that oft caressed you –
    Must she now plead, arid plead in vain?
How oft o'er you her lone watch keeping,
    She bathed with tears your burning brow;
She wept and prayed while all were sleeping –
    Can you forget her anguish now?

O mother dear! have you forgotten
    The child you once so fondly loved?
Ah! now he weeps in pain and sorrow –
    Can you, then, hear his plaint unmoved?
Friends may forget the ties of friendship;
    And fondest hearts ungrateful prove;
But can a mother's heart, so tender,
    Forget her child, her first-born love?

O friends so kind, so tender-hearted!
    The poor, the stranger at your door,
Receives your alms, your care, your blessing,
    And *we,* are we then yours no more?
The little bird that feebly flutters
    Against your pane 'mid winter's snow,
The flower 'mid summer's ardor drooping,
    Receive your care, awake your woe:

And we, your friends, your own, your kindred,
    Can we no more your pity share?
Has your love with the cold grave ended?
    Can you refuse a heartfelt prayer?
Relieve, O God! this thirst, this hunger,
    This longing, yearning, wild unrest:
Receive the home-sick soul to heaven,
    Where dwell, 'mid light and joy, the blest!

How would this spectacle affect us? Would not their pains alone plead more pathetically than any human tongue? Would not our eyes stream with tears, and our hearts be moved with compassion at beholding innumerable holy and illustrious servants of God suffering more than any human being can conceive? But, unable to let us witness their tears and hear their moans, they borrow a voice from the Church, their mother, and her priests, who, to express their moans and inconceivable distress, and to excite our compassion and charity, cry to the words of Job: "Have pity upon me, have pity upon me, at least you, my friends, for the hand of the Lord hath smitten me" (Job 19:21).

Just and holy souls, illustrious servants of the Lord, noble sons of the Heavenly Father, heirs of his celestial glory, chosen vessels of election, enriched with precious gifts and ornaments of divine grace laden with the merits of so many good works, confirmed in grace, and no longer in a condition to offend God, dear spouses of Christ but victims to the Divine justice, shall we be so dead to compassion, so steeled to feelings of humanity, as to refuse you our sympathy? Shall we be as deaf and unmerciful to you as the just God who punishes you? *"Quare me persequimini sicut Deus?"* Oh! what a cruelty. A sick man weeps on his bed and his friend consoles him; a baby cries in his cradle, and his mother at once caresses him; a beggar knocks at the door for an alms, and receives it; a malefactor laments in his prison, and comfort is given him; even a dog that whines at the door is taken in; but these poor, helpless souls cry day and night from the depths of the fire in Purgatory: "Have pity upon me, have pity upon me, at least you, my friends, because the hand of the Lord hath smitten me" – and there is no one to listen!

It seems as though we heard these poor souls exclaim; Priest of the Lord, speak no longer of our sufferings and pitiable condition. Let your description of it be ever so touching, it will not afford us the least relief. When a man has fallen into the fire; instead of considering his pains, you try at once to draw him out or quench the fire with water. This is true charity. Let Christians do the same for us.

Indeed, it seems to be a kind of folly to reflect long upon the pains of the souls in Purgatory by way of inducing ourselves to assist them. To know that they are tormented by fire ought to be enough to bring us to their relief at once, especially as we can do so with so little inconvenience to ourselves.

We read in the Acts of the Apostles that the faithful prayed unceasingly for St. Peter when he was imprisoned, and that an angel came and broke his chains and released him. We, too, should be good angels to the poor souls in Purgatory, and free them from their painful captivity.

Now, one of the easiest, yet one of the most powerful, means to procure relief for the souls in Purgatory is to say the beads for them with fervor. To say the Rosary for the souls in Purgatory is to offer up to God for their relief all the labors, fatigues, prayers, tears, contempt, sufferings, blood, and death – all the merits of the life of our dear Savior. Next to Mass, no more efficacious offering can be made to God than this for the relief of the souls in Purgatory. Our Lord himself taught St. Mary Magdalene often to make this offering of his blood and merits for the suffering souls in Purgatory, and she accustomed herself to make it fifty times a day. Our dear Savior showed her repeatedly multitudes of souls thus delivered from Purgatory.

In a monastery of the Dominicans of Milan a young lay-sister, named Angela, died in the odor of sanctity in the year 1673. This virtuous young sister observed to the letter the words of Jesus Christ: "I give you a new commandment, that you love one another: the mark by which you shall be known to be my disciples is, that you love one another." Angela took for her leading virtue charity, which she extended to all; particularly did she apply it to the souls in Purgatory. She offered for them most fervent prayers, all her labor, sought humiliations, imposed on herself penances, practiced mortifications, and submitted to many painful sacrifices for obtaining their deliverance. One day, being transported in spirit to Purgatory, she recognized a religious of her convent, Sister Constantine Marie, for whom she had entertained a devoted love. This poor soul avowed to her that her greatest suffering arose from the confusion and shame she felt in having offended a God so good, who had done so much and suffered such intense torture for her, and how badly she had corresponded with his innumerable graces. Angela was deeply moved at her beloved sister's sad recital; and, knowing the great virtue of the Rosary, she instantly recited it for the benefit of this poor suffering soul. Before the termination of the Rosary the holy sister was ravished into ecstasy, and she perceived the soul of Constantine Marie quitting her dreary prison, all resplendent in glory, and taking a seat on a throne of light in the midst of angels and saints. ("Month of the Rosary.")

Another reason why the Rosary is a most powerful prayer to obtain relief for the souls in purgatory is, because we offer up for them not only the prayers of the Rosary, but also all the indulgences attached to these prayers, and these indulgences are another means to relieve the suffering souls.

A very pious nun had just died in the convent in which St. Mary Magdalene of Pazzi lived. Whilst her corpse was exposed in the church, the saint lovingly looked upon it, and prayed fervently that the soul of her sister might soon enter eternal rest. Whilst she was thus rapt in prayer, her sister appeared to her, surrounded with great splendor and radiance, in the act of ascending into heaven. The saint, on seeing this, could not refrain from calling out to her "Farewell, dear sister! When you meet your heavenly Spouse, remember us, who are still sighing for him in this vale of tears!" At these words our Lord himself appeared, and revealed to her that this sister had entered heaven so soon on account of the indulgences gained for her ("Vita S. Magd. de Pazzi," 1. i. c. 39).

The third reason why the Rosary is a most powerful prayer to obtain relief for the souls in Purgatory is, because we offer it up for them in honor of the Blessed Virgin, that she may intercede for them. Mary is not only the powerful and merciful mother of the just, and even of sinners on earth, but she is also a most tender and compassionating mother of the suffering souls in Purgatory. This divine Mother, in her revelations to St. Bridget, said: "I am the mother of all the souls in Purgatory; and all the suffering which they deserve for the sins committed in life are every hour, while they stay there, alleviated in some measure by my prayers ("Rev. C.," 1. iv. 132). "Oh! how kind and beneficent is the Holy Virgin to those who are suffering in Purgatory," says St. Vincent Ferrer: "through her they receive continual consolation and refreshment" ("Serm. 2 de Nat.") The Blessed Virgin said to St. Bridget, that as a poor sick person, suffering and deserted on his bed, feels himself refreshed by some word of consolation, so those souls feel themselves consoled in hearing only her name. If the name alone of Mary is for these souls a great comfort, what relief must they not experience when we say the Rosary for them, in which we offer up the blood of Jesus Christ, the indulgences attached to each Hail Mary, and in which we ask the Mother of God to pray for them!

Father Eusebius Nieremberg relates that there lived in the city of Aragona a girl, named Alexandra, who, being noble and very beautiful, was greatly loved by two young men. Through jealousy, they one day fought and killed each other. Their enraged relatives, in return, killed the poor young girl as the cause of so much trouble, cut off her head, and threw her into a well. A few days after, St. Dominic was passing through that place, and, inspired by the Lord, approached the well and said: "Alexandra, come forth," and immediately the head of the deceased came forth, placed itself on the edge of the well, and prayed St. Dominic to hear its confession. The saint heard its confession, and also gave it communion in presence of a great concourse of persons, who had assembled to witness the miracle. Then St. Dominic ordered her to speak, and tell why she had received that grace. Alexandra answered, that when she was beheaded she was in a state of mortal sin, but that the most holy Mary, on account of the Rosary which she was in the habit of reciting, had preserved her in life. Two days the head retained its life upon the edge of the well, in the presence of all, and then the soul went to Purgatory. But fifteen days after the soul of Alexandra appeared to St. Dominic, beautiful and radiant as a star, and told him that one of the principal sources of relief to the souls in Purgatory is the Rosary which is recited for them, and that, as soon as they arrive in Paradise, they pray for those who apply to them these powerful prayers. Having said this, St. Dominic saw that happy soul ascending in triumph to the kingdom of the blessed. ("Troph. Marian.," 1. iv, c. 29.)

The relief, however, which the souls in Purgatory receive from the Rosary is in proportion to the fervor with which we say it. This was one day expressly declared by our Lord to St. Gertrude, when asking him, "How many souls were delivered from Purgatory by her and her sisters' prayers?" "The number," replied our Lord, "is proportionate to the *zeal and fervor* of those who pray for them. Although the souls of the departed are much benefited by these vigils and other prayers, nevertheless a few words said with affection and devotion are of far more value to them." And this may be easily explained by a familiar comparison: it is much easier to wash away the stains of mud or dirt from the hands by rubbing them quickly in a little warm water, than by pouring a quantity of cold water on them without using any friction; so a single word said with fervor and devotion for the souls of the departed is of far greater efficacy than many vigils and prayers coldly and negligently offered.

Dinocrates, the brother of St. Perpetua, died at the age of seven years. One day, when St. Perpetua was in prison for the sake of the faith, she had the following vision: "I saw Dinocrates," she says, "coming out of a dark place, where there were many others, exceedingly hot and thirsty; his face was dirty, his complexion pale, with the ulcer in his face of which he died, and it was for him that I prayed. There seemed a great distance between him and me, So that it was impossible for us to come to each other. Near him stood a vessel full of water, whose brim was higher than the stature of an infant. He attempted to drink, but though he had water, he could not reach it. This mightily grieved me, and I awoke. By this I knew my brother was in pain, but I trusted I could by prayer relieve him; So I began to pray for him, beseeching God with tears, day and night, that he would grant me my request, as I continued to do till we removed to the camp prison. The day we were in the stocks I had this vision: I saw the place which I had beheld dark before now luminous; and Dinocrates, with his body very clean and well-clad, refreshing himself, and instead of his wound a scar only. I awoke and I knew he was relieved from his pains" ("Butler's Lives of the Saints.")

After St. Ludgardis had offered up many fervent prayers for the repose of the soul of her deceased friend Simeon, abbot of the monastery of Soniac; our Lord appeared to her, saying: "Be consoled, my daughter; on account of thy prayers I will soon release this soul from Purgatory." "O Jesus! Lord and Master of my heart," she rejoined, "I cannot feel consoled so long as I know that the soul of my friend is suffering so much in the Purgatorial fire! Oh! I cannot help shedding most bitter tears until thou hast released this soul from her sufferings." Touched and overcome by this tender prayer, our Lord released the soul of Simeon, who appeared to Ludgardis all radiant with heavenly glory, and thanked her for the many *fervent* prayers which she had offered up for his delivery. He also told the saint that had it not been for her fervent prayers he would have been obliged to stay in Purgatory for eleven years ("Life," 1. i. c. 4). "It is, therefore, a holy and wholesome thought" says Holy Writ, "to pray for the dead, that they may be loosed from their sins" (2 Mach. 12:46).

St. Gertrude never felt happier than on the days on which she had prayed much for the relief of the souls in Purgatory. Once she asked our Savior why it was that she felt so happy on those days. "It is," he replied, "because it would not be right for me to refuse the *fervent* prayers which you on these days pour out to me for the relief of my suffering spouses in Purgatory." "It is not right for me," says Jesus Christ, "to refuse the prayers which you address to me in behalf of my captive spouses." How consoling, then, and at the same time how encouraging, must it be to remember in our prayers the poor sufferers of Purgatory, especially to say the holy Rosary for them often. Christians should pray earnestly for the souls of deceased priests whose lives have been passed in the service of the faithful. This great and true charity a false charity often prevents. People say, "Oh! the soul of this or that priest is certainly in heaven." Ah! how long and how much does this false charity cause souls to suffer in Purgatory! Let us say rather with St. Bernard, "I will forthwith come to the relief of the suffering souls in Purgatory; with sobs and sighs I will conjure the Lord; with tears I will entreat him; I will be their advocate by my prayers; I will especially offer up for them, or have offered for them, the holy sacrifice of the Mass and the prayers of the Rosary, in order that the Lord, with the eyes of his unspeakable mercy, may look down upon them, changing their desolation into comfort, their misery into joy, and their pains into everlasting glory and bliss."

CHAPTER 13

THE ROSARY: THE BEST PRAYER BOOK

One day two beggars came to a millionaire. One of them said to the rich man: "How magnificent your palace is! how splendid your furniture! how elegant your grounds! how vast your wealth!" The rich man, however, was not induced by these expressions of admiration to give an alms to the poor beggar. The other beggar spoke to the millionaire thus: "My good sir, be kind enough to assist me in my poverty; please give me some money, some clothes, some provisions." The rich man, being charitably disposed, complied with the beggar's request, giving him even more than he had asked for.

We are all beggars before God. But some obtain more by their prayers than others. Many, like the first beggar just mentioned, pray by way of exclamation and affectation, for instance: "O excess of love! One heart is too little to love thee, my Jesus; one tongue is not enough to praise thy goodness. O my Jesus! How great are my obligations to thee. No, I will no longer live in myself; but Jesus alone shall live in me; he is mine, and I am his. O love! O love! No more sins! I will never forget the goodness of God and the mercies of my Savior. I love thee, O infinite Majesty! My God, I wish to love nothing but thee," and so on. Expressions like these are called devout affections of the heart; but as they do not contain the least petition for any particular grace, the soul will not become over-rich with the gifts of God if this manner of prayer alone be adopted. Although devout affections are good in themselves, and often quite natural to the soul, yet, strictly speaking, our Lord is not bound to bestow graces upon us merely because we admire his perfections, goodness, or other attributes. But if we, like the other beggar, ask for positive favors, if we say to him: "Lord, make me understand better the excess of thy love; grant that my heart may never love anything but thee, that it may ever be thine; make me always seek only thee; let everything else be distasteful to me" – expressions like these, being petitions or prayers in which we ask for particular graces, our Lord Jesus Christ, on account of his promise, feels bound to grant them.

The venerable Paul Segneri, S.J., used to say that at one time he was in the habit of employing the time of prayer in reflections and affections; "but God (these are his own words) afterwards enlightened me, and thenceforward I endeavored to spend my time in making petitions; and if there is any good in me, I ascribe it to this manner of recommending myself to God."

We must do the same. St. Alphonsus, that most zealous doctor of the Church, who is justly called the Apostle of Prayer, tells us that our prayers should be petitions rather than affections, especially for the grace of divine love and final perseverance. Hence that prayer book whose prayers are put up in the *form of petitions,* is to be especially recommended. Now, there is but one prayer book, one grand devotion, the prayers of which are all put up in the form of petitions, and that is the Rosary. Almost every word of its prayers is a petition for particular favors. What great graces do we not ask of God in that short prayer called the Lord's Prayer, which, shortly paraphrased, runs thus: "Our Father," most blessed, most holy, our Creator, Redeemer, and Comforter – "who art in heaven" where thou dwellest with the angels and the saints, whom thou enlightenest and inflamest with thy love, so that they may know thee; for thou, O Lord, art the life and love that dwell in them; thou art their everlasting happiness, communicating thyself to them; thou art the supreme and eternal source from which all blessings flow, and without thee there is none –

"Hallowed be thy name"; enlighten us with thy divine wisdom, that we may be able to know thee, and to comprehend the boundless extent of thy mercies to us, thy everlasting promises, thy sublime majesty, and thy profound judgments –

"Thy kingdom come"; so that thy grace may remain in our hearts and prepare us for thy heavenly kingdom, where we shall see thee clearly and perfectly love thee, rejoicing with thee and in thee through all eternity –

"Thy will be done on earth as it is in heaven," that, being occupied with thee, we may love thee with our whole heart, with our whole soul, desiring nothing but thee; with our whole mind, referring all things to thee, and ever seeking thy glory in all our actions; with our whole strength, employing all our faculties, both of body and soul, in thy service, applying them to no other purpose whatsoever than to promote thy kingdom; endeavoring to draw all men to thee, and to love our neighbor as ourselves, rejoicing at his welfare and happiness as at our own sympathizing with his necessities, and giving no offence to him –

"Give us this day our daily bread": Thy dearly beloved Son, our Lord Jesus Christ; him we ask of thee as our daily bread, in order that we may be mindful of the love he has testified for us, and of the things he has promised, done, and suffered for us; grant us the grace always to keep them in our mind, and to value them exceedingly –

"Forgive us our trespasses," through thy unspeakable mercy, through the merits of the passion and death of thy most dearly beloved Son, through the intercession of the holy Virgin Mary, and of all the saints -- " as we forgive them that trespass against us," grant us the grace that we may sincerely and truly forgive our enemies, and pray earnestly to thee for them; that we may never return evil for evil, but seek to do good to those who injure us –

"And lead us not into temptation," whether it be concealed, manifest, or sudden – " but deliver us from evil," past, present, and future. Truly no man, no angel, the Lord alone, could give us so simple and yet so exalted, so celestial, a form of prayer, in which we ask all, even more than is asked in the prayers of the longest prayer book, all the good prayers of which are but paraphrases or expositions of this.

Next in sublimity comes the Hail Mary, which we so often repeat in the Rosary, because, as it contains a form of praise for the Incarnation, it best suits a devotion instituted to honor the principal parts of that great mystery. In the Hail Mary we are, above all, not to pass over as insignificant those words of the evangelist, "And the name of the virgin was Mary" (Lk. 1:28). For her very name is not without a mystery, and ought to be to us most amiable, sweet, and awful. "Of such virtue and excellency is this name that the heavens exult, the earth rejoices, and the angels sound forth hymns of praise when Mary is named," says St. Bernard. She is truly the star which arose from Jacob, and which, being placed above this wide, tempestuous sea, shines worth by the merits and examples of her life. "Oh! you who find yourself tossed in the tempests of this world, turn not your eyes from the brightness of this star if you would not be overwhelmed by storms. If the winds of temptations rise; if you fall among the rocks of tribulations, look up at the star, call on Mary. If you are tossed by the waves of pride, ambition, detraction, jealousy, or envy, look up at the star, call on Mary. If anger, covetousness, or lust beat on the vessel of your soul, look up to Mary. If you begin to sink in the gulf of melancholy and despair, think of Mary. In dangers, in distresses, in perplexities think of Mary, call on Mary; let her not depart from your lips; let her not depart from your heart; and that you may obtain the suffrage of her prayers, never depart from the example of her conversation. Whilst you follow her, you never go astray; whilst you implore her aid, you never sink in despair; when you think on her, you never wander; under her patronage you never fall; under her protection you need not fear; she being your guide, you are not weary." Such are the sentiments of confidence, devotion, and respect with which the name of Mary ought always to inspire us.

Next to this holy name, the words of the salutation come to be considered. "Hail" is a word of salutation, congratulation, and joy. The archangel addressed it with profound reverence and awe to this incomparable and glorious virgin. It was anciently an extraordinary thing if an angel appeared to one of the patriarchs or prophets, and then he was received with great veneration and honor, being by nature and grace exalted above them; but when the Archangel Gàbriel visited Mary, he was struck at her exalted dignity and pre-eminence, and approached and saluted her with admiration and respect. He was accustomed to the luster of the highest heavenly bodies, but was amazed and dazzled at the dignity and spiritual glory of her whom he came o salute Mother of God, whilst the attention of the whole heavenly court was fixed with ravishment upon her. With what humility ought we, worms of the earth and base sinners, to address her in the same salutation. The devout Thomas a Kempis gives the following paraphrase of the Angelic Salutation: "With awe, reverence, devotion, and humble confidence do I suppliantly approach you, bearing on my lips the salutation of the angel, humbly to offer you. I joyfully present it to you, with my head bowed out of reverence to your sacred person, and with my arms expanded through excessive affection of devotion; and I beg the same may be repeated by all the heavenly spirits for me a hundred thousand times and much oftener; for I know not what I can bring more worthy your transcendent greatness, or more sweet to us who recite it. Let the pious lover of your holy name listen and attend. The heavens rejoice, and all the earth ought to stand amazed when I say 'Hail Mary.' Satan and hell tremble when I repeat 'Hail Mary.' Sorrow is banished, and a new joy fills my soul when I say 'Hail Mary.' My languid affection is strengthened in God and my soul is refreshed when I repeat 'Hail Mary.' So great is the sweetness of this blessed salutation that it is not to be expressed in words, but remains deeper in the heart than can be fathomed. Wherefore, again I most humbly bend my knees to you, O most holy Virgin, and say: 'Hail Mary, full of grace.' Oh! that, to satisfy my desire of honoring and saluting you with all the powers of my soul, all my members were converted into tongues and into voices of fire, that I might glorify you, O mother of God, without ceasing! And now, prostrate in your presence, invited by sincere devotion of heart, and all inflamed with veneration for your sweet name, I represent to you the joy of that salutation when the Archangel Gabriel, sent by God, entered your secret closet, and honored you with a salutation unheard from the beginning of the world, saying: 'Hail, full of grace, the Lord is with thee'; which I desire to repeat, were it possible, with lips pure as gold, and with a burning affection, and I desire that all creatures now say with me, *Hail.*"

In like sentiments of profound respect and congratulation with the angel, we style her *full of grace.* Though she is descended of the royal blood of David, her illustrious pre-eminence is not derived from her birth or any other temporal advantages, but from that prerogative in which alone true excellency consists, the grace of God, in which she surpasses all other mere creatures. To others, God deals out portions of his grace according to an inferior measure; but Mary was to be prepared to become mother of the Author of grace. To her, therefore, God gave every grace and every virtue in an eminent degree of excellency and perfection. "Mary was filled with the ocean of the Holy Ghost poured upon her," says Venerable Bede (in Mt. c.1). It was just that the nearer she approached to the fountain of grace, the more abundantly she should be enriched by it; and, as God was pleased to make choice of her for his Mother, nothing less than a supereminent portion of grace could match her transcendent dignity. The Church, therefore, applies to her that of the Canticles: "Thou art all fair, and there is no spot in thee" (Cant. 4:7).

In the words "the Lord is with thee" we repeat with the angel another eulogium, consequent of the former. God, by his immensity or omnipotence, is with all creatures, because in him all creatures have their being. He is much more intimately with all his just, inasmuch as he dwells in them by his grace, and manifests in them the most gracious effects of his goodness and power; but the Blessed Virgin, being full of grace and most agreeable in his eyes above all other mere creatures, having also the closest union with Christ as his Mother, and burning with more than seraphic divinity, she is his most beloved tabernacle, and he favors her with the special effects of his extraordinary presence, displaying in her his boundless munificence, power, and love.

The following praise was given to her in the same words both by the Archangel Gabriel and St. Elizabeth: "Blessed art thou amongst women." Mary is truly called blessed above all other women, she having been herself always preserved from the least stain of sin, and having been the happy instrument of God in converting the maledictions laid on all mankind into blessings. When Judith had delivered Bethulia from temporal destruction, Ozias, the prince of the people, said to her: "Blessed art thou, daughter, above all women upon the face of the earth" (Judith 13:23). And "the people all blessed her with one voice, saying: Thou art the glory of Jerusalem, thou art the joy of Israel, thou art the honor of our people." How much more emphatically shall we, from our hearts, pronounce her blessed above all women who brought forth Him who is the author of all manner of spiritual and eternal blessings to us. She most justly said of herself, in the deepest sense of gratitude to the divine goodness, "Behold, from henceforth all generations shall call me blessed" (Lk. 1:48).

By bestowing these praises on Mary, we offer principally to God a profound homage of praise for the great mystery of the Incarnation. The pious woman mentioned in the Gospel who, upon hearing the divine doctrine of our Redeemer, cried out with admiration, "Blessed is the womb that bore thee, and blessed are the breasts which gave thee suck" (Lk. 11:27), meant chiefly to commend the Son. In like manner, the praises we address to Mary in the Angelical Salutation are reflected in the first place on her divine Son, from whom and by whom alone she is entitled to them; for it is for his gifts and graces and for his sake that we praise and honor her. On this account, this prayer is chiefly an excellent doxology for the great mystery of the Incarnation. Whence, having styled the Mother blessed above all women, we pronounce the Son infinitely more blessed, saying: "And blessed is the fruit of thy womb." He is the source and author of all her graces and blessings; she derives them only from him; and to him we refer whatever we admire and praise in her. Therefore, in an infinitely higher sense of praise, love, and honor, and in a manner infinitely superior to her, we call him blessed for ever by God, angels, and men: by God, as his well beloved Son, and in his divinity coequal and coeternal with the Father; by the angels, as the author of their being, grace, and glory, inasmuch as he is their God; by men, in his Incarnation as the repairer of their losses and their Redeemer. We, considering attentively the infinite evils from which he has delivered us, the pains and labors which he sustained for us, the ransom which he has paid with his precious blood to redeem us, the everlasting and infinite advantages which he has purchased for us with the boundless felicity of heaven, the excess of his goodness, love, and mercy, and his infinite majesty and perfection – we, I say, bearing all this in mind, ought, in a spirit of love and praise ever to call her blessed through whom we receive so great a Savior; but him infinitely more blessed, both for his own adorable sanctity and for all the graces of which he is the source.

The most holy and glorious name of Jesus, which is added to this doxology, is a name of unspeakable sweetness and grace – a name most comfortable and delightful to every loving soul, terrible to the wicked spirits, and adorable with respect to all creatures. So that at its very sound every knee in heaven, on earth, and in hell shall bend, and every creature be filled with religious awe and profound veneration and respect.

The last part of this prayer is a supplication. The prayer of the blessed spirits in heaven consists chiefly in acts of adoration, love, praise, thanksgiving, and the like. We, in this vale of tears and miseries, join sighs even to our hymns of praise and adoration. So extreme are our spiritual wants and trials, that we never present ourselves in prayer before Almighty God without imploring his mercy and graces with the greatest earnestness possible and the deepest sense of our needs. It is in this sincere feeling of our necessities and the most humble and earnest cry of our heart that the fervor and very soul of our prayer consist. God knows, and with infinite tenderness compassionates, the depth of our wounds and the whole extent of our numberless and boundless spiritual miseries. But our insensibility under them provokes his just indignation. He will have us sincerely feel and acknowledge the weight of our evils; our extreme spiritual poverty and total insufficiency, the baseness of our guilt, the rigor of his judgments, the frightful torments of an unhappy eternity which we deserve for our sins, and the dangers from ourselves and the invisible enemies with which we are surrounded. He requires that we confess the abyss of miseries in which we are sunk, and out of it raise our voice to him with tears and groans, owning our total dependence on his infinite mercy and goodness. If a beggar ask an alms of us, his wants make him eloquent – he sums them all up to move us to compassion; sickness, pains, hunger, anguish of mind, distress of a whole family, and whatever else can set off his miseries in the most moving manner. In like manner, when we pray we must feel and lay open before our Heavenly Father our deep wounds, our universal indigence, inability, and weakness, and with all possible earnestness implore his merciful aid. We must beg that God himself will be pleased to form in our hearts and sustain such sincere desires, that he inspire us with a deep sense of our wretchedness, and teach us to lay this before him in such a manner as will most powerfully move him to pity and relieve us.

We have recourse to the angels and saints to beg their joint intercession for us. For this we address ourselves in the first place to the Blessed Virgin, as the refuge of the afflicted and of sinners. In this prayer we repeat her holy name to excite ourselves to reverence and devotion. By calling her Mother of God we express her most exalted dignity, and stir up our confidence in her patronage. For what can she not obtain for us of God, who was pleased to be born of her! We at the same time remember that she is also spiritually *our Mother;* for, by adoption, we are brothers and coheirs of Christ. She is to us a mother of more than maternal tenderness; incomparably more sensible of our poverty and weakness, and more ready to procure for us all mercy and assistance, than mothers according to the flesh can be, as in charity she surpasses all other mere creatures. But to call her mother, and to deserve her compassion, we must sincerely renounce and put an end to our disorders, by which we have too often trampled upon the blood of her Son.

These words, "Holy Mary, Mother of God," are a kind of preface to our petition, in which we humbly entreat her to pray for us. We do not ask her to *give* us grace; we know this to be the most precious gift of God, who alone can bestow it on us. We only desire her to *ask* it for us of her Son, and to join her powerful intercession with our unworthy prayers. We mention our quality of sinners to humble ourselves in the deepest sentiments of compunction, and to excite her compassion by laying our extreme miseries and wants before her, which this epithet of sinners expresses beyond what any created understanding can fathom. Mary, from her fuller and more distinct knowledge of the evil of sin, and the spiritual needs of a soul infested with it, forms a much clearer and more exact idea of the abyss of our evils than we can possibly do; and, in proportion to them and to the measure of her charity, is moved to compassionate us under them. But we must mention our sins with sincere sentiments of contrition and regret; for the will which still adheres to sin provokes indignation, not compassion, in God and in all the saints, who love his sanctity and justice above all things. We must, therefore, mention our guilt with the most profound sentiments of confusion and compunction. In proportion to their sincerity and fervor, we shall excite the pity and mercy of God and the tender compassion of his Mother. Mary, having borne in her womb the Author of grace and mercy, has put on the bowels of the most tender compassion for sinners. By this mention of our quality of sinners, we sufficiently express what it is that we beg of God – namely, the grace of a sincere repentance, the remission of all our sins, and strength to resist all temptations to sin. We ask also for all graces and virtues, especially that of divine charity. All this is sufficiently understood by the very nature of our request without being expressed: for what else ought we to ask of God through the intercession of her who is the Mother of the Author of grace? We beg this abundance of all graces, both *at present*, because we stand in need of it every moment of our lives, and for the hour of our death, that great and most dreadful moment, which must be a principal object in all our prayers. The whole life of a Christian ought to be nothing else than a constant preparation for that tremendous hour which will decide our eternal lot, and in which the devil will assail us with the utmost effort of his fury; and our own weakness in mind and body, the lively remembrance of our past sins, and other alarming circumstances and difficulties, will make us stand in need of the strongest assistance of divine grace and the special patronage of her who is the protectress of all in distress, particularly of her devout clients in their last and most dangerous conflict.

Amen, or, *so be it,* expresses an earnest repetition of our supplication and praise. As the heart, in the ardor of its affections, easily goes far beyond what words can express, so neither is it confined by them in the extent and variety of its acts. In one word it often comprises perfect acts of faith, hope, and charity, adoration, praise, and other such virtues. Thus, by *amen* it repeats with ardor all the petitions and acts of the Lord's Prayer and Angelical Salutation. Some devout persons have made this short but energetic and comprehensive word one of their most frequent aspirations to God during the course of the day – meaning thereby to assent to, confirm, and repeat, with all possible ardor and humility, all the hymns and perfect acts of profound adoration, humility, love, praise, zeal, thanksgiving, oblation of themselves, total resignation, confidence in God, and all other virtues, which all the heavenly spirits offer to God, with all their power and strength, and with the utmost purity of affection, without intermission to eternity. In these acts we join by the word *Amen*, and desire to repeat them all with infinite fervor, were it possible, for ever; and with them we join the most sincere sentiments and acts of compunction and a particular humility, condemning ourselves as infinitely unworthy to join the heavenly choirs or faithful servants of God in offering him a tribute of praise; most unworthy even to pronounce his most holy name or mention any of his adorable perfections, which defiled lips and faint, divided affections rather profane and depreciate than praise and honor.

Such are the sentiments of faith, hope, charity, gratitude, humility, and sorrow which we express in reciting the Hail Mary; such are the graces and favors which we ask in the few words of which the Hail Mary is composed. Were we to say the prayers of all prayer books we could not express deeper sentiments of religion than we do in the Hail Mary, nor ask for greater favors than we pray for in the Angelic Salutation. No wonder, therefore, that all good Christians always delighted in repeating most frequently the Our Father and the Hail Mary. From these heavenly prayers they drew greater delight, strength, and courage, greater sentiments of religion than from all other prayers, even the most excellent.

In saying, line by line, the prayers contained in a prayer book, we use other men's words to express our own feelings. Now the Church does not forbid this kind of prayer. By no means; on the contrary, the very best books of devotion are found precisely in the Catholic Church.

But this method of devotion has one serious defect, it requires us to use the words of another, and these words do not always fully express our feelings. Sometimes the words express a sense of sorrow and abasement which we do not feel, and again the words are full of joy and fervor, while our heart is perhaps crushed and humbled under the intolerable weight of sin. Moreover, the wants of the heart are so various that we cannot find prayers to express them all. Sometimes our wants are quite distinct. They grow out of the crosses and troubles of daily life. They are, perhaps, temptations and difficulties that may seem slight and unimportant to others, but are very real and serious to us. Then, again, there are feelings of the soul that are *not* so clear and definite. There are feelings and desires which others cannot understand, and which even we ourselves cannot clearly understand. It is perhaps nothing but a sense of weariness, a sense of some great need. It is not that we have any particular want to ask for, but we feel weak, and fearful, and unhappy. We would wish to kneel down in the presence of God and let him see our heart. At such a time the best chosen phrases of other men seem stiff and cold and meaningless. We may try at such a time to use our own words, but we cannot find the right words to express our feelings, and then there is great danger of becoming annoyed and distracted, and giving up prayer altogether. Now, at such times, especially, we need something like an outline of prayer which will keep us recollected, and at the same time give full liberty to our thoughts and affections, and this is exactly what we find in the Rosary.

The Rosary has enough of outward form to keep us from distraction, and at the same time the prayers of which it is composed are such that we can adapt them to whatever state of mind we may be in at the time. Take again, for instance, the Lord's Prayer. How far superior it is to any human composition! It asks for definite blessings, and yet its words can express every desire of our heart. When, for instance, we say, "Thy kingdom come," we may pray for the kingdom of his holy Church, which has so many enemies on earth, or we may be weary of this sinful life, and pray that we may be soon admitted into the kingdom of the blessed.

When we say, "Forgive us our trespasses," we may mean the forgiveness of that sin especially which at the moment presses so heavily on our heart. When we say: "Lead us not into temptation, but deliver us from evil," we may pray that God would deliver us from that particular temptation that harasses us, or from that misfortune that has befallen us.

Thus the prayers of the Rosary, which are in themselves so plain and simple, are full of a deep and varied meaning, and become really the prayer of the heart. We may say these wonderful prayers every day, and every hour of the day, and they never grow old, never grow wearisome; they have always a new meaning, they always express the desires of our heart. The same may be said of the Hail Mary.

The words of the Hail Mary, "Pray for us," are very simple, and yet into these words we may put all the feelings that fill our heart. The words "Pray for us" may be repeated over and over again, and yet each time we may say them with a different intention and the words will have an entirely different meaning.

Let us suppose, for instance, that we meditate on the mystery of the Annunciation. We first try to form in our mind a picture of the little room in which Mary is praying all alone. We gaze on her in silence. We think of her purity, her lowliness, of all the graces which adorn her soul, and make her a living temple of God. Suddenly there steals through the open casement a ray of soft, glorious light; it shines around this sweet virgin, growing brighter and brighter the longer it shines. She raises her head and sees standing before her the beautiful form of one of God's angels. His silvery voice breaks the solemn stillness. He announces the glad tidings that she is to be the Mother of God. Now, surely, such a scene, were we to witness it in reality, would make a deep impression on us. It would make us wish to have the same graces which made the Blessed Virgin Mary so pleasing to God. We would feel naturally inclined to love and honor that holy virgin, and especially we would love and honor God for sending his dearly beloved Son to become man's sufferer, and die for our redemption. And then whilst repeating the Hail Mary, the prayer would naturally come to our lips: "Holy Mary, pray for us, that we may be humble like thee. Pray for us, that we may be always resigned to the will of God, as thou wert. Pray that God may always dwell in our hearts, as he dwelt in thee." Thus, the Hail Mary may take any sense we choose to put upon it, and will always express the various desires of our heart.

Suppose, again, we desire to pray for those whom we love, and who are suffering either in mind or body. We meditate on the first sorrowful mystery – the agony of Jesus Christ in the garden. Now, will not the thought "that his soul was sorrowful unto death," give us great confidence in praying for them in their sorrows? The depths of his agony no human heart will ever know. In like manner the griefs of even our best friends are in a great part hidden from us. At such a time, when we say the Hail Mary, it is as if we said, "Holy Mary, pray for us, that God's angel may come down from heaven and strengthen these poor suffering souls. Pray for us, that no matter what happens, we may always say with Jesus, "Thy will, not mine, be done."

In this way the words and mysteries of the Rosary are connected.

Let us take another kind of trouble which good people find to be their greatest hindrance and torment – distractions or dryness in prayer; that painful feeling, as if we had no comfort in good thoughts, as if we were tired of religion, and were out of God's favor. This, perhaps, often happens to us, and while the feeling lasts, we seem to ourselves to be very wicked, though we are not conscious of any particular sin. There is a general indefinite sense of being shut out of God's presence, and of being left entirely to ourselves. Now, in such a state of mind long prayers are sure to be wearisome. We could not keep our thoughts from wandering, even if we were to follow the words of the most excellently written form of prayer. Now, the Rosary supplies a form of devotion which is full of comfort to any one so suffering. Let us take, for instance, when thus tempted, the fifth joyful mystery, "The finding of the child Jesus in the temple." We try, first, to think a little about the mystery before saying any prayers at all. For twelve happy years Mary and Joseph had our Blessed Lord always with them. Day and night he had been always near them; and we can hardly imagine the joy and consolation which his presence must have given them. Now they have lost him, and the loss is agonizing. They seek him everywhere, but in vain. The world is blank, for Jesus is not with them. Everything around is empty and desolate. Is not this precisely the way we also feel when deprived of God's sensible presence? Our heart, which was yesterday full of consolation, is now sad and sorrowful. At last Mary and Joseph find Jesus in the temple. Oh! how great is their joy. They teach us by their example that if we wish to find Jesus again, we must seek him in the temple, in prayer, in the reception of the sacraments, in a good confession, in a worthy communion. Ah! then, the little words, " Pray for us," are full of meaning. They mean, "Pray for us, O holy Mother of God! that like thee we may find Jesus whom we have lost. Pray for us, that our sinfulness and coldness may never again drive him away from us."

We kneel in spirit in the stable of Bethlehem. With the eyes of our soul we behold the divine Infant and his blessed Mother. We see St. Joseph and the shepherds, and we kneel in their midst. There we feel how good and joyful a thing it was for our Lord to be born in the world that night, and there is so much meaning in the words: "Blessed art thou amongst women, and blessed is the fruit of thy womb, Jesus."

Or, perhaps, a more awful picture rises before us. We see a darkened sky and an uplifted cross. There is one dying upon that cross, and he is dying for love of us. The work which was begun in lowly poverty, is finished in agony and death; and, still, beneath the cross, there is the mother's form. She was a mother of joy; she is now a mother of sorrow. Yet, still, among her tears, we call her "blessed among women," and still, in childlike accents, we entreat her to "pray for us now, and at the hour of our death."

The courts of heaven are lying open before our sight. The spot we kneel on, the thoughts of the day or yesterday are passed away, nay, earth itself is forgotten, and we see nothing but the crystal sea and the dazzling white throne, and the ineffable brightness of God's infinite majesty. Around that ineffable glory we see the folded wings of the seraphim, in its very center we see the form of the divine humanity bright with unutterable beauty. Nearest to him in glory, as she was once in suffering, is she who is truly the "Blessed among women"; and then, more than ever trusting to the power of her intercession, we say with a confident heart: "Holy Mary, Mother of God, pray for us now, and at the hour of our death." In this way the words and mysteries of the Rosary are connected with our own cares and anxieties. There is always some part of the life of our Blessed Lord which will give us strength and comfort, and we can thus make a far more earnest, heartfelt form of prayer than we can find in the best of prayer books. This form accommodates itself to all times and to all persons. It is clear and comprehensible to the unlearned, and yet it contains an inexhaustible source of strength and meditation to the learned. It contains within itself an immeasurable depth, and embraces all the regions of the doctrines of faith and of moral truth. It declares and regulates the highest duties of human life. It is sufficiently evident that so simple, and yet so exalted and celestial, a form of prayer must be descended from heaven, and will never be surpassed by any human composition.

There is a countless variety of prayer books; but not one of them can be better than the Rosary. What book is so convenient to carry with us as our beads? It can always be about us; in going to our work we can take it in our hands, and say a decade; at night we can put it around our neck or on the arm, and before falling asleep offer to our Mother another decade of prayer. And if we happened to lose it? Why, our dear Lord has provided each of us a living pail of beads; we can count our ten Hail Mary's on our ten fingers, and accommodate ourselves thus until we have provided ourselves with another. The Rosary is a prayer book for all. From the hour it was made known, it found its way through millions of lowly homes, even to the most distant countries. It has been used in every language throughout the wide world; its prayers have been said by the lips of little children who can barely lisp the name of mother; by the lips of old age that trembles with weakness and grief; they have been said by the sailor on the deep, by the ploughman at his work in the field, by the scholar at his books, by the soldier battling bravely for his altars and firesides, by peasant girls singing in sunny vineyards, by the lips of those whose brows flashed the gems of royal diadems. The book of the Rosary is in use in the cottage and in the hall; at the wayside shrine and under the fretted roof of the grand cathedral; in the hour of joy and in the hour of anguish. It is a book blest and approved by twenty-five Popes, and recommended by the many indulgences they attached to its prayers; a book which the little child and aged man, the rich and the poor, the learned and the uninstructed can use with the same fervor, the same love, the same efficacy; a book in which the good Christian glories as the living testimony of Catholicism, and a mark of tenderness towards Jesus Christ and the most holy Mother of God.

CHAPTER 14

WE MUST SAY THE ROSARY FOR
A LAWFUL OBJECT

God is our Father. Now, a father will not give to his children what he knows to be hurtful to them. Should we, then, say the Rosary to obtain of our Heavenly Father something that is detrimental to us, especially to our salvation, he will not hear our prayer. The object of our prayer, then, must be lawful, and conducive to our spiritual welfare, as otherwise it would be displeasing to God; and it would be unreasonable for us to expect that God would grant us something which is displeasing to him. Accordingly, God will not hear us –

1. If we ask for something that is detrimental to our salvation. "A man," says St. Augustine, "may lawfully pray for the goods of this life, and the Lord may mercifully refuse to hear him." As a physician who desires the restoration of his patient will not allow him those things which he knows will be hurtful to him, so, in like manner, the Lord will turn a deaf ear to our devotion of the Rosary when we ask for such things as he knows will be detrimental to us. It is not forbidden, however, to pray for the necessaries of this life: "Give me only the necessaries of life" (Prov. 30:8); nor is it wrong to be solicitous about such things, provided our anxiety with regard to them be not inordinate, and we do not set our hearts upon them so absolutely as to make them the chief objects of our desires. We must always ask for them with resignation, and on condition that they be of advantage to our souls. We read in the life of St. Thomas of Canterbury, that a sick man had recovered his health through the saint's intercession; reflecting afterwards that sickness might have been better for him than health, he prayed again to the holy bishop, saying that he would prefer being sick, if sickness were better for him than health; and immediately his sickness returned.

2.   God will not hear our prayer of the Rosary, if we pray to be delivered from a particular temptation or cross (as St. Paul

prayed for deliverance from the temptations of the flesh), which God knows to be useful to our advancement in humility, and other virtues.

3.   Nor will God hear us if we ask for something from motives of ambition, like the sons of Zebedee, who prayed to obtain the principal offices in the kingdom of Christ.

4.   God will not hear our prayer of the Rosary if we ask for something from indiscreet zeal, as the Apostles did, when they asked our Lord to send fire from heaven upon the Samaritans, who had rejected Christ our Savior.

5.   God often delays hearing the prayer of the Rosary, if the object of it is not profitable to us at the time, but is so only at a later period. One day St. Gertrude complained to our Lord because she had not obtained from him a certain favor for her relatives, notwithstanding the promise he had made to her to hear all her prayers. Our Lord told her that he had heard her prayer, but would grant the favor she had asked for at some future time, when it would be more useful to her relatives.

6.   If the prayers of the Rosary are said, as it were, at random, without asking any particular grace, they are also more or less defective and inefficacious. "You know not what you ask" (Mk. 10:38), said our Lord Jesus Christ to the sons of Zebedee, when they asked of him that they might sit, one on the right hand and the other on his left, in his glory. Alas! how many Christians are there not to whom our Lord could address the same words: "You do not know what you ask of God in the Rosary." But it is self-deception to say the beads merely at random. This is to be like a person who is sick and goes to a druggist to buy medicine, without reflecting whether or not it will suit his particular disease. Such a manner of saying the beads is certainly injudicious, because it is not adapted to the spiritual wants of our souls. Hence we must say the beads to obtain some particular grace which we stand in need of; for instance, to be more patient and charitable towards such and such a person, or to overcome a certain temptation, or to do away with certain occasions of sin or dangerous objects, to obtain an increase of faith, hope, love for God, sorrow for our sins, perseverance in God's grace and friendship, and the like.

CHAPTER 15

WE MUST SAY THE ROSARY WITH HUMILITY

"Two men went up into the temple to pray; the one a Pharisee, the other a publican. The Pharisee, standing, prayed thus to himself: O God, I give thee thanks that I am not as the rest of men, extortioners, unjust, adulterers, as also is this publican. I fast thrice in the week; I give tithes of all I possess. And the publican, standing afar off, would not so much as lift up his eyes towards heaven, but struck his breast, saying: O Lord, be merciful to me a sinner! I say to you, this man went down to his house justified, rather than the other" (Luke 18:10-14).

In this parable of the Pharisee and the publican our Lord Jesus Christ teaches us that prayer without humility obtains nothing. As the Pharisee left the temple just as bad and as sinful as he entered, so shall we not improve much by the devotion of the Rosary if we perform it with the same sentiments of pride and self-conceit. Even common sense tells us that prayer, to be good, must be humble. Should a poor man beg alms in a haughty and impudent manner, he would be despised by every person; for to beg and to be proud at the same time is an abominable thing. All beggars know this but too well; hence many of them study different ways and manners to show themselves humble; they take the last place; they adopt humble language; they fall prostrate before you, if you meet them, asking alms with joined hands and with tears in their eyes. Should they have a good suit of clothes, they will put on ragged and tattered ones when they go out begging. How many humble reasons do they not allege to obtain an alms, such as not having eaten anything for the whole day. They pretend to suffer innumerable infirmities, and so lamentably do they sigh as even to move the hardest hearts to pity. No one blames them for this conduct; every one, on the contrary, approves of their manner of acting.

If humility, then, is required from men when asking a favor of their fellowmen, how much more will it not be required from us by the Lord of heaven and earth, when we address him in the prayer of the Rosary? To know that we are sinners, and that we have so often offended the divide majesty; that we have crucified our Lord Jesus Christ by our heinous sins; to know that if God did not assist us every day we would commit the most shameful crimes, and become even worse than the brute – all this should, undoubtedly, be a sufficient reason for us always to remain humble, and to say the beads with sentiments of exterior and interior humility, saying, with the publican, "Lord, be merciful to me a sinner!" in order that we, like him, may always come forth from prayer more acceptable, more justified, and more sanctified in the sight of the Lord of heaven and earth. "From the beginning have the proud not been acceptable to thee," said Judith," but the prayer of the humble and the meek hath always pleased thee" (Judith 9:16).

How great was not the wisdom which Solomon received in prayer! But in what manner, and with what sentiments, did he pray? Holy Writ says that Solomon, when praying, "had fixed both knees on the ground, and had spread his hands towards heaven" (3 Kings 8:54). St. Stephen effected by his prayer the conversion of St. Paul the Apostle, and of many others of his enemies. But how humble was not his prayer? "Falling on his knees," says Holy Scripture," he cried with a loud voice, saying: Lord, lay not this sin to their charge" (Acts 7:59). How humble must not have been the prayer of St. James the Apostle, who used to pray so long on his knees that the skin of them became as hard as that of a camel. St. John Chrysostom adds that the skin of the forehead of this Apostle had also become quite hard, from lying with it prostrate on the ground whilst at prayer. Ribadeneira and others relate the same of St. Bartholomew the Apostle.

The good thief received the forgiveness of his sins, but, before asking it, he humbled himself, avowing before the whole world what he was, and what he had deserved. "We receive the due reward of our deeds" (Lk. 23:41). The woman of Chanaan suffers herself to be compared to a dog by our Lord Jesus Christ; she does not feel herself insulted by this comparison, believing, as she did, that she deserved this name. Our dear Savior wondered at this, saying : "O woman! great is thy faith" (Mt. 15:28). Her faith was so great, because her humility was so profound. Hence she heard, from the mouth of our Lord, these consoling words: "Be it done to thee as thou wilt." The prodigal son says: "Father, I have sinned against heaven and before thee; I am not now worthy to be called thy son; make me as one of thy hired servants" (Luke 15:18). The father, seeing this great humility and sorrow in his son, pardoned him, and even received him as one of his best children.

God will treat us in the same manner, if we present ourselves before him with the same sentiments of humility and unworthiness. When our Lord Jesus Christ said to the Centurion: "I will come and heal thy servant," the centurion answered: "Lord, I am not worthy that thou should enter under my roof" (Mt. 8:8). This humility and faith of the centurion pleased our Savior so much that he said to him: "Go, and as thou hast believed, so be it done to thee; and the servant was healed at the same hour" (Mt. 8:13).

And in what manner did our Lord Jesus Christ himself pray? "Kneeling down, he prayed" (Lk. 22:47). Nay, he did more : "He fell upon his face, praying and saying: My Father, if it be possible, let this chalice pass from me" (Mt. 26:39). St. Thais, after her conversion from her sinful life, did not even dare so much as pronounce the name of God when praying. She used to say: "Thou who madest me, have pity on me." St. Paul the Hermit was so much accustomed to pray on his knees, and with his hands lifted up to heaven, that he died in this posture. Is it, then, astonishing that the saints have received so many and such great favors from God, since their humility was so great and so pleasing to him? "To the humble God giveth grace," says the Apostle St. James. "Their prayer shall pierce the clouds" (Eccles. 35:21).

"Yes," says St. Alphonsus, "should a soul have committed ever so many sins, yet the Lord will not reject it if she knows how to humble herself." "A contrite and humble heart, O God, thou wilt not despise" (Ps. 1:19). As he is severe and inexorable to the proud, so is he bountiful, merciful, and liberal to the humble. "Know, my daughter," said Jesus Christ one day to St. Catherine of Sienna, "that whosoever shall humbly persevere in asking graces of me, shall obtain all virtues." "Never did I," said St. Teresa," receive more favors from the Lord than when I humbled myself before his Divine Majesty."

CHAPTER 16

WE MUST SAY THE ROSARY WITH FERVOR

"Well hath Isaias prophesied of you, saying: This people honoreth me with their lips: but their heart is far from me" (Mt. 15:8). In these words our Savior gives us to understand that a prayer which proceeds not from the heart, or which is not devout and fervent, is not heard by the heavenly Father. There are many Christians who recite their prayers without thinking of what they say. Should they be required to tell what they asked of our Lord, they would be at a loss for an answer. The prayers of such Christians are quite powerless with God. One "Our Father," said with fervor, is better, and obtains more from God, than the entire Rosary recited a dozen times in a careless manner.

St. Bernard once saw how an angel of the Lord wrote down in a book the divine praises of each of his brethren when they were reciting the Divine Office; some were written in letters of gold, to express the devotion and fervor with which they were recited; others in letters of silver, on account of the pure intention with which they were performed; others were written with ink, to signify that they were said by way of routine and in a slothful manner; others, again, were written with watercolor, to indicate that they had been performed with great lukewarmness, and without devotion or fervor.

The divine praises of some of St. Bernard's brethren were not written down at all; but instead of the chanted psalms, the following words were written: "This people honoreth me with their lips, but their heart is far from me", (Is. 29:13), to signify that the angel of the Lord was much displeased with this kind of prayer.

Holy angels! show us once your book, that we may see in what colors the prayers of the Rosary of so many Christians are written down, especially in time of prosperity, when no calamity forces them to have recourse to God. There is good reason to fear that the prayers of the Rosary of many are written down in letters of ink, others in watercolor, and the greater number of them, I fear, are not written down at all; so that the devil himself must rejoice and laugh at them, as he did at the prayers of two Christians, of whom Jourdanus speaks: "They recited their prayers in so careless a manner that, at the conclusion of it, the devil appeared and cast an intolerable odor around, at the same time exclaiming, with great laughter: 'Such incense is due to such prayer!'"

Moreover, how many are there not who say the Rosary without being at all in earnest to obtain what they ask? They recite, for instance, the "Our Father" repeatedly, without wishing at all that any of its seven petitions should be granted. Let us examine them briefly. The first petition is, "Hallowed be thy name"; that is "Give me, and to all men, the grace to know thee always better and better; to honor, praise, glorify, and love thee; to comprehend the greatness of thy blessings, the duration of thy promises, the sublimity of thy majesty, and the depth of thy judgments." These are the graces which we ask in the first petition of the "Our Father." But who are those that earnestly ask for these graces, either for themselves or for others? Certainly these blessings are not asked for by any of those who, when entering the church, do not even think of bending the knee to express their faith in the name of God.

Nor are these graces asked for by those who do not desire to listen to the divine word in sermons and Christian instructions, that they may better learn their duty towards God, themselves, and their fellowmen.

Nor are these graces asked for by those who never think of praying fervently for the conversion of sinners, heretics, Jews, or heathens; or by those who dishonor the name of God by cursing and swearing, thus teaching others the language of the devil; nor by those who are ashamed of giving good example, who think, speak, and act badly, when others do the same; nor by all those who grievously transgress any of the commandments of God, and thus dishonor, despise, and insult the name of God. All such men certainly do not praise and honor God's name, and yet with their lips they will always pray, "Hallowed by thy name," without contributing anything at all towards the glory of the Lord of heaven and earth. Of these we must think that they know not what they ask, or do not wish to obtain what they ask.

The second petition is, "Thy kingdom come." Where are those who truly wish that God alone should reign in their hearts, and that no creature should have any part in it? Alas! most men feel provoked at the least temporal loss, at the slightest harsh word. And what account do the generality of men make of the grace and friendship of God? The readiness with which they commit sin tells it sufficiently. How difficult is it not for the priest to prevail upon them so far as to make them go to Confession and Holy Communion! How seldom do they pray! Shall we, then, believe that those who neglect and refuse the means to acquire the grace of God are in earnest when they pray, "Thy kingdom come"?

And where are those who truly desire to leave this world for a better one? Alas! should death knock at their door, what mourning, what alarm, what tears would it produce. Nay, many even are so much attached to this life that, should God offer them the choice between heaven and earth, they would prefer the latter. Let them pray, sigh, and exclaim, "Thy kingdom come"; their prayer is not true, because they do not wish for God's kingdom.

And where are those who are in earnest when they pray: "Thy will be done on earth, as it is in heaven"? Were God to say to them: "Well, it is my will that you should undergo humiliations and contempt on the part of your neighbor, of your friend, of your companion; like Job, you shall lose your good name, your honor among your fellowmen, or your children, and all your earthly goods," how soon would every one of them change his prayer and say: "Lord, be it otherwise done to me, as I do not mean this when I pray: 'Thy will be done on earth, as it is in heaven."

The fourth petition is, "Give us this day our daily bread — that is, give us everything necessary for the support of our temporal and spiritual life. Of course no one refuses the temporal, but where are those who truly hunger and thirst after the food of their souls, after prayer, the Word of God, Confession, and Holy Communion?

As this food is relished but by the smallest number of men, it is evident that the greater part of them do not wish to be heard when they make this petition.

"And forgive us our trespasses, as we forgive those who have trespassed against us." Neither does this fifth petition of the "Our Father" proceed from the heart of most men. They all, of course, wish that God should forgive them every sin, guilt, and punishment, but they themselves do not like to forgive. How long do they not harbor in their hearts a certain aversion, rancor, even enmity, against those of their fellowmen who offended them by a little harsh word! To salute them, to speak to or pray for them, seems too hard. How can they be sincere in saying "Forgive us our trespasses, as we forgive them that have trespassed against us"? As they ask forgiveness of God in the same way as they forgive others, they cannot be in earnest when they pray for forgiveness; their prayer is untrue; otherwise, they would forgive their fellowmen.

"Lead us not into temptation" – that is, Lord, preserve us from the temptations of the devil, of the flesh, and of the world. But, alas! most men love the occasion of temptations, and betake themselves willfully unto it. How should the Lord, then, preserve them from temptations? Most assuredly they do not wish at all to be heard in making this petition.

"And deliver us from evil" – that is, preserve us from sin; but the greater number of men commit sins deliberately every day, not doing the least violence to themselves by trying to avoid the occasions of sin, or to have recourse to prayer in the moment of temptation, or to receive the sacraments frequently. As they do not make use of the means which God has given us to be preserved from sin, how can they pray in truth or in earnest: "Deliver us from evil"? They do not mean it.

Such a prayer is worthless in the eyes of the Lord; he will never hear us, unless we are in earnest to obtain what we pray for. "Wilt thou be made whole?" (Jn. 5:6) said our Lord to the man languishing thirty – eight years. "What will ye that I do to you?" (Mt. 29:32) our Lord asked the two blind men. Had he noticed that they were not in earnest in their petition for health, he would have left them alone. Holy Scripture says of those who pray to God in earnest and with fervor that they *cry* to the Lord. Thus holy David says of himself: "In my trouble I *cried* to the Lord, and he heard me" (Ps. 119:15). And the Lord has promised to hear such a prayer. "He shall *cry* to me, and I will hear him" (Ps. 59:15). Now, to cry to the Lord means, according to St. Bernard, to pray with a great desire to be heard. The greater this desire is, the more piercing is this cry of prayer to the ears of God.

In vain do we hope that God will hear our Rosary prayer, if it be destitute of this earnest desire, fervor, sighing, crying, and effusion of the heart. Hence the prophet Jeremias says; "Arise give praise in the night, in the beginning of the watches; pour out thy heart like water before the face of the Lord; lift up thy hands to him for the life of thy little children that have fainted for hunger" (Jer. 2:19). Now, what is it to pour out our heart before the Lord? It is to pray, to sigh, to cry with a most vehement desire to be heard by our Lord. Hence St. Bernard says: "A vehement desire is great crying in the ears of the Lord," for God considers more the ardent desire and love of the heart than the cries of the lips. And St. Paul says, in his Epistle to the Romans: "The Spirit himself asketh for us with *unspeakable groanings*" (Rom. 8:26). Hence the royal prophet says of his prayer: "In his sight I pour out my prayer" (Ps.140:3); and in Ps. 61:9 he says: *"Pour out your heart before him."* It was thus that Anna poured out her heart before the Lord, and obtained the holy child Samuel (1 Kings 1:15). "As Anna had her heart full of grief, she prayed to the Lord, shedding many tears; and it came to pass, as she multiplied prayers before the Lord," etc.

Here the holy Fathers ask what is meant by this long prayer of Anna, since she besought the Lord only in a few words to grant her a child. St. John Chrysostom answers and says: "Although her prayer consisted of but few words, yet it was long, on account of the interior fervor and ardent desire with which she poured out her heart before the Lord; for she prayed more with her heart than with her lips, according to what is related in Holy Scripture: 'Now Anna spoke from her heart, whilst her lips only moved, but her voice was silent'" (1 Kings 1:13). Our Lord will, therefore, hear us, provided we understand how to pour out our hearts in prayer – that is, to lay open before him all the wishes and desires of our soul, its griefs, sufferings, cares, solicitudes, and anxieties, laying them, as it were, into his paternal heart, and into the bosom of his divine Providence, in order that he may come to aid, relieve, and comfort us.

Nay, according to St. Paul, we ought to do still more. In his Epistle to the Ephesians (Eph. 6:18) we read: "By all prayer and supplication, praying at all times in the spirit." In these words the Apostle gives us to understand that we should pray so earnestly and fervently to God as to sigh, cry, strike our breast, falling prostrate on the ground; nay, even conjure the Lord, by the death and blood of Jesus Christ, and by everything sacred, thus to move him to grant our prayer. Should we experience, in our will, a certain languor, sloth, and tepidity, nay, even a certain repugnance and resistance to ask favors of God with fervor and earnestness, we must beseech our dear Lord, as the Holy Church does in one of her prayers, to compel our rebellious wills, by means best calculated to enkindle this holy fervor in our hearts, in order that we may make sure of being heard, and of receiving what we pray for.

In order to produce this holy fervor in our hearts, God often sends us troubles, crosses, sickness, and adversities of every description, nothing being better calculated to make us pray with fervor than afflictions, tribulations, and crosses. Let the soul be under heavy sufferings, which it would like to cast off – surely it will not need a prayer book. It is then that, like hungry beggars, it finds a flow of words to produce the most heartfelt and fervent prayer. In prosperous times the prayer book is recurred to, but in the hour of adversity it is the heart that speaks, from an over – great desire to be relieved and comforted. It is then that men say, with David: "All the day I cried to thee, O Lord! I stretched out my hands to thee" (Ps. 87:10) "Consider and hear me, O Lord my God!" (Ps. 12:4.) Such prayers are most pleasing to God, and he cannot help hearing them, according to what David says: "In my trouble I cried to the Lord and he heard me" (Ps. 119:1).

When the prophet Jonas was swallowed by the whale, and carried about in the depths of the ocean, he prayed most fervently to the

161

Lord his God, saying: "Thou hast cast me forth into the heart of the deep sea, and a flood hath encompassed me; all thy billows and waves have passed over me" (Jonas 2:4). He then said: "I cried out in my affliction to the Lord, and *he heard me*. I cried out of the belly of hell, and *thou hast heard my voice*" (verse 3). How great was the affliction of Sara, on being accused of having murdered seven husbands, who had been killed by a devil named Asmodeus at their first going in unto her! At this reproach, says Holy Scripture, she went into an upper chamber of her house, and for three days and three nights did neither eat nor drink, but, continuing in prayer with tears, besought God to deliver her from this reproach. "And her prayers were heard in the sight of the glory of the Most High God" (Job 3:10-11). With what fervor did not the apostles cry out to our Lord Jesus Christ amidst the storms of the sea: "Lord, save us, we perish!" And he heard their cry, and commanded the winds and the sea, and there came a great calm (Mt. 7:25-26). Yes, in tribulation is truly verified what is related of the ruler in the Gospel: "And he himself believed, and his whole house" (Jn. 4:53). It is then that not only one member of the family will pray; nay, father, mother, children, servants, relatives, will unite in beseeching the Lord for assistance, because grief and affliction have come upon the whole house. Thus the Latin proverb is verified: "Qui nescit orare, eat ad mare" – Let him who does not know how to pray with fervor make a voyage at sea. There the storms and dangers of death will teach him to pour forth most fervent prayers. Such prayers are most powerful with, and they are heard by, the Lord.

I cannot omit remarking that tears shed during prayer are most powerful with God to obtain our petitions. The Fathers of the Church are profuse in bestowing praises upon the humble tears of the soul. The Holy Scriptures and the lives of the saints abound in examples to prove their power with God. "Oh! how great is the power which the tears of sinners exercise with God," exclaims St. Peter Chrysologus (Serm. 93). "They water heaven, wash the earth clean, deliver from hell, and prevail upon God to recall the sentence of damnation pronounced over every mortal sin. "Yes," says Anselmus Laudunensis, commenting on the words of the Book of Tobias (Tob. 3:11) "Continuing in prayer, with tears he besought God." Prayer appeases God, but, if tears are added, he feels overcome, and unable to resist any longer. The former is for him an odoriferous balm; the latter is a sweet tyranny.

Hence Julianus (Lib. de Ligno Vitae, chap. 9) exclaims, with truth: "O humble tears! how great is your power, how great is your reign. You need not fear the tribunal of the Eternal Judge; you silence all your accusers, and no one dares prevent you from approaching the Lord; should you enter alone, you will not come out empty. Moreover, you conquer the unconquerable, you bind the Omnipotent, you open heaven, you chase all the devils." "Indeed," says Peter Cellensis (Lib. de Panibus, ch. 12), "the infernal spirits find the flames of hell more supportable than our tears." Cornelius a Lapide says: "One tear of the sinner, produced by the sorrow of his heart, is capable of making God forgive and forget many, even the most atrocious, crimes." For this reason St. Leo, the Pope, says of the tears of St. Peter (Serm. 9, de Passione): "O happy tears of thine, O holy Apostle St. Peter! which were for thee a holy baptism to cancel thy sin of denying the Lord." St. Magdalen asks of our Lord the forgiveness of her numerous and great sins; but in what manner? "She began to wash his sacred feet with her tears" (Lk. 7:38); these tears moved his compassionate heart, and made him say: "Many sins are forgiven her, because she hath loved much."

Why was it that the holy patriarch Jacob, when wrestling with the angel of the Lord, received his blessing? (Gen. 32.) It was because he asked it with tears in his eyes: "He *wept*, and made supplication to him" (Osee 12:4). In the fourth Book of Kings (ch. 20) we read as follows: "In these days Ezechias was sick unto death, and Isaias the Prophet came to him and said: Thus saith the Lord God: Give charge concerning thy house, for thou shalt die, and not live. And he turned his face to the wall, and prayed to the Lord, saying: I beseech thee, O Lord, remember how I have walked before thee in truth, and with a perfect heart, and have done that which is pleasing before thee. And Ezechias *wept with much weeping*." What did he obtain by his tears? Holy Writ says: "And before Isaias was gone out of the middle of the court, the word of the Lord came to him, saying: Go back and tell Ezechias: Thus saith the Lord: I have heard thy prayer and I have seen thy *tears;* and behold, I have healed thee;

on the third day thou shalt go up to the Temple of the Lord. And I will add to thy days fifteen years."

Our Lord Jesus Christ himself often prayed with tears in his eyes, according to what St. Paul the Apostle writes: "Who, in the days of his flesh, with a strong cry *and tears, offering up prayers and supplication, was heard* for his reverence" (Heb. 5:7). In his comment on Zacharias (ch. 12), Cornelius a Lapide relates that St. Dunstan, after the death of King Edwin, from whom he had received much ill-treatment, saw, whilst at prayer, several black men running off with the soul of the king in their hands. Forgetting all the injuries and ill-treatment which he had received from Edwin, he took pity on him in his miserable condition, shedding *torrents of tears* before the face of the Lord for the deliverance of the king's soul, and he did not cease weeping and praying until the Lord heard him. Soon after he saw the same black men again, but their hands were empty, and the soul of the king was no longer in their possession. They then commenced to curse and swear, and utter the most abominable imprecations against the servant of God, to which St. Dunstan paid no attention, but thanked God for the extraordinary great mercy shown to the king.

Let us, then, with Judith (Judith 8:14), pray to the Lord, and ask with tears his pardon, his graces, and all his favors; and let us rest assured that as a mother cannot help consoling her weeping child, neither will our dear Lord refuse to hear the petitions of weeping souls.

CHAPTER 17

THE PRAYER OF THE ROSARY MUST BE FOLLOWED BY AMENDMENT OF LIFE

The sinner who says the Rosary without having the desire to quit the state of sin must not expect to be heard. "There are," says St. Alphonsus, "some unhappy persons who love the chains with which the devil keeps them bound like slaves. The prayers of such are never heard by God, because they are rash, presumptuous, and abominable." The prayer of him who turns away his ears so as not to hear what God commands is detestable and odious to God: "He who turneth away his ears from learning the law, his prayer shall be an abomination" (Prov.28:9). To these people God says: "It is of no use your praying to me, for I will turn my eyes from you, and will not hear you; when you stretch forth your hands I will turn away my eyes from you, and when you multiply prayer I will not hear" (Is. 1:15).

Why was the Lord so severe to the Jews, his chosen people, inflicting upon them the hardest punishments, such as the Egyptian bondage, in which they suffered for so many years? How often did they not pray for their deliverance? And why did the Lord not hear them? The prophet Ezechiel says: "And they committed fornication in Egypt; in their youth they committed fornication" (Ez. 23:3). Hence they prayed and cried to God in vain. But no sooner had they done away with their sins of idolatry and fornication than the Lord graciously heard them: "And the children of Israel, groaning, cried out because of the works; and their cry went up unto God from the works, and he heard their groaning, and remembered the covenant which he had made with Abraham, Isaac, and Jacob; and the Lord looked upon the children of Israel, and he knew them" (Ex. 2:23-25).

The Ark of the Covenant was a great treasure for the Jews. When it was carried around the city of Jericho, the walls of the city fell down; when the Jews had arrived with it at the river Jordan, the waters of the river divided, the lower part flowing off, and the upper part rising like a mountain. Now, after the Jews had lost four thousand men in one day, in a war against the Philistines, they had the Ark brought into the camp, hoping that, for its sake, the Lord would protect them and deliver their enemies into their hands. And the ancients of Israel said: "Why hath the Lord defeated us today before the Philistines? Let us fetch unto us the Ark of the Covenant of the Lord from Silo, and let it come in the midst of us, that it may save us from the hands of our enemies. And when the Ark of the Covenant of the Lord was come into the camp, all Israel shouted with a great joy, and the earth rang again" (1 Kings 4.) Now they thought they had no more to fear from their enemies, who, at the sight of the Ark of the Covenant, were panic-stricken; so much so that they cried out "God is come into the camp. And sighing they said, Woe to us; who shall deliver us from the hands of these high gods?"

With new courage the Jews began to fight again. Were they victorious? By no means; they were defeated worse than ever, losing thirty thousand men, besides the Ark of the Covenant. One might ask here: Did God then cease to love the Israelites? Most assuredly not. His love still remained the same as before. Why, then, were they defeated in the presence of the Ark of the Covenant, which was given to them as a sign of the divine blessing and protection? "But for the love of his Ark" says Theodoret," God did not wish to protect his people, because, after having previously offended him, they did not repent of their sins. It was with sinful hearts they paid outward honor to the Ark. They shouted with great joy as soon as they beheld it, but there was not one who shed a tear of repentance, no one prayed and sighed with a sorrowful heart. Hence the Ark brought down no blessing upon them at that time."

"Why, then, should we wonder," said Dionysius the Carthusian, "if we see miseries and calamities increase among the Christians, notwithstanding their saying the Rosary to avert them? It is because they pray with sinful and criminal hearts, not being sorry in the least for their evil deeds, nor showing the slightest desire to amend their lives." Let them wear upon their person as many Rosaries, Agnus

Deis, Relics of the Saints, Gospels of St. John, as they may wish; let them pray, nay, even cry to heaven as much as they will – all these articles of devotion, prayers, and cries will avail them nothing, if, at the same time, they are given up to the devil, and do not wish to give up his worship and service. Instead of being heard, they will, according to St. Augustine, be so much the more severely punished. "Punishments," says the saint, "become more frequent every day, because the number of sins is daily increasing."

If we, then, wish that God should hear our prayers, we must be sorry for our sins, and endeavor to amend our lives. "Above all" says St. Ambrose, "we must weep, and then pray." The Lord himself has declared this quite distinctly by the prophet Isaias "I will not hear you" – why not? – "for your hands are full of blood" (Is. 1:15) – full of sins and iniquities.

But, on the contrary, the Lord has promised, by the same prophet, that he will hear the prayers of those who truly amend their lives: "Loose the bands of wickedness; undo the bundles that oppress.... Then shalt thou call, and the Lord shall hear; thou shalt cry, and he shall say: Here I am" (Is. 58) – that is, to help you. God commanded the prophet Jonas to announce to the Ninivites that within forty days their city would be destroyed. The Ninivites at once began to pray to God, and ask his pardon. God heard their prayers. Why? Because they repented of their sins, did penance for them, and amended their lives.

The prayers of the Rosary of a true and sincere penitent are acceptable in the sight of God, and are heard by him. Hence, according to the advice of St. Paul, we must endeavor always to pray to God with a contrite heart: "I will, therefore," says this Apostle, "that men pray in every place, lifting up pure hands" (1Tim. 2:8). When are our hearts pure? "When they are free from sin," says St. Ambrose.

From what has been said, the sinner should, however, not infer that, as he is a sinner and in disgrace with God, his devotion of the Rosary could not be acceptable to God, and that therefore he should cease saying the beads. No, it would be entirely wrong for a sinner to argue thus; for as long as he does not sin unto death

-- that is, if he has not the will to live and die in sin but desires to amend his life and prays for this grace – God will listen to his prayer, and hear it, if he perseveres in his petition. "There are others," says St. Alphonsus, "who sin through frailty, or by the violence of some great passion, who groan under the yoke of the enemy, and desire to break these chains of death, and to escape from their miserable slavery. Let such ask the assistance of God; for their prayer, if persevered in, will certainly be heard, Jesus Christ having said: 'Every one that asks receives, and he who seeks finds'" (Mt. 7:8).

His prayer, it is true, is not heard on account of his meritorious works, which he does not possess, but it is heard on account of the merits of Jesus Christ, and because our Savior has promised to hear every one that asks. "Therefore, when we pray," says St. Thomas, "it is not necessary to be friends of God in order to obtain the grace that we ask; for prayer itself restores us to his friendship." Hence St. Bernard says: "The desire of the sinner to escape from sin is a gift which is certainly given by no other than God himself, who most undoubtedly would not give this holy desire to the sinner unless he intended to hear him." Witness the publican in the Gospel, who went into the temple to pray "And the publican standing afar off, would not so much as lift up his eyes towards heaven, but struck his breast, saying: O God, be merciful to me a sinner! I say to you, this man went down into his house justified" (Lk. 8:13-14).

But the sinner may say, I have no sorrow for my sins, and I do not desire to amend my life; therefore, according to what you have said, God will not hear my prayer; consequently I may abandon the devotion of the Rosary. I answer, By no means give up saying the beads, although God will not hear you so long as you persevere in these dispositions of heart; yet for the sake of your prayer God spares you, waiting patiently for your conversion. "No sinner," says St. Alphonsus, "should ever give up his prayer, as otherwise he would be lost forever. God would send sinners to hell sooner if they ceased praying, yet, on account of their perseverance in prayer, he still spares them."

But let him who has no sorrow for his sins, no desire for the amendment of his life, let him ask of God this sorrow and grace of a thorough conversion, and let him persevere in saying the beads to obtain it. If he does, he may rest assured that God will finally enlighten his mind by making him understand the miserable state in which he is living, and touch his heart with sorrow for it; besides, God will also strengthen the will of the sinner, so as to be able to make serious efforts to rise from this fatal state.

Another will say, I have not only no sorrow for my sins, but I have not even the least desire to ask God's grace to be sorry for them. How can I, then, pray, not having the least desire to obtain anything? This, I must confess, is a pitiable but not a desperate state; for, if you will pray with perseverance, God will give you the desire to pray for the grace of contrition. Has he not declared: "I desire not the death of the wicked, but that he be converted and live"? God has the greatest desire to see all sinners saved, and he is ready at any time to give them the graces necessary for their salvation; but he wishes that they should pray for every good thought and desire, and for efficacious grace to put their good desires into execution. Let such a sinner say the beads to obtain a true desire to pray for his salvation; let him persevere in thus praying, and then let him rest assured that he will not be lost.

The conversion of King Manasses is a most striking proof of this truth. Manasses was twelve years old when his father died. He succeeded him on the throne, but not in his piety and fear of the Lord. He was as impious as his father was pious towards God and his people. He introduced again all the abominations of the Gentiles, which the Lord had extirpated from among the children of Israel; he apostatized from the Lord; he brought in again, and encouraged, idolatry; even in the temple of the Lord he erected an altar to Baal; he introduced into the temple of the true God such abominations as were never heard of before, and which are too shameful to relate. To crown his impiety, he made his son pass through fire in honor of Moloch; he used divination, observed omens, appointed pythons, and multiplied soothsayers to do evil before the Lord, and to provoke him (4 Kings 21:1-7). The Lord often warned him through his prophets, but in vain. At last "the Lord spoke to his prophets, saying: Because Manasses, King of Juda, hath done these most wicked abominations, beyond all that the Amorrhites did before him, and hath made Juda to sin with his filthy doings, therefore thus saith the Lord the God of Israel: Behold, I will bring evils upon Jerusalem and Juda, that whosoever shall hear of them, both his ears shall tingle. I will stretch over Jerusalem the line of Samaria and the weight of the house of Achab, and I will efface Jerusalem, as tables are wont to be effaced; . . . and I will deliver them into the hands of their enemies, and they shall become a prey and a spoil to all their enemies" (4 Kings 21:10-14).

Manasses, instead of entering into himself, added cruelty to idolatry. He shed so much innocent blood that, to use the words of Holy Writ, "he filled Jerusalem up to the mouth" (4 Kings 21:16). According to Josephus (Ant. 10:13), "he went so far in his contempt for God as to kill all the just of the children of Israel, not sparing even the prophets, but taking away their lives day by day, so that streams of blood were flowing through the streets of Jerusalem. "Now do you think so impious a wretch could be converted? O wonderful power of prayer! so great is thy efficacy with God that, should a man be ever so impious and perverse, he will not fail to obtain forgiveness of the Lord, if he pray for it with a sincere heart." "And the Lord," says Holy Writ, "brought upon Jerusalem the captains of the army of the King of the Assyrians, and they took Manasses and carried him, bound with chains and fetters, to Babylon. In this great distress and affliction he entered into himself, and he prayed to the Lord his God and did penance exceedingly before the God of his fathers, and he entreated him and he besought him earnestly; and the Lord heard his prayer, and brought him again to Jerusalem unto his kingdom. From that time forward he endeavored to serve the Lord the more fervently, the more grievously he had offended him. He abolished idolatry, destroyed the temples, altars, groves on the high places, put up in honor of heathenish deities; repaired the altar of Jehovah in the temple of Jerusalem, and sacrificed upon it victims and peace offerings, and offerings of praise, and he commanded Juda to serve the Lord the God of Israel" (Parlip. 33.)

I again repeat what I have said elsewhere: How great will be the pain and misery of the damned, seeing that they might have been saved so easily, provided they had prayed to God for their salvation! How true is it not what St. Alphonsus says: "All spiritual writers in their books, all preachers in their sermons, all confessors in their instructions to their penitents, should not inculcate anything more strongly than continual prayer; they should always admonish, exclaim, and continually repeat: Pray, pray, never cease to pray; for if you pray, your salvation will be secure; but if you leave off praying, your damnation will be certain. All preachers and directors ought to do this, because, according to the opinion of every Catholic school, there is no doubt of this truth, that he who prays obtains grace and is saved; but those who practice it are too few, and this is why so few' are saved" (Ch. 4, on Prayer).

CHAPTER 18

THE PRAYER OF THE ROSARY MUST BE UNITED WITH FORGIVENESS OF INJURIES

"And when you shall stand to pray, forgive, if you have aught against any man" (Mk. 11:25. "Leave thy offering before the altar, and go first to be reconciled to thy brother, and then coming, thou shalt offer thy gift" (Mt. 5:23).

In these words our Lord Jesus Christ teaches us that our prayer will not be heard by his Heavenly Father so long as we entertain in our hearts feelings of dislike towards any of our fellowmen. If you say the beads, he says, and at the same time have aught against any man, go first and be reconciled to your brother, or at least forgive him from the bottom of your heart, and then come and offer up your devotion of the Rosary; otherwise I will not listen to you. He has made every man his representative on earth by creating him according to his own image and likeness; he has redeemed all men with his most precious Blood; he has, therefore, declared that whatever we do to the least of our fellowmen for his sake we do it to him. Now, by commanding us to love our enemies, to do good to those that hate us, and to pray for those who persecute and calumniate us (Mt. 5:44), he asks of us to give to him in the person of his representatives that which we can give so easily. It would be great presumption to ask his gifts and favors without being willing, on our part, to give him what he requires of us in all justice. To refuse this request of our Lord would, indeed, on our part, be great injustice. We ask of him the greatest gifts, such as the pardon of innumerable and most grievous offences, final perseverance, deliverance from hell, everlasting glory, and so many other countless favors for both body and soul. What he asks of us is little or nothing compared with his graces.

I will give you what I can, says he, if you give me what you can; if you will not, neither am I bound to give anything to you. Hence I have said "that if two of you shall consent upon earth concerning anything, whatsoever they shall ask, it shall be done to them by my Father who is in Heaven" (Mt. 17:19). Our Savior means here to say that our Heavenly Father is so much pleased with the prayers of those who have no willful feelings of hatred towards one another, that he will grant to them whatsoever they ask of him; but if, on the contrary, they willfully entertain feelings of hatred, their prayer will not be heard." As singing is not pleasing or attractive to any one if the voices are not in perfect harmony, so neither, says Origen, "will the prayers of Christian congregations give any pleasure to God, if they be not of one heart and one soul, nor will he hear their petitions."

We must, then, whenever we betake ourselves to say the Rosary, banish from our hearts all willful enmity, hatred, rancor, and all uncharitable sentiments which may arise in our soul, by saying a short but fervent prayer for all those towards whom such feelings arise, or by offering up to God for each one of them the precious Blood of Jesus Christ, and all his merits, in union with those of his Blessed Mother and of all his saints.

To pray for those who wish us evil is an extremely difficult act, and one of the most heroic charity. It is an act free of self love and self interest, which is not only counseled, but even commanded, by our Lord (Mt. 5:44). The insults, calumnies, and persecutions of our enemies relate directly to our own person; wherefore, if we forgive, nay, even beg God also to forgive our enemies, we give up our claim to our right and honor, thus raising ourselves to the great dignity of true children of God – nay, even to an unspeakably sublime resemblance to his Divinity, according to what Jesus Christ says: "If you pray for those who hate, calumniate, and persecute you, you will be children of your Father who is in heaven, who maketh his sun to rise upon the good and bad, and raineth upon the just and the unjust" (Mt.5:45). For with God nothing is more characteristic, nothing more honorable, than to have mercy and to spare; to do good to all his enemies, thus converting them to become his friends, his children, and heirs of his everlasting glory.

Now, by imitating his goodness in a point most averse to our nature, we give him the greatest glory, and do such violence to his tender and meek heart as to cause it not only to forgive the sin of our enemies, but even to constrain it to grant all our prayers; because he wishes to be far more indulgent, far more merciful, and far more liberal than it is possible for us ever to be. Holy Scripture and the lives of the saints furnish us with the most striking examples in proof of this great and most consoling truth.

The greatest persecutor of St. Stephen was St. Paul the Apostle before his conversion: for, according to St. Augustine, he threw stones at him by the hands of all those whose clothes he was guarding. What made him, from being a persecutor of the Church, become her greatest Apostle and Doctor? It was the prayer of St. Stephen; "for, had he not prayed," says St. Augustine, "the Church would not have gained this Apostle." St. Mary Oigni, whilst in a rapture, saw how our Lord presented St. Stephen with the soul of St. Paul, before his death, on account of the prayer which the former had offered for him; she saw how St. Stephen received the soul of this Apostle the moment of his death, and how he presented it to our Lord, saying: "Here, O Lord, I have the immense and most precious gift which thou gavest me; now I return it to thee with great usury" ("Life," by Cardinal Vitriaco, lib. 2, Ch.11.) Oecomen is of the opinion that, on account of St. Stephen's prayer, not only St. Paul, but many others, most probably received the forgiveness of their sins and life everlasting.

In many instances St. Stephen has proved to be a most powerful intercessor and patron of all those who wish to convert, not only their enemies, but also other obstinate sinners. God granted him this power for his zeal, his example, and his martyrdom. Let us often invoke him to pray for our enemies, as he did for his.

Most touching is that which Father Avila relates of St. Elizabeth of Hungary. One day this saint prayed to God to give great graces to all those who had in any way injured her; nay, even to give the greatest graces to those who had injured her the most. After this prayer, our Lord Jesus Christ said to her: "My dear daughter, never in your life did you make a prayer more pleasing to me than the one which you have just said for your enemies; on account of this prayer, I forgive not only all your sins, but even all temporal punishments due to them." Let us be sure that the greater injuries we forgive for God's sake, the greater graces we shall receive in answer to our prayer.

We read in the life of St. John Gualbertus that he met one day with the murderer of his only brother in a very narrow street. Fearing that John would take revenge on him, and seeing no possibility of escape, the murderer fell on his knees, asking forgiveness for the sake of our Lord Jesus Christ, who forgave his murderers, and prayed for them on the cross. John forgave him at once, and embraced him as one of his best friends. Afterwards he went to a church, there to pray before a crucifix; but Oh! how pleasing was his prayer now to our Lord, and how powerful was it with him! Whilst praying, he saw how our Lord bowed his head towards him, thanking him, as it were, for the great offence he had forgiven. At the same time, he felt a most extraordinary change in his own soul, to such a degree that he renounced the world and became the founder of a religious order.

But some might say: I have no enemies; hence I have nothing to forgive, and thus I cannot use this means to make my prayer efficacious. In this case, say to God: Had I, O Lord, a thousand enemies, for thy sake I would forgive, love, and pray for them. Thus you will practice, at least in desire, the highest degree of charity, and our Lord will take the will for the deed. But you must remember that, if you have no opportunity to practice this degree of charity in reality, you will always find plenty of occasions to practice the degree next to it, which consists in bearing with your neighbors' whims, weaknesses, faults of character, disagreeable manners, and the like, trying to make yourself all to all. The practice of this kind of charity will equally move our Lord graciously to listen to your prayers.

In proof of this, we have but to consider the example of Moses. Notwithstanding the frequent murmurs of the Jewish people, their reproaches, their rebellion, their apostasy, he acted towards them with the same unvarying kindness; instead of taking revenge, he poured forth fervent prayers to God for their temporal and spiritual welfare. Hence it was that his prayer was so powerful with God as to prevent him from punishing the Jews for their sins so long as Moses interceded and asked him to pardon them. On this account, St. Jerome, St. Thomas, Hugo, Theodoret, and others, say that when this meek and forbearing charity is praying, it forces God, as it were, to listen to and hear its prayer. Let this be remembered by those especially who guide and direct others.

CHAPTER 19

THE PRAYER OF THE ROSARY
MUST BE UNITED WITH GOOD WORKS

"And thy justice shall go before thy face" (Is.58:8). St. Cyprian, commenting on these words of Isaias, says "that God will listen to and hear those prayers which are joined to good works." The angel of the Lord said to Tobias: "Prayer is good with fasting and alms" (Tob. 12:8); and by the prophet Isaias the Lord says: "Deal thy bread to the hungry, and bring the needy and the harborless into thy house; when thou shalt see one naked cover him, and despise not thy own flesh" (Is. 58:8). "Seek judgment, relieve the oppressed, judge for the fatherless, defend the widow" (Is. 6.) "Then shalt thou call, and the Lord shall hear; thou shalt cry, and he shall say: Here I am" (Is. 58.)

And again it is said: "Blessed are the merciful, for they shall obtain mercy" (Mt. 5); especially when they pray, for whosoever is good and liberal to the brethren of Jesus Christ on earth, to him Jesus Christ must be good and liberal also; for he is, and he desires to exhibit himself, infinitely better than any one possibly could be. We read in the life of the Bishop St. Julian that he distributed among the poor and needy everything he possessed. Hence the Church says of him that, being inflamed with a great paternal charity for his fellowmen, he obtained from God many wonderful things. When the people were once suffering very much from a want of corn, he began to pray to God with tears in his eyes; at once several wagon loads arrived, and no sooner were they unloaded than the men who brought the corn disappeared. Another time, when an epidemic spread rapidly throughout the diocese of this holy bishop, God caused it suddenly to cease, on account of the prayer of his holy servant. The Lord also heard his prayer for many who suffered from incurable diseases.

But many a one may say: It is not in my power to give alms, to fast, to wait upon the sick, or perform any such good works; hence the means just given to make prayer efficacious is for me not practicable.

In this case you must remember that, besides these so-called exterior good works, there are others called interior ones, which are better calculated to make prayer very powerful with God. Of these latter I will mention but one, viz.: the denial of your own will, in order to do God's will in the most perfect manner. "If thou hear the voice of the Lord thy God" (Deut. 30:10), or, as Isaias says, "If thou turn away thy foot from doing thy own will" (Is. 58:13), in order to follow mine, as it is expressed in my commandments, in the doctrine of my Son, and thy Redeemer, and in thy rules, if thou art a religious, in the precepts of those who keep my place with thee on earth, and in my inspirations, I also will listen to thy voice when thou prayest to me. Hence Cornelius a Lapide says: "If you wish that God should do your will when praying, you must first do what he wishes and commands you. If you wish that he should turn to you, you must go to meet him; if you desire that he should delight in you, you must delight in him." "Delight in the Lord," says the Psalmist, "and he will give thee the requests of thy heart" (Ps. 36:4).

Now, who can be said in truth to go and meet the Lord and delight in him? He only who, with a cheerful heart, does the Lord's will. "His petitions," as the royal prophet says, "shall be granted." Hence our Lord said one day to St. Gertrude, when she was praying for one of her sisters in religion who wished that God should grant her prayer for divine consolations: "It is she herself who puts obstacles to the consolations of my grace by the attachment to her own will and judgment. As one who closes his nostrils cannot enjoy the fragrance of fresh flowers, so, in like manner, the sweet consolations of my grace cannot be experienced by him who is attached to his own will and judgment."

Our Lord Jesus Christ expressed this also very clearly in his last discourse to his disciples, wherein he dwells particularly upon the three most essential virtues of Faith, Hope, and Charity; of Faith, by saying, "You believe in God, believe also in me" (Jn.14:1); of Hope, by saying, in verse 13: "Whatsoever you ask the Father in my name, that I will do" (prayer being an Act of Hope); of Charity, by saying: "If you love me, keep my commandments" (verse 15). These three virtues are most intimately connected with one another;

for Faith produces Hope, and Hope generates Charity. The meaning, then, is this: If you wish to obtain what I promised you, and to receive what you ask in my name; nay, if you wish that I may ask it for you of my heavenly Father, or may even give it myself to you, you must love me, who have loved you so very much, and you must persevere and increase in love of me. Now you will accomplish this by keeping my commandments. If you faithfully and perseveringly comply with this wish of mine, I promise you an immense reward, viz., the Paraclete, the Holy Ghost: "And I will ask the Father, and he will give you another Paraclete" (Jn.14:16).

The grant of our petitions in prayer depends, then, on our faithful fulfillment of the will of God. "You ought to know, brethren, that God will comply with our wishes in prayer only in proportion as we try to comply with his commandments" (Auct Serm. Ad Frat. in Eremo, apud St. Aug. tom. 10, Serm. 61) Hence we must not be astonished if we see or hear how the saints obtained everything from God. "He who honoreth his father, . . . in the day of his prayer he shall be heard"(Eccles. 3:6). The saints honor their Heavenly Father most perfectly, by an exact compliance with his divine will, and he honors the saints by doing their will.

St. Francis of Assisi would often stop on his journey suddenly, as soon as he perceived within himself an interior inspiration of God, and, giving it all his attention, he would say: "Speak, O Lord! for thy servant heareth."He would stop as long as the inspiration lasted, listening to it in all humility, and promptly executing whatever our Lord would inspire him to do. Hence he became so great and powerful with God. One day, as he was praying in these words, "Lord, have compassion on poor sinners,"Jesus Christ appeared to him, saying: "Francis, thy will is one with mine; I am therefore ready to grant all thy prayers."

For this reason it is that Cornelius a Lapide exclaims "Oh! how powerful should we be with God, were we always to find a ready ear and an obedient heart to his voice!"Like St. Dominic, we would experience that there is nothing that could not be obtained by prayer. Indeed, so good is our Lord to those who do his will perfectly that he not only grants their prayers, but even anticipates them. Tauler relates (Serm 1. De Circumcis.) of a pious virgin, whose spiritual director he was, that many people used to come and recommend their affairs to her prayers. She always promised to pray for them, but often forgot to do so. Nevertheless, the wishes of those who had recommended themselves to her prayers were fulfilled. These persons then came and thanked her, feeling persuaded that through her prayers God had helped them. The pious virgin blushed, and confessed that although she had intended to pray for them, she had forgotten to do so. Wishing to know the reason why our Lord blessed all those who recommended themselves to her prayers, she said to him: "Why, O Lord! is it that thou dost bless all those who recommend themselves to my prayers, even though I do forget to pray for them?" Our Lord answered her: "My daughter, from that very day on which you gave up your will, in order always to do mine, I gave up mine to do yours, wherefore I even comply with the pious intentions which you forget to carry out."

Thus is verified what the Lord promised by the Prophet Isais (Is. 65:24): "And it shall come to pass that before they call I will hear." Would to God that all men would understand what has just been said, and practice it most faithfully! How happy would they make themselves and others! Let us often say the Rosary to obtain the grace to love and do what God commands, and then we shall obtain what he promises.

CHAPTER 20

WE MUST SAY THE ROSARY
WITH CONFIDENCE

According to the Apostle St. James, one of the principal defects of prayer is a want of confidence in God that he will hear our petition. "Let him," says the Apostle, "who wavereth (that is, he who has no confidence in the Lord) not think that, when he prays, he will receive anything of him." "A diffident prayer," says St. Bernard, cannot penetrate into heaven"; because immoderate fear restrains the soul so much that, when she prays, she not only has no courage to raise herself to heaven, but she dares not even so much as stir. Now she hopes to be heard, then she doubts, saying to herself: "I shall obtain what I ask, no, I shall not. God will grant what I pray for, no, he will not do so, or he will do so when too late. He will give it sparingly. I deserve to be heard; no, I do not deserve it; I am worthy of it; no, I am unworthy of it. God is merciful and liberal; but he is also a just God. His mercy is great, but my sins are too numerous and too great to be heard."

Hence it happens that, in this fluctuation of thoughts and doubts, a diffident soul at one time prays to God with the patience, then complains of and murmurs against him with impatience; again she is resolved to wait until God is pleased to hear her; at another time she loses courage, and feels angry because she is not heard at once. She is, as St. James says, "like the waves of the sea, which are moved and carried about by the wind," giving herself up to these thoughts and doubts, without making any serious efforts to combat them; especially so when she meets with any troubles, adversity, cross, or the like. Thus, Moses began to doubt, on account of the unworthiness of the rebellious Jews, saying: "Hear, ye rebellious and incredulous: Can we bring forth water out of this rock?" (Num.20:10). In punishment for his want of confidence, he had to die in the desert. "And the Lord said to Moses: Because you have not believed me, you shall not bring this people into the land which I will give them."

St. Peter, also, when walking upon the water at the command of Jesus, and perceiving the great wind, began to doubt and lose confidence in the word of his Master. Our Lord reproached him for it, saying: "O thou of little faith! why didst thou doubt?"(Mt. 14:31.) Therefore, if we wish to be heard in prayer, we must, as the Apostle says, "pray with faith." But this faith, to be good, must have three qualities: first, it must be the right faith in its true meaning, free from hesitation or doubt, as otherwise it would be infidelity or heresy; secondly, it must include confidence, or certain, firm hope, free from diffidence or despair; and, thirdly, it must comprise a firm conviction of obtaining what we ask, excluding all wavering or the fear of not obtaining what we ask.

First. The Apostle St. James requires, for prayer, the right faith in its true bearing; and not only a general faith in God's omnipotence, providence, munificence, veracity, paternal care and love for us all – that as God he is able, and as Father inclined, to do good to us, his children – but also a particular faith; that is, that he will give us what we ask, provided it be not detrimental to us. This is the very promise of him who is truth itself, and who can neither deceive nor be deceived: "And all things whatsoever you shall ask in prayer, believing, you shall receive"(Mt. 21:22, Mk. 11:23.)

We believe with a divine faith that God is faithful to his promises, giving us what we ask of him in prayer, and as it is impossible for God to deny himself, so in like manner is it impossible for him to break his promises. This faith our Lord often required of those who asked of him their health or the like. To the blind, for instance, he said: "Do you believe that I can do this unto you?" And when they said: "Yea, Lord," he said to them: "According to your faith be it done unto you. And their eyes were opened "(Mt. 9:29-30.)

Secondly. This faith produces hope and confidence, on which account St. Paul calls it "the substance of things to be hoped for" (Heb. 11:1), because faith in the omnipotence and veracity of God is the strong pillar and ground of hope, and of all things to be hoped for. For this reason St. Augustine says: "If this faith is gone, prayer is gone with it" (Serm. 36, De Verbo Dom.) It is for this very reason that the Apostle said, when exhorting to prayer: "Whosoever shall call upon the name of the Lord shall be saved" (Rom. 10:13); thus giving us to understand that prayer necessarily supposes, not only true faith, but also hope by a natural consequence, because hope is the nurse of prayer.

As a river will cease to flow if its source will be dried up, so, in like manner, there can be no longer any prayer, if its source -that is, hope and confidence – is gone. This confidence was likewise demanded by Jesus Christ when he said to the man sick of the palsy: "Be of good heart, son, thy sins are forgiven thee" (Mt. 9:2); and again to the woman: "Be of good heart, daughter, thy faith hath made thee whole" (Mt. 9:22). From this it is evident that Jesus Christ requires not only faith, but confidence proceeding from faith. Hence St. Thomas Aquinas says: "Prayer derives its efficacy of meriting from charity; but its efficacy for obtaining, from faith and confidence."

Thirdly. As faith produces hope and confidence, so in like manner do these produce a certain persuasion in the mind that God will grant what we ask of him. Now, the greater the hope and the confidence of the heart, the stronger will be this persuasion in the understanding to obtain the granting of our prayer.

This threefold faith makes prayer efficacious. It is, indeed, a great gift of the Lord to a soul, and almost a certain sign that he will hear her prayer, even though a miracle should be necessary to that effect, should this be for our good, or for the manifestation of the truth, and the glory of the Church. This is that wonder-working faith – that is, faith joined to a firm confidence in God's aid for the working of the miracle. This confidence is produced by an interior impulse of the grace of God, who animates the thaumaturgus (the performer of the miracle), promising him, as it were, his assistance for the miracle which he intends to work. Of this confidence Jesus Christ speaks and exhorts to it when he says: "Amen I say to you, if you shall have faith and stagger not, not only this of the fig tree shall you do, but also if you shall say to this mountain: Take up and cast thyself into the sea, it shall be done. And all things whatsoever you shall ask in prayer, believing, you shall receive "(Mt. 21:21-22.)

During the late war, a Sister of Charity went to an officer of the Union army to obtain a pass to go South. "Please, sir,"said she to the officer, "give me a pass, for the love of God." "I have no love for God," replied the officer. "Give me one, then, for the love of your wife," she asked again. "I have no love for my wife," answered the officer. "Well, then, give me a pass for the love of your children," urged the good Sister. "I have no love for my children," was the officer's reply. "Give me one for the love of your best friend." "I have no such friend," said the officer. "Well," said the Sister, "is there nothing in the world that is dear to you and which you love much? Please reflect awhile." "Oh! yes," said the officer, after a moment's reflection, "I have a dear little child that I love most tenderly." "Well, please, then," said the Sister, "give me a pass for the love of this dear child." At these words the officer relented, and gave a pass to the good Sister.

Now, God bears an infinitely greater love to his beloved Son than this officer did to his child. He is, then, also infinitely more inclined to hear the prayers which we address to him in the name of his Son. Ah! Pardon me, my God, my Heavenly Father, for having compared thy infinite love for thy Son to that of an earthly father for his child! What favor and grace canst thou refuse, if asked in the name of thy beloved Son? Thou didst hear the prayers of the Jews when they asked thee anything in the name of thy servants Abraham, Isaac, and Jacob; and shall it be said that thou wilt not hear a Christian who asks of thee in the name and through the merits of thy beloved Son? "So great and so powerful is the name of the Son with the Father," says St. John Chrysostom, "that, for the sake of this name alone, the Father grants most wonderful gifts." Oh! great, St. John Chrysostom, great indeed is the praise which you bestow upon the power of the name of Jesus!

But were you to unite with all the angels and saints of heaven in describing the power of this holy name, you could not say anything more admirable than what Jesus Christ has said in these few words: "Amen, amen I say to you, *whatsoever* you ask the Father in my name, he will give it to you." My Father, says Jesus Christ, grants *everything – nothing excepted –* that is asked in my name; and in order to take away all doubt from your heart, and make your confidence unwavering, I swear to you: "Amen, amen I say to you, whatsoever you ask the Father in my name, he will give it you." These words, "Amen, amen," are equivalent, in the Hebrew language, to a solemn oath.

Who, then, knowing that God has promised so solemnly to hear our prayer, can still harbor the least doubt when he prays in the name of Jesus Christ? Who does not see that such want of confidence would be a great offence against the omnipotence, the goodness, and fidelity of God? No! God, who is infinite holiness and justice itself, cannot deceive us; he will not make a promise unless he intends to fulfil it.

Do not say that it is presumption to believe that God is bound to hear our prayers. It would, indeed, be presumption to believe that he was bound to hear us on account of our merits; but it is far from presumption to believe that he is bound to hear us on account of the merits of his divine Son, on account of his own infinite goodness, and especially on account of the solemn promise he has made to give us whatever we ask in the name of our Lord Jesus Christ.

Palladius relates that Paul the Hermit one day exorcised a young man who was possessed by an evil spirit. The devil cursed during the entire exorcism, and said: "Whatever you may do, I shall not leave this young man." The hermit then commenced to pray to God most confidently: "Why, O Lord! I dost thou not force the devil to obey me? I have now been praying for half a day, and yet he will not depart. Now, O Lord! I am resolved neither to eat nor to drink anything until I see this young man delivered from the evil spirit." No sooner had the hermit uttered this prayer, so full of confidence, than the devil left the young man, howling and blaspheming.

Surius relates that the mother of St. Catherine of Sienna died suddenly, without receiving the last sacraments. Catherine then began to pray with unusual fervor and unlimited confidence in God, saying: "Is it thus, O Lord! that thou keepest thy promise that none of our family should die an unprovided death? How couldst thou permit my mother to die without the sacraments? Now, O Lord! I will not rise from this place until thou hast restored my mother to life. And behold, her mother instantly arose from the dead, and lived for several years.

Most wonderful, indeed, is what St. Ananias obtained by confident prayer. The King of Babylon commanded the Christians to prove the truth of their religion by causing a mountain to move from its place; should they not be able to perform this miracle, they must either renounce their faith or suffer death. The Christians represented to the king that it would be a sin to ask a miracle of God merely to gratify idle curiosity. But the tyrant still insisted. St. Ananias, Bishop of Jerusalem, hearing of the distress of the Christians, went to the king, and, full of confidence in God's promises, said to him: "To show you, O king! that the promises of the God whom we worship are infallible, that huge mountain that you see yonder shall not only move, but it shall even move rapidly." The holy bishop then said in a loud voice: "In the name of that God who has promised to him who prays with confidence the power even to move mountains, I command thee, O mountain! to rise, and move instantly towards the city." No sooner had the bishop spoken these words than the mountain rose, in the presence of the king and the people, and moved swiftly towards the city, like a vessel sailing before a fair wind. It swept away houses, trees, and everything before it. The king was filled with terror and amazement; and fearing that it would destroy the city, he requested the holy bishop to cause the mountain to stand still. The bishop then prayed, and in an instant the mountain became fixed and immovable as before (Petr. de Nat. in Cat. Sanct. I. 9, Ch. 19.)

Let us, then, be assured that God will never refuse a confident prayer. Our hope and confidence are, as it were, the coin with which we can purchase all his graces; he bestows his gifts upon us in proportion to our confidence, God himself values our confidence exceedingly. We give him great honor by placing our confidence in him; for we show thereby that we distrust ourselves, and that we stand in need of his assistance. Whenever we betake ourselves to say the beads, let us reanimate our confidence in the Lord; let us imagine to ourselves that we hear the voice of Jesus Christ saying to us: "Whatsoever you ask believing, you shall receive."

Yes, let us say the Rosary, but let us say it with confidence for great things, and great things will be given us. Let us say it especially to be delivered from darkness and blindness of the understanding, from attachment to sensual pleasures, from our sins and punishments due to them, and the Lord will deliver us from these evils. Let us say it for a lively faith, for an ardent divine love, and the great gift of confidence in the divine promises, and God will bestow these gifts upon us. "The hand of the Lord is not shortened, that it cannot save, neither is his ear heavy, that it cannot hear" (Is. 59:1). "God is able of the stones to raise up children to Abraham" (Mt. 3:9). Can we doubt this truth without being guilty of blasphemy? O the great goodness of God! Did he not change, in a moment, the heart of Saul, and make him, from a persecutor of the Christians, a most zealous defender and propagator of the Gospel? Did not God change the heart of the good thief, of St. Augustine, of St. Mary of Egypt, of St. Margaret of Cortona, and of thousands of other notorious sinners, and make them models of virtue and ornaments to the Church? Now, God will bestow the same graces upon us, if we pray to him with confidence. "If you, then," says our divine Redeemer in the Gospel, "being evil, know how to give good gifts to your children, how much more will your Father from heaven give the *good spirit* to them that ask him!" (Lk. 11:12). "Hitherto you have not asked anything in my name. Ask, and you shall receive, that your joy may be full" (Jn. 16:24).

CHAPTER 21

WE MUST PERSEVERE
IN THE DEVOTION OF THE ROSARY

When Holofernes was besieging the city of Bethulia, all men, women, and children began to pray and to fast, crying to the lord, with tears in their eyes: "Have thou mercy on us, because thou art good " (Judith 7:20). But as the Lord deferred to come to their aid, they began to despair. Ozias, their leader, rising up all in tears, said: "Be of good courage, my brethren, and let us wait these five days for mercy from the Lord; but if, after five days be past, there comes no aid, we will do the things which you have spoken"; that is, deliver up the city into the hands of the enemy. Now, it came to pass that when Judith heard of this she came and said to them: "What is this word by which Ozias hath consented to give up the city to the Assyrians, if within five days, there come no aid to us? And who are you that tempt the Lord? . . . . And you have appointed him a day, according to your pleasure" (Judith 8:10-13). Thus Judith reproaches the Jews and their leader for their rashness in having fixed upon the time within which God was to come to their aid. This is not the way to obtain mercy from God, but rather to excite his indignation. "This is not a word that may draw down mercy, but rather that may stir up wrath and enkindle indignation " (Judith 8:12).

Jesus Christ has, it is true, promised to give us everything we ask of him, but he has not promised to hear our prayers immediately. The holy Fathers assign many reasons for which he often defers the grant of our petitions:

1.   That he may the better try our confidence in him.

2.   That we may long more ardently for his gifts, and hold them in higher esteem. "He defers the granting of them," says St. Augustine, "in order to increase our desire and appreciation of them."

3.   "That he may keep us near him," as St. Francis de Sales says, "and give us occasion to pray with greater fervor and vehemence. He acted thus towards his two disciples at Emmaus, with whom he did not seem willing to stay, before they forced him, as it were, to do so."

4.   He delays because, by this means, he wishes to unite himself more closely to us. "This continual recourse to God in prayer," says St. Alphonsus, "and this confident expectation of the graces which we wish to obtain from God-oh! how great a spur and chain of love are they not to inflame us and to bind us more closely to God!" We must not, therefore, imitate the Jews by appointing the time within which God is to hear our prayer, as otherwise we would deserve the above reproach of Judith; but let us humble ourselves before the Lord, and pray to him with tears, that, *according to his will*, so he would show his mercy to us. If we are patient, resigned, and determined to persevere in prayer until he will be pleased to hear us, we shall not be disappointed in our hope and expectation to receive what we ask of him.

Our Lord Jesus Christ taught us this when he said: "Ask, and you shall receive; seek, and you shall find; knock, and it shall be opened to you" (Lk. 11:9). It might seem that he would have said enough by simply saying "*ask*," and that the words "*seek*" and "*knock*" would be superfluous. " But no," says St. Alphonsus; "by them our Savior gave us to understand that we must imitate the poor when they ask for alms. If they do not receive the alms at once, they do not, on that account, cease asking; they return to ask again; and if the master of the house does not show himself, they begin to *knock* at the door, until they become so troublesome and importunate for him that eo prefers to give them an alms rather than to suffer their impunity any longer." If we pray again and again in like manner, and do not give up, God will at last open his hands and give us abundantly. "When thou openest thy hand they shall all be filled with good" (Ps. 103:28).

If men sometimes give alms to poor beggars merely for the sake of ridding themselves of their importunity, "how much more," says St. Augustine, "will our dear Lord give, who both commands us to ask, and is angry if we do not ask!" Hence St. Jerome, commenting on the parable of the man who would not give bread to his friend in the middle of the night, until he became importunate and annoying in his demands, says: " Not only once but twice, yea, three times, must we knock, and we must continue to do so until the door of God's mercy be opened." Perseverance is a great thing; if it become importunate, it will prove a better friend to us than the friend mentioned in the parable.

"Let us humbly wait for the consolations of the Lord our God" (Judith 8:20), and imitate the perseverance of the servants of God in prayer. Moses was a very great servant of the Lord, who would not have granted him a complete victory over the Amalekites had it not been for his perseverance in prayer. "By perseverance in prayer," says St. John Chrysostom (in his sermon on Moses), "he rendered the victory complete." Isaac was very dear to the Lord, and yet, in order to obtain a child, he had to pray for twenty years. "Isaac persevered in praying and sighing to the Lord for twenty years," says the same saint, "and finally he obtained what he asked" (Hom. 94, in Gen.)

And how did the Lord treat the woman of Chanaan? "And behold a woman of Chanaan, who came out of those coasts, crying out, and said to him: Have mercy on me, O Lord! thou son of David, my daughter is grievously troubled by a devil" (Mt. 15:22). And what does our Lord reply? He does not so much as even look at her, nor does he give her any answer- "Who answered her not a word." Still, she continues to pray with great humility: "Lord, help me." But our Lord seems not to hear her; so much so that even his disciples, being annoyed by her incessant supplication, "came and besought him, saying: Send her away, for she crieth after us." Instead of hearing her, he rejects her like a dog, saying: "It is not good to take the bread of the children and to cast it to the dogs." Who can discover, in this conduct of our Lord, anything of his usual kindness and condescension which he deigned to show even to the greatest sinners? Will he not, by his manner of acting, intimidate or discourage this woman so as to make her give up all hopes of being heard? But no; Jesus Christ had his wise designs in thus treating her. He knew her faith, and was much pleased with her confidence, which he wished to make shine forth more brilliantly. "But she said: Yea, Lord, for the whelps also eat of the crumbs that fall from the table of their masters." True, indeed, she wished to say, I am but a poor dog; but as such I beg you to help me, O Lord! And the liberal hand of Jesus opens and gives her what she wants. "Then Jesus answering, said to her: O woman! great is thy faith: be it done to thee as thou wilt; and her daughter was cured from that hour." Had this woman been discouraged by the first answer of our Lord, her daughter would never have been cured.

St. Monica (mother of St. Augustine) was treated in like manner: she had to pray to God for seventeen years before she could obtain of him the grace of conversion for her son Augustine. Had she become tired with pouring out prayers and shedding tears before the face of the Lord, in all probability the name of Augustine would not now he shining with so great a luster in the calendar of the saints. For twenty years did St. Philip Neri pray for a high degree of the love of God. After that time, this gift was granted him in such a measure as has seldom been granted to man.

Not only were the servants of God, but even Jesus Christ himself, was thus treated by his Heavenly Father. Prostrate on his face, he prays to him, but receives neither relief nor comfort. He prays a second time in a most lamentable voice: "Father, if it be possible, let this chalice pass away from me"; neither is he heard this time. He prays a third time with greater intensity, and not till then did the angel come to comfort and console him.

Poor miserable creatures, wretched sinners, that we are! How exalted an opinion have we not of ourselves! The Heavenly Father lets his only-begotten, well-beloved, most innocent, and afflicted Son, like a poor beggar, knock three times at his door before he opens; and we think we have done enough when we have petitioned a few times at the gate of heaven! We complain so readily of being unmercifully treated by God if he does not come at once to our aid, and, almost despairing of being heard, we give up praying altogether. "Truly, this is not the right way to pray," says St. John Chrysostom. "Let us bewail our indolence in praying; for thirty-eight years did the sick man spoken of in the Gospel (John 4) wait to be cured, and yet his desire was not fulfilled. Nor did it happen thus through his negligence, yet, for all that, he did not despair; but if we pray for ten days, perhaps, and are not heard, we think it is of no use to pray any longer" (Homil. 35, in Joan.)

We must, then, follow the advice of St. Gregory: "Let us be assiduous in prayer and importunate in asking; let us beware of growing remiss in it when it appears the Lord will not hear us; let us be robbers, as it were, doing violence to heaven. What robbery can be more meritorious, what violence more glorious? Happy violence, by which God is not offended but appeased; by which sin is not multiplied but diminished" (Comments in Ps. 129.)

If we wish, then, to pray aright, we must not only commence but must also continue our prayer; especially if we ask something conducive to our own spiritual welfare or to that of our neighbor. Most men fail in this point, and this is the reason why their prayer is of so little efficacy. Never allow yourself to become guilty of voluntary despondency. " Keep firm to the promise of Jesus Christ," says St. John Chrysostom; "never cease praying until you have received. If you present yourself before the Lord with this firm determination, saying, I will not leave thee till thou hast granted my prayer, you will receive most assuredly" (Hom. 24, in Mt. 7.)

Let us say with the Apostle: "Why should I not be able to do what others have done?" What so many could obtain by their perseverance in prayer, why should we not be able, by our perseverance, to obtain likewise? What a shame will it not be for us to see, on the judgment day, how the saints of heaven, by their perseverance in prayer, have become what they are; whilst we, for our want of perseverance in prayer, shall appear so very unlike unto them! Most assuredly Almighty God will manifest his power, goodness, and mercy in us as much as he has done in all the saints, provided we pray for it with the perseverance of the saints.

A priest was once travelling in Scotland. No one could tell that he was a priest. It happened one day that as he was on his journey he passed by a house that stood alone in the country. At the moment when he was passing the door a person came out of the house and asked him if he would come in. The priest did not wish to stop, so he asked what was the matter; why did they wish him to come in? The person at the door answered that the old man of the house was dying; but the old man would not believe that he was dying, although the doctor and every one had told him that he was dying. The priest then went into the house, and walked upstairs into the room where the old man was. The priest looked at him, and saw that he was certainly dying, so he spoke to him. "My good man," he said, "you had better get yourself ready for death; you are certainly dying." "Oh! no," answered the old man, " I am sure I shall not die now." "But," said the priest, "many deceive themselves about death. They die when they do not think that they are dying. Believe me, for I have seen many die." "No," he answered; "I am quite sure that I shall not die *now*." "Tell me," said the priest, "what makes you think so?" "I will tell you the truth," said the old man; "I do not know who you are, but I am a Catholic. For thirty years I have prayed every day to God that before I died a priest might come to hear my confession; but there is no priest in this part of the country. After praying to God for thirty years not to die without a priest, God makes me feel sure that I shall not die till a priest comes here." "What you say," said the priest "is true. If you have prayed to God every day for thirty years not to die without a priest, it is not likely that God will let you die without a priest. I am happy to be able to tell you that a priest is here now: I am a priest." Great was the joy of the old man, and many tears did he shed. Well might he say with the good old Simeon (Lk. 2): "Now, O Lord! thou dost dismiss thy servant, according to thy word, in peace: because my eyes have seen thy salvation." The old man then made his confession, received the holy Sacraments, and died a very happy death.

Perhaps you might say that it was only by chance that the priest passed the house just when the old man was dying. It is true the priest did not go that way to help the dying man, for he knew nothing about the dying man; but God put it into the mind of the priest to go that way, and to go past that house just at that moment when the old man was dying. God has said, "Ask, and it shall be given to you: for every one that asketh receiveth" (Mt. 7.) For thirty years the old man had *asked* of God to receive the sacraments at his death. So he who gives to every one who asks took care that the sacraments should be given to him before he died.

So let us say the Rosary every day for a happy death. "If we pray for a happy death till the end of our lives, we shall die a happy death" (Bellarmine). "You must pray every day for a happy death, and God will grant your prayer every day" (Suarez). Now, we pray particularly for a happy death whenever we say: "Holy Mary, Mother of God, pray for us sinners, now *and at the hour of our death.*"

We repeat this prayer fifty-three times every day if we say but five decades of the Rosary. To say five decades every day for a whole year is to repeat this prayer, "Holy Mary, Mother of God," etc., nineteen thousand and eighty times. If you, then, persevere in saying the beads every day of your life, behold what an immense number of cries for mercy ascend from your lips to heaven in the course of your earthly career-cries for mercy that, in the hour of death, will carry your soul to the gates of heaven and obtain admission into the joys of the heavenly kingdom.

CHAPTER 22

I MANNER OF SAYING THE ROSARY

1. Begin with the sign of the cross.

2. Say the Creed, or "I believe in God the Father,'" etc.

3. Say one Our Father and three Hail Marys for an increase of faith, hope, and charity.

4. Glory be to the Father, etc., once, in thanksgiving for God's blessings.

6. "Meditation on the Mysteries," or events of the life of our Lord and of the Blessed Virgin.

1. THE FIVE JOYFUL MYSTERIES

(To be said on Mondays and Thursdays throughout the year, and daily from the first Sunday in Advent until the feast of the Purification.

The First Joyful Mystery – The Annunciation

Meditation: In this mystery let us meditate how the Angel Gabriel saluted Our Blessed Lady with the title "Full of Grace," and how she was to conceive and bear a Son, our Lord Jesus Christ.

One Our Father, ten Hail Marys, and one Glory be to the Father, etc.

The Second Joyful Mystery – The Visitation

Meditation: Let us contemplate in this mystery how the Blessed Virgin Mary, understanding from the angel that her cousin St. Elizabeth, had conceived, went with haste into the mountains of Judea to visit her, and remained with her three months.

One Our Father, ten Hail Marys, and one Glory be to the Father, etc.

The Third Joyful Mystery – The Birth of Our Lord

Meditation: Let us contemplate in this mystery how the Blessed Virgin Mary, when the time of her delivery was come, *brought forth our Redeemer Jesus Christ at midnight, and laid him in a manger,* because there was no room for him in the inns at Bethlehem.

One Our Father, ten Hail Marys, one Glory be, etc.

The Fourth Joyful Mystery – The Presentation

Meditation: Let us contemplate in this mystery how the most Blessed Virgin Mary, on the day of her purification, presented the child Jesus in the temple, where holy Simeon, giving thanks to God with great devotion, received him into his arms.

One Our Father, ten Hail Marys, and one Glory be, etc.

The Fifth Joyful Mystery – The Finding of Our Lord in the Temple

Meditation: Let us contemplate in this mystery how the Blessed Virgin Mary, having lost, without any fault of hers, her beloved Son in Jerusalem, sought him for the space of three days, and at length found him in the Temple, in the midst of the doctors, disputing with them, being of the age of twelve years.

One Our Father, ten Hail Marys, and one Glory be, etc.

After each 5th decade is said:

Hail, Holy Queen, Mother of Mercy, our life, our sweetness, and our hope; to thee we cry, poor banished children of Eve; to thee we send up our sighs, mourning and weeping in this vale of tears; turn, then, most gracious advocate, thine eyes of mercy towards us, and, after this our exile, show unto us the blessed fruit of thy womb, Jesus – O! Clement, O! pious, O! Sweet Virgin Mary!

V.   Queen of the most holy Rosary, pray for us.

R.   That we may be made worthy of the promises of Christ.

Let us pray:

O God, whose only-begotten Son, by his life, death, and resurrection, has purchased for us the rewards of eternal life, grant, we beseech thee, that meditating upon these mysteries, in the Most Holy Rosary of the Blessed Virgin Mary, we may imitate what they contain, and obtain what they promise, through the same Christ our Lord. Amen.

V.   May the divine assistance remain always with us.

R.   Amen.

V.   May the souls of the faithful departed, through the mercy of God, rest in peace.

R.   Amen.

2. THE FIVE SORROWFUL MYSTERIES

(To be said on Tuesdays and Fridays throughout the year, and daily from Ash Wednesday until Easter-Sunday.)

The First Sorrowful Mystery – The Agony in the Garden

Meditation: Let us contemplate, in this mystery, how our Lord Jesus was so afflicted for us in the garden of Gethsemani that his body was bathed in a bloody sweat, which ran trickling down in great drops to the ground.

One our Father, ten Hail Marys, one Glory be, etc.

The Second Sorrowful Mystery – The Scourging at the Pillar

Meditation: Let us contemplate, in this mystery, how our Lord Jesus Christ was most cruelly scourged in Pilate's house; the number of stripes they gave him being above five thousand.

One our Father, ten Hail Marys, and one Glory be, etc.

The Third Sorrowful Mystery – The Crowning with Thorns

Meditation: Let us contemplate, in this mystery, how those cruel ministers of Satan made a crown of sharp thorns, and most cruelly pressed it on the head of our Lord Jesus Christ.

One Our Father, ten Hail Marys, and one Glory be, etc.

The Fourth Sorrowful Mystery – The Carrying of the Cross

Meditation: Let us contemplate, in this mystery, how our Lord Jesus Christ, being sentenced to die, bore, with the most amazing patience, the Cross-It was about fifteen feet in length-which was laid upon him for his greater torment and ignominy.

One our Father, ten Hail Marys, and one Glory be, etc.

The Fifth Sorrowful Mystery – The Crucifixion of our Lord Jesus Christ

Meditation: Let us contemplate, in this mystery, how our Lord and Savior Jesus Christ, being come to Mount Calvary, was stripped of his clothes, and his hands and feet most cruelly nailed to the Cross, in the presence of his most afflicted Mother.

One our Father, ten Hail Marys, and one Glory be, etc.

Hail, Holy Queen, etc., as above at the end of the joyful mysteries.

3. THE FIVE GLORIOUS MYSTERIES

(To be said on the Ordinary Sundays, and the Wednesdays and Saturdays throughout the year; and daily from Easter Sunday until Trinity Sunday.)

The First Glorious Mystery – The Resurrection

Meditation: Let us contemplate in this mystery how our Lord Jesus Christ, triumphing gloriously over death, rose again the third day, immortal and impassible.

One our Father, ten Hail Marys, and one Glory be, etc.

The Second Glorious Mystery – The Ascension

Meditation: Let us contemplate in this mystery how our Lord Jesus Christ, forty days after his resurrection, ascended into heaven, attended by angels, in the sight of his most holy Mother, and his apostles and disciples, to the great admiration of them all.

One our Father, ten Hail Marys, and one Glory be, etc.

The Third Glorious Mystery – The Descent of the Holy Ghost

Meditation: Let us contemplate in this mystery how our Lord Jesus Christ, being seated on the right hand of God, sent, as he had promised, the Holy Ghost upon his apostles; who, after he was ascended, returning to Jerusalem, continued in prayer and supplication with the Blessed Virgin Mary, expecting the performance of his promise.

One Our Father, ten Hail Marys, and one Glory be, etc.

The Fourth Glorious Mystery – The Assumption of the Blessed Virgin Mary into Heaven

Meditation: Let us contemplate in this mystery how the glorious Virgin Mary, twelve years after the resurrection of her Son, passed out of this world unto him, and was by him assumed into heaven, accompanied by the holy angels.

One Our Father, ten Hail Marys, and one Glory be, etc.

The Fifth Glorious Mystery – The Coronation of the Blessed Virgin

Meditation: Let us contemplate in this mystery how the glorious Virgin Mary was, with great jubilee and exultation of the whole court of heaven, and particular glory of all the saints, crowned by her son with the brightest diadem of glory.

One Our Father, ten Hail Marys, and one Glory be, etc.

Hail! Holy Queen, Mother of Mercy, our life, our sweetness, and our hope. To thee do we cry, poor banished children of Eve. To thee do we send up our sighs, mourning and weeping in this vale of tears. Turn, then, most gracious advocate, thine eyes of mercy towards us; and after this our exile, show unto us the blessed fruit of thy womb, Jesus. O! Clement! O! Pious! O! Sweet Virgin Mary!

V.   Pray for us, O Holy Mother of God.

R.   That we may be made worthy of the promises of Christ.

Let us Pray

O! God, whose only-begotten Son, by his life, death, and resurrection, has purchased for us the rewards of eternal life, grant, we beseech thee, that meditating upon these mysteries, in the most holy Rosary of the Blessed Virgin Mary, we may imitate what they contain, and obtain what they promise, through the same Christ our Lord. Amen.

II.   A METHOD OF SAYING THE BEADS WITH THE MYSTERIES WITHOUT A BOOK

Begin as usual:

1. With the sign of the cross.
2. Say the Creed, the Our Father, and three Hail Marys, and the Glory be to the Father, for an increase of faith, hope, and charity.
3. Then go on with the recitation of the decades as follows:

When you choose for your devotion the *joyful mysteries*, say the Hail Marys of the first decade in this manner: "Hail Mary, full of grace, the Lord is with thee; blessed art thou amongst women, and blessed is the fruit of thy womb, Jesus, *whom thou didst conceive at the message of an angel*: Holy Mary, Mother of God, pray for us sinners, now and at the hour of our death. Amen."

In the second decade, instead of the words, *"Whom thou didst conceive,"* say, *"Whom thou didst carry in thy womb on they visit to Elizabeth."* Holy Mary, Mother of God, etc. In the third decade, after the word Jesus, say: *"Who was born of thee at Bethlehem."* In the fourth decade: *"Whom thou didst present in the Temple."* In the fifth: *"Whom thou didst find in the Temple."* Having thus recited the five decades, end with the following

PRAYER

O God! whose only-begotten Son, by his life, death, and resurrection, has purchased for us the reward of eternal life: grant, we beseech thee, that, while we meditate upon these mysteries in the most holy Rosary of the Blessed Virgin Mary, we may imitate what they contain, and obtain what they promise, through the same Christ, our Lord. Amen.

When you select for your devotion the sorrowful mysteries, in the first decade, after the word Jesus in the Hail Mary, say: *"Who sweat blood for us in the garden."*

In the second decade: *"Who was scourged for us."*

In the third: *"Who was crowned with thorns for us."*

In the fourth: *"Who has carried his cross for us."*

In the fifth: *"Who was crucified for us."*

For the glorious mysteries:

In the first decade: *"Who arose from the dead."*

In the second: *"Who ascended into heaven."*

In the third: *"Who sent the Holy Ghost."*

In the fourth: *"Who took thee up into heaven."*

In the fifth: *"Who crowned thee Queen of heaven."*

INDULGENCES ATTACHED TO THE ROSARY OF THE BLESSED VIRGIN.

In order to animate all the faithful often to have recourse to the Blessed Virgin by the devotion of the Rosary, Pope Benedict XIII granted, by his Brief *Sanctissimus*, of April 13, 1726, to all who say with contrition the whole Rosary of fifteen decades, or a third part of it of five decades –

1. THE INDULGENCE OF 100 DAYS for every *Pater noster* and every *Ave Maria*.

2. THE PLENARY INDULGENCE to all who shall have said the third part of it once every day for a year, on any one day in the year, after Confession and Communion.

   The present Sovereign Pontiff, Pius IX, by a decree of the Sacred Congregation of Indulgences of May 12, 1851, confirmed these indulgences, and granted besides –

3. THE INDULGENCE OF SEVEN YEARS AND SEVEN QUARANTINES to every one who with contrition shall say a third part of the Rosary in company with others, either in public or private.

4. THE PLENARY INDULGENCE, on the last Sunday in every month, to all who are in the habit of saying with others, at least three times a week, the said third part of the Rosary; provided that on that Sunday they shall, after Confession and Communion, visit a church or public oratory, and pray there for a time according to the mind of his Holiness.

To gain these indulgences, it is requisite that the Rosaries should be blessed by a priest having power to attach indulgences to them; and that, whilst the prayers are being said, meditation be made on the mysteries of the Birth, Passion, Death, Resurrection, etc., of our Lord Jesus Christ, according to the decree of the Sacred Congregation of Indulgences of August 12, 1726, approved by the above named Pope Benedict XIII. Note, however, that he declared, in his Constitution *Pretiosus* of May 26, 1727, $ 4, that simple people who could not meditate might obtain the indulgence by merely saying the Rosary devoutly.

Observe also that all persons enrolled in the Confraternity of the Rosary, wherever it has been canonically erected, gain many more indulgences when they say the Rosary or do any other pious work.

CHAPTER 23

THE LIVING ROSARY

About the year 1825 the devotion of the Rosary was greatly neglected in many parts of Catholic countries in Europe. To revive it again, two pious priests established at Lyons, in France, the so-called devotion of the Living Rosary. In this devotion fifteen persons unite to say the whole Rosary every day, each saying the decade allotted to him. The devotion is called "living" because if a member dies another is chosen to take his place, and the devotion is thus constantly kept up by the circle of those fifteen persons. A number of circles united under a clergyman as director form a sodality.

A few years after the devotion had been established, it attracted the attention of Cardinal Lambroschini, who was then Nuncio of the Holy See in France. On his way through Lyons, the Cardinal had an opportunity of making himself acquainted with the forms and rules of the devotion, and was delighted to witness the abundant fruits of virtue which it had already produced. Having returned to Rome, he gave an account of it to his late Holiness, Pope Gregory XVI, who was graciously pleased to give it his solemn sanction and approbation in his brief of January 27 and February 2, 1832, and to issue, in confirmation of it, a brief containing the following indulgences:

They who belong, to a society of the Living Rosary, and recite the part of the Rosary assigned to them, may gain a plenary indulgence

1. On the first festival after their admission.

2. On the third Sunday in each month.

3. On the solemn feasts of Christmas, the Epiphany, the Circumcision, Easter, the Ascension, Corpus Christi, Pentecost, and Trinity Sunday; also upon all the festivals of the Blessed Virgin, provided on those days they approach devoutly the sacraments of Penance and the Holy Eucharist, and offer up some prayers in a church.

These indulgences may be gained by those who are lawfully prevented from going to church, provided they perform some other work of piety substituted by their confessor.

4.   An indulgence of one hundred days, every time they recite their part of the Rosary during the week; and an indulgence of seven years and seven times forty days, every time they recite it on Sundays and festivals.

The above plenary indulgences are applicable to the souls in Purgatory.

N.B.   The indulgences attached to the recital of the Rosary are also attached to the Living Rosary.

RULES FOR THE ESTABLISHMENT AND DIRECTION OF THE LIVING ROSARY

Fifteen persons unite, and divide amongst them the fifteen Mysteries of the Rosary.

Thus by reciting each a decade, or *one Pater* and *ten Aves,* with a *Gloria Patri*, every day, the daily recitation of the entire Rosary is constantly kept up by the circle. A number of circles united under a clergyman as director constitutes a sodality.

The following observances have been drawn up for the direction of such sodalities:

1.   A clergyman purposing to establish a sodality should explain the devotion to his flock and procure a few pious persons, to give their assistance in forming the circles, and remain afterwards the *representatives* of them.

2   Each *representative* is then to find two other associates, and the three thus associated obtain each four additional members, thus completing the circle of fifteen.

3.   The representatives take a list of the members of their respective circles, which they hand in to the secretary of the sodality, in order to be entered in a registry kept for the purpose.

4.   The secretary should be careful to keep the circles distinct in the register, and to note down the representatives of each.

5.   For the correct keeping of the register, the representatives should give notice to the secretary of any changes or substitution of names that may occur in their circles.

6.   A number of circles being thus formed, there is a mystery of the Rosary, together with the corresponding virtue, allotted to each member on the first Sunday of each month.

7.   Each member receives one of the mysteries which is drawn for each member by the representatives.

8.   The members, having received their tickets, take a few moments every day during the month to reflect on the mysteries assigned them respectively. They then recite one decade of the Rosary in honor of these mysteries, and to obtain of God, through the intercession of the Blessed Virgin, the grace of the corresponding virtues.

9.   The reflections on the mysteries may be greatly facilitated, particularly in the case of persons not accustomed to meditation, by reading the reflections; or, if a person cannot read, by looking at the engraving of the mystery.

10. The members conclude this daily devotion by invoking their patrons and imploring their intercession.

11. The persons to whom the first joyful mystery is allotted recite, moreover, the Creed, Our Father, and three Hail Marys before their decade.

12. The adorable Sacrifice of the Mass is offered for the spiritual and temporal welfare of the members and for the extension of the sodality on the third Sunday of every month, the day of the monthly plenary indulgence.

13   The representatives on delivery of the tickets receive the monthly donations of the members, and hand in the amount to the secretary on the second Sunday of each month.

11. The donations are applied to defray the necessary expenses of the sodality.

CHAPTER 24

LITTLE ROSARY OF
THE IMMACULATE CONCEPTION

In the name of the Father, etc.

1.   I thank thee, Eternal Father, because thou hast by thy omnipotence preserved the most holy Virgin Mary, thy daughter, from original sin. One Our Father and four Hail Marys, adding after each Hail Mary: "Blessed be the holy, most pure, and Immaculate Conception of the Blessed Virgin Mary."

2.   I thank thee Eternal Son, because thou hast by thy wisdom preserved the most holy Virgin Mary, thy mother, from original sin. Our Father, etc., as above.

3.   I thank thee, Eternal Holy Ghost, because thou hast by thy love preserved the most holy Virgin Mary, thy spouse, from original sin. Our Father, etc., as above. Finish by reciting once Glory be to the Father, etc., in honor of the purity of St. Joseph, spouse of the Blessed Virgin Mary.

INDUGENCES

1.   An indulgence of one hundred days for reciting the above Little Rosary with a contrite heart – *(Pius IX, Jan. 9, 1852.)*

2.   A plenary indulgence once a month, on the ordinary conditions, for reciting it every day for a month – (Idem.)

3.   An indulgence of one hundred days as often as the versicle, "Blessed be the holy," etc., as above, is recited with a contrite heart – *(Pius VI, Nov. 21, 1793.)*

4.   An indulgence of one hundred days for devoutly kissing the medal of the Immaculate Conception, and saying: "Mary, conceived without sin, pray for us who have recourse to thee."

CHAPTER 25

CHAPLET OF THE SEVEN DOLORS

It was about the year 1233 that seven holy men of noble birth, by name Bonfiglio, Monaldio, Bonagiunta, Manetto, Amadeo, Uguccio, and Alessio Falconieri, withdrew from the city of Florence into the solitude of Mount Senario, afterwards receiving from the Church the appellation of the "Seven Blessed Founders." For it was in that solitude that, passing their days in the constant exercise of prayer, penitence, and other virtues, they, by a special revelation from the Blessed Virgin, instituted the Order called "Servants of Mary," taking for the object of their institution meditation on the bitter pains she suffered in the Life, Passion, and Death of her Son Jesus, and undertaking to promulgate this devotion amongst Christian people. One of the devout practices which they made use of for their purpose was a Chaplet or Rosary of seven divisions, in remembrance of the seven principal Dolors of the Blessed Virgin, which were to form the subject of the reciter's meditation according to his ability; the prayers to be said during such meditation being one *Pater noster* and seven *Ave Marias* for each division, with three more *Ave Marias* at the end of all, in honor of the tears shed by the same most holy Virgin in her Dolors.

This devout prayer, so acceptable to our most holy Sorrowful Mother, and so useful to Christian souls, was propagated throughout the Christian world by these Servants of Mary; and it afterwards received much encouragement from Pope Benedict XIII, who, in order to induce more of the faithful to adopt it, granted, by his Brief *Redemptoris,* of September 26, 1724 —

1. THE INDULGENCE OF 200 DAYS for every *Pater noster*, and the same for every *Ave Maria*, to every one who, having confessed and communicated, or at least made a firm resolution to confess, should say this Chaplet in the churches of the Order of the Servants of Mary.

2. THE SAME INDULGENCE OF 200 DAYS may be gained by saying it everywhere on Fridays, and –

3. THE INDULGENCE OF 100 DAYS on any other day; and, lastly, the same Pope added –

4. THE INDULGENCE OF SEVEN YEARS AND SEVEN QUARANTINES to any one who says this Chaplet either alone or in company with others. Afterwards Pope Clement XII, "that the faithful might often recollect and sympathize with the Dolors of Mary," confirmed lay his Bull of *Unigeniti*, December 12, 1734, the before-named indulgences, adding also the following:

5. THE PLENARY INDULGENCE and remission of all sins to every one who shall say this Chaplet daily for a month together, and shall then, after having confessed and communicated, pray for holy Church, etc.

6. THE INDULGENCE OF 100 YEARS, every time it is said, to all who say this Chaplet, being truly penitent and having confessed, or having at least a firm resolution to confess.

7. THE INDULGENCE OF 150 YEARS, every Monday, Wednesday, Friday, and Feast of Obligation of the holy Church, after having confessed and communicated.

8. THE PLENARY INDULGENCE to all who say it four times a week, on any one day in the year when, after having confessed and communicated, they shall say the said Chaplet of Seven Dolors.

9. THE INDULGENCE OF 200 YEARS also to those who shall say it devoutly after their confession.

10. THE INDUGENCE OF 10 YEARS to those who keep one of these Chaplets about them, are in the habit of saying it frequently, every time that, after having confessed and communicated, they shall hear Mass, be present at a sermon, accompany the Blessed Sacrament to the sick, make peace between enemies, bring sinners to confession, etc., etc.; or whenever, saying at the same time seven *Pater nosters* and seven *Ave Marias*, they shall do any spiritual or temporal good work in honor of our Lord Jesus Christ, the Blessed Virgin, or their Patron Saint.

All these indulgences were confirmed by decrees of the Sacred Congregation of Indulgences issued at the command of Pope Benedict XIV, on January 16, 1747, and Clement XIII, March 15, 1763. It is, however, requisite, in order to gain these indulgences, that these Chaplets should be blessed by the Superiors of the Order of the Servants of Mary, or by other priests of the Order deputed by them. And when blessed, they cannot be sold or lent for the purpose of communicating these indulgences to others, in which case they would be deprived of their blessing. See the above-named Brief of Benedict XIII.

WAY OF SAYING THE CHAPLET

Act of Contrition.

Savior, my sole and only love, see me before the divine presence standing all confusion by reason of the many grievous injuries I have done thee. With my whole heart I ask thy pardon for them; repenting of them out of thy pure love, and at the thought of thy great goodness hating and loathing them above every other evil of this life. I would that I had died a thousand times ere ever I had offended thee; but now most firmly am I resolved rather to lose my life by every death than offend thee again. My Jesus crucified, I firmly purpose to cleanse my soul forthwith by thy most precious Blood in the sacrament of penance. And thou, most tender Virgin, Mother of Mercy and Refuge of the sinner, do thou by thy bitter pains obtain for me the pardon of sins; whilst I, praying according to the mind of so many holy Pontiffs for the indulgences granted to this holy Rosary of thine, hope thereby to obtain remission of all pains due to my many sins.

1. With this trust laid up within my heart, I begin my meditation on the *First* Sorrow, when Mary, Virgin Mother of my God, presented Jesus, her only Son, in the Temple, laid him in the arms of holy, aged Simon, and heard his word of prophecy: "This, thy Son, shall be a sword of pain to pierce thine own heart," foretelling thereby the Passion and Death of her Son Jesus.
    One Pater noster and *seven* Ave Marias.

2. The *Second* Sorrow of the Blessed Virgin was when she had to fly into Egypt by reason of the persecution of cruel Herod, who impiously sought to slay her well-beloved Son.
One Pater noster *and seven* Ave Marias.

3. The *Third* Sorrow of the Blessed Virgin was when, after having gone up to Jerusalem at the Paschal Feast with Joseph her spouse and Jesus her beloved Son, she lost him on her return to her poor house, and for three days bewailed the loss of her sole-beloved One.
One Pater noster and *Seven* Ave Marias.

4. The *Fourth* Sorrow of the Blessed Virgin was when she met her most loving Son Jesus carrying on his tender shoulders the heavy cross whereon he was to be crucified for our salvation.
One Pater noster and *seven* Ave Marias.

5. The *Fifth* Sorrow of the Blessed Virgin was when she saw her Son Jesus raised upon the cross's tree, and all his Sacred Body pour forth Blood; and then, after three long hours' agony, beheld him die.
One Pater noster and *seven* Ave Marias.

6. The *Sixth* Sorrow of the Blessed Virgin was when she saw the lance cleave the Sacred Breast of Jesus, her beloved Son, and then received his Holy Body, laid in her purest bosom.
One Pater noster and *seven* Ave Marias.

7. The *Seventh* and last Sorrow of the Blessed Virgin, Queen and Advocate of us her servants, miserable sinners, was when she saw the Holy Body of her Son buried in the grave.

One Pater noster *and seven* Ave Marias.

Then say three Ave Marias in veneration of the tears which Mary shed in her sorrows, to obtain thereby true sorrow for sins and the holy indulgences attached to this pious exercise.

V: Pray for us, Virgin most sorrowful.

R: That we may be worthy of the promises of Christ.

Let us pray.

GRANT, we beseech thee, O Lord Jesus Christ! that the most Blessed Virgin Mary, thy Mother, may intercede for us before the throne of thy mercy, now and at the hour of our death, through whose most holy soul in the hour of thine own Passion the sword of sorrow passed. Through thee, Jesus Christ, Savior, of the world, who livest and reignest with the Father and the Holy Ghost for ever and ever. Amen.

CHAPTER 26

CHAPLET OF THE PRECIOUS BLOOD OF JESUS

Pope Pius VII, in order to inflame the hearts of the faithful with devotion to the Precious Blood of Jesus Christ, granted by two Rescripts, one of May 31,1809, kept in the acts of the Congregation of Rites, the other October 18,1815, in the Archivium of the Archconfraternity of the Precious Blood, erected at St. Nicholas in Carcere, in Rome –

1. THE INDULGENCE OF SEVEN YEARS AND SEVER QUARANTINES, once a day, to all who shall say with devotion the Chaplet in honor of the Precious Blood of Jesus Christ.

2. THE PLENARY INDULGENCE, once a month, to all who, having said it every day for a month, shall confess and communicate, and pray for the holy Church, etc.

3. THE 300 DAYS' INDULGENCE, daily, to all who say the prayer "Most Precious Blood, etc.," for which see page [215].

This Chaplet is made up of seven mysteries, in which we meditate upon the seven times on which Jesus Christ for love of us shed blood from his most innocent body; at each mystery except the last we are to say five *Pater nosters* and one *Gloria Patri,* and at the last three *Pater nosters* only and one *Gloria Patri,* in remembrance of the thirty-three years during which the Precious Blood of Jesus was enclosed in his veins before it was all poured out for our salvation. The Chaplet ends with the devout prayer, "Most Precious Blood, etc."

THE CHAPLET

V: Incline unto my aid, O God.

R: O Lord, make haste to help me.

V: Glory be to the Father, etc.

R: As it was, etc.

FIRST MYSTERY

The first time our loving Savior shed his precious Blood for us was on the eighth day after his birth, when, to accomplish the law of Moses, he was circumcised. While, then, we think on all that Jesus did to satisfy God's justice for our wanderings, let us excite ourselves to true sorrow for them, and promise, with the help of his all-powerful grace, to be henceforth truly chaste in body and in soul.

Five Pater nosters *and one* Gloria Patri.

V: We beseech thee, therefore, help thy servants, whom thou hast redeemed with thy Precious Blood.

SECOND MYSTERY

Next, in the Garden of Olives, Jesus shed his Blood for us in such streams that it bathed the earth around. This did Jesus at the vision he then had of the ingratitude with which men would meet his love. Oh! Let us, then, repent sincerely for the past, considering how poorly we have met the countless benefits of our God, and henceforth resolving to make good use of his graces and holy inspirations.

Five Pater nesters *and one* Gloria Patri.

V: We beseech thee, etc.

THIRD MYSTERY

Then, in his cruel scourging, Jesus again shed his Blood, when from his lacerated skin and wounded flesh on every side there flowed the precious streams, the while our gentle Lord kept offering it to his Eternal Father in payment of our impatience and our wantonness. How is it, then, we do not curb our wrath and our self-love? But henceforth we will indeed try our very best to bear our little trials, and, despisers of ourselves, take peacefully the injuries men do us.

Five Pater nosters *and one* Gloria Patri.

V: We beseech thee, etc.

FOURTH MYSTERY

Then, too, the sacred Head of Jesus poured forth Blood when it was crowned with thorns, all for our pride and evil thoughts. Oh! Shall we never cease to nurture haughtiness, foster foul imaginations, and feed the wayward will within us? Henceforth let there be ever before our eyes our utter nothingness, our misery, and our weakness; and with generous hearts let us combat bravely the temptations of our wicked foe.

Five Pater nosters *and one* Gloria Patri.

V: We beseech thee, etc.

FIFTH MYSTERY

But oh! it was on the mournful way to Calvary that, laden with the heavy wood of the cross, our loving Jesus poured forth his precious Blood in torrents from his veins; then were the very streets and ways of Jerusalem, through which he passed, bathed with it; and all this was done in satisfaction for the scandals and bad examples by which his own creatures had led others astray on the way to ruin. Ah! Who can tell how many of us are of this unhappy number! Who is he that can say how many he alone, by his own bad example, has thrust down to hell? And have we done nothing to remedy this evil? Alas! Let us henceforth at least endeavor all we can to save souls by word and by example, making ourselves to all a pattern of good and holy life.

Five Pater nosters *and one* Gloria Patri,

V: We beseech thee, etc.

SIXTH MYSTERY

More and yet more Blood there flowed from the Redeemer of mankind in his most barbarous crucifixion; then were veins rent and arteries broken, and in torrents there welled from out his hands and feet that saving balm of life eternal which cancelled all the crimes and enormities of a whole world. What man is he who still will choose to continue in his sin, renewing thus the cruel crucifixion of the Son of God? Bitterly, bitterly will we weep then for our bad deeds done,

214

and at the feet of God's own minister detest them. Now will we mend our evil ways, and henceforth begin a truly Christian life, with the thought ever in our hearts of all the Blood which our eternal salvation cost the Savior of men.

Five Pater nosters *and one* Gloria Patri.

V: We beseech thee, etc.

SEVENTH MYSTERY

Last of all, when he was dead, and the lance opened his sacred Side and cleft his loving Heart, Jesus still shed Blood, and with the Blood there came forth water, to show us how the Blood was all poured out to the last drop for our salvation. O goodness infinitely great of our Redeemer! Who will not love thee? What heart not melt away for the very love of thee, which has done all this for our redemption? The tongue wants words to praise thee; wherefore we invite all creatures upon earth, all angels and all saints in Paradise, and, most of all, our dearest Mother Mary, to bless, to praise, and to hymn thy most precious Blood. Glory to the Blood of Jesus! Glory to the Blood of Jesus now and ever throughout all ages. Amen.

At this last Mystery three Pater nosters and one Gloria Patri are to be said, to make up the number of thirty-three.

V: We beseech thee, etc.

Then say the following:

PRAYER

Most Precious Blood of life eternal! price and ransom of the world! the soul's drink and the soul's bath, ever pleading man's cause before the throne of heavenly mercy, from the depths of my soul I adore thee; faint would I, were I able, make thee some compensation for the outrages and wrongs thou dost ever suffer from thy creature man, and most from those who in their rashness dare to blaspheme thee. Who will not bless this Blood of value infinite? Who will not burn for love of Jesus, who shed it all for us? What were I but for this Blood, which has redeemed me? Who drew thee out of my Jesus' veins to the last drop? Love, of a surety, love! O boundless love, which gave to us this saving balm! O balm beyond all price, welling from the fount of immeasurable love! Give to all hearts, all tongues, power to praise, hymn, and thank thee, now and ever, and throughout all eternity. Amen.

V: Thou hast redeemed us, O Lord! with thy blood

R: And made us a kingdom to our God

Let us pray:

Almighty and everlasting God, who has appointed thine only-begotten Son, the Savior of the world, and has willed to be appeased with his Blood, grant us, we beseech thee, so to venerate this price of our salvation, and by its might so to be defended upon earth from the evils of this present life, that in heaven we may rejoice in its everlasting fruit. Who liveth and reigneth with thee in the unity of the Holy Ghost, world without end. Amen.

SHORT CHAPLET OF THE PRECIOUS BLOOD.

By a grant of Pope Gregory XVI, of July 5, 1843, the Indulgences mentioned above at page [   ] for saying the Chaplet of the Precious Blood, may all be gained by saying the following short Chaplet; and any one who cannot meditate may gain them by only saying devoutly the thirty-three Pater nosters which make up the Chaplet.

THE SHORT CHAPLET

V: Incline unto my aid, O God!

R: O Lord, make haste to help me. Glory be to the Father, etc.

First Mystery

Jesus shed Blood in his Circumcision.

Five Pater nosters, *one* Gloria, *and*

We beseech thee, therefore, help thy servants, whom thou had redeemed with thy precious Blood.

Second Mystery

Jesus shed Blood in the Agony in the Garden.

Five Pater nosters, *one* Gloria.

We beseech thee, etc.

Third Mystery

Jesus shed Blood in his Scourging.

Five Pater nosters, *one* Gloria.

We beseech thee, etc.

Fourth Mystery

Jesus shed Blood in his crowning with thorns.

Five Pater nosters, *one* Gloria.

We beseech thee, etc.

Fifth Mystery

Jesus shed Blood in carrying his Cross.

Five Pater nosters, *one* Gloria.

We beseech thee, etc.

Sixth Mystery

Jesus shed Blood in his Crucifixion.

Five Pater nosters, *one* Gloria.

We beseech thee, etc.

Seventh Mystery

Jesus shed Blood and Water from his wounded Side.

Five Pater nosters, *one* Gloria.

We beseech thee, etc.

PRAYER

Most Precious Blood, etc., *as above,* p. [215].

CHAPTER 27

CHAPLET OF OUR LORD

This chaplet, instituted by divine inspiration about the year 1516, by the Blessed Michael of Florence, a Camaldolese monk, who used to say it every day until his death, January 11, 1522, is called the Chaplet of our Lord, because it is said in honor of Jesus Christ, and is composed of thirty-three *Pater nosters*, in remembrance and veneration of the thirty-three years which he lived on the earth; to these are added five *Ave Marias* in honor of his five most holy wounds, three of which are said, one at a time, at the beginning of each of the three sets of ten *Pater nosters*, and of the two remaining the first is said previous to saying the three concluding *Pater nosters*, and the last after them. The Chaplet finishes with the Credo in honor of the holy Apostles who composed it, and which itself contains an epitome of the Birth, Life, Passion, and Death of our Divine Lord Jesus Christ. Pope Leo X, at the prayer of the above-named Blessed Michael, granted by a Bull dated February 18, 1516, several indulgences to any one who should keep about him the said Chaplet or say it. Gregory XIII did as much by means of a Brief dated February 14, 1573; and Sixtus V by another Brief dated February 3, 1589. These indulgences were all confirmed anew by Clement X, in a special brief, *De salute Dominici gregis,* dated July 20, 1674, who also added several more indulgences, as follows:

1. INDULGENCE OF 200 YEARS every time to any one who shall say it, being penitent and having confessed, or who at least shall firmly resolve to confess.

2. INDULGENCE OF 150 YEARS to any one who, having confessed and communicated, shall carry about him one of these Chaplets, and say it every Monday, Wednesday, and Friday, and also on all festivals of obligation.

218

3. PLENARY INDULGENCE ONCE A YEAR on any one day to any one who, having confessed and communicated, shall have made a practice of saying it at least four times a week.

4. PLENARY INDULGENCE once a month to any one who shall have said it every day for a month, and shall then, being penitent, having confessed and communicated, pray to God for the holy Church, etc.

5. PLENARY INDULGENCE to any one who shall die in battle against the infidels, having been previously accustomed to say the said Chaplet three times a week, and having said it on the day of his death and the day previous to it; provided he be penitent for his sins, and ask pardon of God for them.

6. PLENARY INDULGENCE and remission of all sins in the article of death to any one who, being penitent and having confessed, shall then invoke, at least with the heart if he cannot do so with his lips, the most holy name of Jesus; provided he has said the above-named Chaplet once during his illness with the intention of gaining this Indulgence; in the event of his recovery, he may gain the 200 years' indulgence.

7. INDULGENCE OF TWENTY DAYS to any one who shall carry about him one of these Chaplets, and invoke the adorable name of Jesus after he has made an examination of conscience with contrition for his sins, and said three *Pater nosters* and three *Ave Marias* for the good estate of the Church.

8. THE INDULGENCE OF TWENTY YEARS to any one who, having examined his conscience and confessed, shall, after his confession, pray to God for the advancement of the Catholic faith, the extirpation of heresy, and the exaltation of the holy Church, etc.

9. THE INDULGENCE OF TEN YEARS to any one who, having about him the said Chaplet, shall say three *Pater nosters* and three *Ave Marias as often as he does any spiritual or temporal good* work in honor of our Lord Jesus Christ, the Blessed Virgin Mary, or some saint.

10. Any one who keeps one of the said Chaplets about him, if he be accustomed to do any good work which is done in any religious Order, shall participate in all the good works which are done in the Order in whose good works he has made the intention of sharing; if he assist at holy Mass by saying five *Pater nosters* and five *Ave Marias*, he shall supply for every defect and distraction which has happened to him through inadvertence in the course of the Mass; moreover, if on days of obligation he has been legitimately hindered from hearing Mass, he shall have the same merit as if he had assisted at it, provided he say the five *Pater nosters* and five *Ave Marias* as above.

11. Any one out of Rome keeping one of these Chaplets about him shall, on the days of the Stations, gain the 200 years' Indulgence on visiting any church he chooses; if hindered from doing so, he shall gain the same indulgence by saying this Chaplet, the seven Penitential Psalms, with the Litanies and Prayers. The same indulgence in Rome may be gained by any one who, being legitimately hindered from visiting the Church of the Station, shall say the Chaplet and Psalms as above.

Pope Benedict XIII afterwards, by a decree of the Sacred Congregation of Indulgences, dated April 6, 1727, confirmed all the above indulgences, and added another –

12. PLENARY INDULGENCE to any one who, after having confessed and communicated, should say this Chaplet on Friday. This Plenary Indulgence can only be gained on the Fridays in March; and that after the works enjoined above have been fulfilled; as was declared by Pope Leo XII, in a decree of the Sacred Congregation of Indulgence dated August 11, 1824.

In order to gain the above-named indulgences, it is necessary that –

1. The Chaplet be blessed by the Reverend Fathers of the Camaldolese Order, either hermits or monks, or else by those who have apostolic authority to bless them; once blessed, they cannot be sold or lent to others for the purpose of communicating

to them the indulgences, in which case they would afterwards be deprived of the indulgences annexed to them according to the said Brief of Pope Clement X.

2. Every one saying the Chaplet must, according to his capacity, meditate on the mysteries of the life of our Lord Jesus Christ. It is not, however, necessary either to read or recite the following short reflections, as they are only added for the greater devotion of any one who might wish to make use of them.

CHAPLET OF OUR LORD

Begin with an Act of Contrition

FIRST DECADE

The Archangel Gabriel makes known to the Blessed Virgin Mary the Incarnation of the Divine Word in her pure womb.

Ave Maria

1. The Son of God made man is born of Mary the Virgin, and laid in a manger.

Pater noster

2. The angels make merry and sing Gloria in excelsis Deo

Pater noster

3. The shepherds hear the angels' tidings, and come and adore him.

Pater noster

4. He is circumcised the eighth day, and called by the most holy name of Jesus.

Pater noster

5. Is adored by the Magi, and receives offerings of gold, frankincense, and myrrh.

Pater noster

6. Is presented in the Temple, and foretold the Savior of the world.

Pater noster

7. Flies from the wrath of Herod, and is carried into Egypt.

Pater noster

8. Herod finds him not, and murders the innocents.

Pater noster.

9. He is carried back by Joseph and his Mother into Nazareth, his country.

Pater noster

10. Disputes in the Temple with the doctors, being twelve years old.

Pater noster

Add the *Rest eternal (if said for the departed)*

SECOND DECADE

Jesus is most obedient to the Blessed Virgin, his Mother, and to St. Joseph.

Ave Maria

1. Thirty years old, he is baptized by John in Jordan.

Pater noster

2. Fasts forty days in the desert, and overcomes the tempter.

Pater noster

3. Practices and preaches his holy law, whereby is life eternal.

Pater noster

4. Calls his disciples, who forthwith leave all and follow him.

Pater noster

5. Works his first miracle of changing water into wine.

Pater noster

6. Heals the sick, makes the lame to walk, gives hearing to the deaf, sight to the blind, life to the dead.

Pater noster

7. Converts sinful men and sinful women, and pardons their sins.

Pater noster

8. When the Jews persecute him even unto death, he chastises them not, but sweetly chides them.

    Pater noster

9. Is transfigured on Mount Thabor, in the presence of Peter, James, and John.

    Pater noster

10. Enters triumphant into Jerusalem, sitting on an ass's colt, and drives the profaners from the Temple.

    Rest eternal, *as above.*

THIRD DECADE

Jesus takes leave of his Mother before he goes to die for our salvation.

Ave Maria

1. Celebrates the Last Supper, washes the Apostles' feet.

    Pater noster

2. Institutes the most holy Sacrament of the Altar.

    Pater noster

3. Prays in the Garden, sweats blood, and is comforted by an angel.

    Pater noster

4. Is betrayed by Judas with a kiss, is taken and bound by the officers of justice as a great malefactor.

    Pater noster

5. Is falsely accused, is buffeted and spit upon, and shamefully used before four tribunals.

    Pater noster

6. Looks tenderly on Peter after he had thrice denied him; whilst Judas despairs, hangs himself, and is lost.

    Pater noster

7. Is cruelly scourged at the pillar, and receives innumerable blows.

Pater noster

8. Is crowned with thorns, shown to the people, who cry, Crucify him, crucify him.

Pater noster

9. Is condemned to die, carries a heavy cross with grievous pain upon his shoulders to Mount Calvary.

Pater noster

10. Is crucified between two thieves, dies after three hours' agony, is wounded in the side with a lance, and is buried.

Pater noster

The Rest eternal, *as above*

Jesus rises the third day, and visits first of all his most holy Mother.

Ave Maria

1. Appears to the three Marys, and bids them tell the disciples they have seen him risen from the dead.

Pater noster

2. Appears to the disciples, shows them his most holy wounds, bids Thomas touch them.

Pater noster

3. The fortieth day after his resurrection, blesses most holy Mary his Mother and all his disciples, then ascends into heaven.

Pater noster

Let us pray to the most holy Virgin to obtain for us also the blessing of her Son Jesus Christ, now and at the hour of our death.

Ave Maria

The Rest eternal, *as above.*

Let us say the Creed in honor of the holy Apostles

End with the prayer said to be St. Augustine's.

Let us pray:

O my Lord Jesus Christ! who, to redeem the world and to free us from the pains of hell, didst vouchsafe to be born amongst men, subject to pain and to death, to be circumcised, rejected and persecuted by the Jews, betrayed by thy disciple Judas with a sacrilegious kiss, and as a lamb, gentle and innocent, bound with cords, and dragged in scorn before the tribunals of Annas, Caiphas, Pilate, and Herod; who didst suffer thyself to be accused by false witnesses, torn by scourges, crowned with thorns smitten with blows, insulted with spittings, to have thy divine countenance covered out of contempt, to be many ways set at naught and outraged, to be filled with reproaches and ignominies, and, last of all, to be stripped of thy clothes, nailed, and raised high upon a cross between two vile thieves, to be drenched with gall and vinegar, and then pierced with a lance, and so to fulfil the mighty work of our redemption: Savior most tender, by thy many cruel sufferings borne by thee out of thy love for me, which I, unworthy as I am, yet dare to contemplate, by thy holy cross and by thy bitter death, free me (and this thy servant, if said for a soul in agony) from the pains of hell, and vouchsafe to gather me into the garden of Paradise, whither thou didst lead the penitent thief who was crucified with thee, my Jesus, who now, with the Father and the Holy Ghost, lives and reignest God for ever and ever. Amen.

CHAPTER 28

THE LITTLE CHAPLET AND PRAYERS OF THE SACRED HEART OF JESUS

Pope Pius VII, that he might extend throughout the Christian world devotion to the Sacred Heart of Jesus, granted, by a decree of the Sacred Congregation of Indulgences, of March 20, 1815, and Rescript of the Segretaria of the Memorials of September 26, 1817–

1.   The Indulgence of 300 Days, once a day, to all the faithful who, with contrition and devotion, say the following little chaplet and prayers to the Sacred Heart of Jesus.

2.   The Plenary Indulgence once a month to all who say them once a day for a month together; to be gained on that day when, after having confessed and communicated, they shall pray for the intention of the Sovereign Pontiff.

THE CHAPLET AND PRAYERS

V: Incline unto my aid, O God! etc.

R: O Lord! make haste to help me.

Glory, etc.

1.   My most loving Jesus, my heart leaps for joy to think upon thy loving Sacred Heart, all tenderness and sweetness for sinful man; and with trust unbounded it never doubts thy ready welcome. Ah! me, my sins, how many and how great! With Peter and with Magdalene, in tears I bewail and abhor them, because they are an offence to thee, my sole and chief good. Grant me, oh! grant me pardon for them all. Oh! might I die or ever I offend thee more; this, too, I ask thy Sacred Heart – to live to love thee.

Say one Pater *and five* Gloria Patris *in honor of the Sacred Heart, then –*

My Jesus' Heart, I thee adore;

Oh! make me love thee more and more.

2.   My Jesus, I bless thy most humble Heart; and I give thanks to thee, who, in making it my model, not only dost urge me with strong pleadings to imitate it, but at the cost of so many humiliations dost thyself stoop to point me out the path, and smooth for me the way to follow thee. Fool and ungrateful that I am, how have I wandered far away from thee! Mercy, my Jesus, mercy! Away, ye hateful pride and love of worldly honor; with lowly heart I would follow thee, my Jesus, amidst humiliations and the cross, so to gain peace and salvation. Only be thou at hand to strengthen me, and I will ever bless thy Sacred Heart.

One Pater *and five* Gloria Patris.

My Jesus' Heart, etc.

3.   My Jesus, I marvel at thy most patient Heart, and I thank thee for all those wondrous examples of unwearied patience thou didst leave me to guide me on my way. It grieves me that these examples still have to reproach me all in vain with my extravagant delicacy, shrinking from the slightest pain. Oh! pour, then, into my poor languid heart, dear Jesus, eager and enduring love of suffering and the cross, of mortification and of penance, that, following thee to Calvary, I may with thee attain to glory and the joys of Paradise.

One Pater *and five* Gloria Patris.

My Jesus' Heart, etc.

4.   Dear Jesus, beside thy gentlest Heart I set my own, and shudder to see how unlike is mine to thine, while at a shadow, look, or word to thwart me I fret and grieve. Oh! then, pardon my excesses, and give me grace, that in every contradiction I may follow the example of thy unvaried meekness, and so enjoy an everlasting, holy peace.

One Pater *and five* Gloria Patris.

My Jesus' Heart, etc.

5.   Sing praise to Jesus for his most generous Heart, the conqueror of death and hell; yet never wilt thou reach his due with

227

all thy praise. Still more than ever am I confounded, looking upon my coward heart, which dreads even a rough word or injurious taunt. Courage, my soul! it shall be so with me no more. My Jesus, I pray thee for such strength that, on earth fighting and conquering self, I may one day rejoice triumphantly with thee in heaven.

One Pater *and five* Gloria Patris.

My Jesus' Heart, etc.

Mary, to thee we turn; Mary, to thee we consecrate ourselves more and yet more, and, trusting in thy mother's heart, we say to thee: By every virtue of thy sweetest heart obtain for me, great Mother of my God, my Mother Mary, a true and lasting devotion to the Sacred Heart of Jesus, thy well beloved Son, that, bound up in every thought and affection in union with that Heart of his, I may fulfil each duty of my state, with ready heart serving my Jesus evermore, but specially this day.

V: Heart of Jesus, burning with love for us.

R: Inflame our hearts with love of thee.

Let us pray:

Lord, we beseech thee, let thy Holy Spirit kindle in our hearts that fire of charity which our Lord Jesus Christ, thy Son, sent forth from his inmost heart upon this earth, and willed that it should burn exceedingly. Who liveth and reigneth with thee in the unity of the same Holy Spirit, God for ever and ever. Amen.

CHAPTER 29

WHY WE SHOULD JOIN THE CONFRATERNITY OF THE ROSARY

During the time that Simon de Montfort was in arms against the Albigenses, St. Dominic undertook a more pacific mode of warfare – the glorious crusade of the Rosary. He earnestly recommended his favorite devotion to all Christians, but particularly to the soldiers exposed to the hazards of war.

A Breton cavalier, a brave warrior, but an indifferent Christian, adopted, like his companions, that holy practice less through a spirit of faith than the desire to escape the dangers of the battlefield. One day, whilst traversing a forest, he was surprised by the enemy, who lay in ambuscade and called upon him to surrender. The Breton drew his sword, to the hilt of which was suspended a Rosary, and, attacking his assailants with great bravery, he soon caused them to retreat. He replaced his sword in the scabbard, and then perceived the Rosary, which he detached with devotion and placed on his arm, so that he could easily recite it while guiding his charger. His enemies, ashamed and humiliated, renewed the attack. Encouraged by his first success, the Breton stood his ground, and, brandishing his sword, wounded several of his antagonists and put the others to flight, without receiving an injury. One of the wounded explained to him the cause of his marvelous victory: "'When you faced us, it seemed to us that you held in your hand a flaming sword, which struck us with terror, and we fled from you in great fear. When we attacked you the second time, you were protected by a shield on which were represented the figure of our Lord crucified, the Blessed Virgin, and a great number of saints, against which our arrows fell harmless, while we felt every stroke of your sword – and even now I see the buckler on your arm." The Breton recognized at once that the marvelous shield was his Rosary. Touched by this significant mark of grace, he amended his life, renounced his warlike career, and became a lay brother in the order of Friar Preachers. ("Month of the Rosary.")

This brave warrior represents every Christian. We are all warriors, soldiers of the militant Church of Christ. We have to fight the numerous and powerful enemies of our salvation under the standard of Jesus Christ. The work of our salvation is an affair of the greatest importance. Once lost, we are lost forever. It is therefore the greatest wisdom to make use of those means and helps which God has been pleased to furnish us through his Church. Amongst those means suggested to the Church by the Holy Ghost, and which are now in practice among good Catholics, that of religious confraternities or sodalities should principally be noted. In these confraternities many persons unite themselves together for God's glory and the salvation of their souls in the practice of virtuous and devout actions. Thus, of many members they become one body. In a well arranged army each soldier singly may easily be defeated by the enemy; but when the soldiers are all well united, the files are rendered compact and the army invincible. The same happens in our warfare with the devil, the world, and the flesh. One who is no member of a confraternity fights singly the enemies of his soul, and may be easily overcome. "Hence there are found," says St. Alphonsus, "more sins in a man who does not belong to the confraternities than in twenty who frequent them" ("Glories of Mary.")

The Confraternity of the Rosary may be said to be the tower of David: "The tower of David: a thousand bucklers hang upon it, all the armor of the valiant men" (Cant. 4:4). And the cause of the good obtained from this and other confraternities is that their members acquire in them many defenses against hell; in them they make use of many means to preserve themselves in divine grace, which is very difficult for persons in the world to practice who are not members of such confraternities.

In the first place, one of the means of salvation is meditating on divine truths: "Remember thy last end, and thou shalt never sin" (Eccles. 7:40). So many are lost because they do not think of the necessity of saving themselves: "With desolation is all the land made desolate, because there is none that considereth in the heart" (Jer. 12:11).

Eternal truths are spiritual, and cannot be discerned by the eyes of the body, but only by the eyes of the mind in thought and consideration. Now, he who does not practice meditation does not consider, and consequently does not see, the importance of eternal salvation, nor the way he should follow to gain it. St. Bernard, writing to Pope Eugenius on this subject, says: "I fear for thee, Eugenius, lest the multitude of affairs, prayer and meditation being intermitted, should bring thee to a hard heart, which does not dread, because it does not know itself." To obtain salvation we must have tender hearts – hearts, that is, docile to receive the impressions of the divine inspirations, and prompt to put them in execution. It was this that Solomon asked of God: "Give, therefore, to thy servant a docile heart" (3 Kings 3:9). It is said in St. John that they who are of God listen to his voice and follow it: "And they shall all be taught of God. Every one that hath heard of the Father, and hath learned, cometh to me" (Jn. 6:45). Our hearts are of themselves hard, because they are wholly inclined to carnal pleasures, and opposed to the laws of the Spirit. They are softened by the influx of grace, and this is communicated to them by means of meditation, in which the soul, by considering the divine goodness and the great love which God has for it, and the immense benefits which he has conferred upon it, becomes inflamed, is softened and made obedient to the divine calls, as David experienced, who said: "In my meditation a fire shall flame out" (Ps. 38:4). Without it the heart remains hard, obstinate, disobedient, and will be lost: "A hard heart shall fear evil at the last; and he that loveth danger shall perish in it" (Eccles. 3:27). And remaining hard, it will be so unhappy as not to know that it is so; because the heart which does not meditate "does not dread, for it does not know itself." Not being sensible of its defects and the impediments which they place in the way of salvation, it does not remove them, but soon comes to love them, and so is lost.

Another reason why meditation is necessary for salvation is because those who do not meditate do not pray, and thus lose their souls. The virtues of those who do not pray cannot be firm and persevering, because perseverance is only to be obtained by prayer, and by persevering prayer. Hence those who pray not perseveringly will not persevere. It was on this account that St. Paul exhorted his disciples to pray always, without intermission: "Pray without ceasing." And for the same reason our Blessed Savior "spoke a parable . . . that we ought always to pray, and not to faint." Meditation, therefore, is *morally necessary* for the preservation of divine grace in the soul: *morally necessary*, because, although the soul, strictly speaking, may, without the aid of meditation, continue in the state of grace, yet, if meditation be laid aside, it will be morally impossible – that is, very difficult – not to fall into grievous faults; and the reason is that when a person does not meditate, being distracted with other affairs, he knows but little of his own wants, of his dangers, and of the means which he ought to adopt to escape them, and, being but little sensible of the urgent necessity of prayer, he neglects prayer, and is lost.

Our Lord, on the other hand, tells us that he who dwells on eternal truths, on death, judgment, and a happy or miserable eternity which awaits him, will avoid sin. "Remember thy last end, and thou shalt never sin" (Eccles. 7:40). Holy David declared that the consideration of eternity induced him to exercise himself in the practice of virtue, and to correct the imperfections of his soul: "I thought upon the days of old, and I had in my mind the eternal years, and I meditated in the night with my own heart, and I was exercised, and I swept my spirit" (Ps. 76:6-7). And if, says a pious author, it were to be asked of the damned: Why are you now in hell? the greater part of them would answer: We are now in hell because we did not think of hell. It is impossible that he who calls to mind, in his spiritual exercises, the eternal truths, and attentively dwells upon them and believes them, should not be converted to God. St. Vincent de Paul said that if, during a mission, a sinner should perform all the spiritual exercises, and should not be converted, it would be a miracle, and yet he who preaches and speaks during such exercises is only man; but in meditation it is God who speaks: "I will lead her into solitude, and I will speak to her heart." Assuredly God speaks better and more powerfully than any preacher. All the saints have become saints by means of meditation; and experience shows us that those who practice meditation very seldom fall into mortal sin; and if they unfortunately do sometimes fall into it, they soon arise by means of meditation, and return again to God. Meditation and sin cannot exist together.

Those who belong to the Confraternity of the Rosary are naturally led to meditate on the great truths of our holy religion and join prayer to their meditations; for, when saying the Rosary, we meditate on the mysteries of the life of our Lord, and join to our meditation the best of all petitions – the petitions of the Our Father and the Hail Mary. It is also part of meditation to thank God for his blessings, spiritual and temporal. This part of meditation is also contained in the Rosary, in the doxology, "Glory be to the Father, and to the Son, and to the Holy Ghost," etc., which we repeat at least six times when we say but the third part of the Rosary. Ah! the more we reflect on the devotion of the Rosary, the more sublime, the more heavenly it appears. The Rosary is, indeed, a book of the most simple yet of the most profound and most useful meditations. What book is there more delightful for souls than the mysteries of the life and Passion of Jesus Christ? It ought certainly to be the principal object of the devotion of every Christian always to bear in mind these holy mysteries, to return to God a perpetual homage of love, praise, and thanksgiving for them, to implore his mercy through them, to make them the ordinary subject of his meditations, and to mould his affections, regulate his life, and form his spirit, his manner of thinking, judging, and speaking, by the holy impressions they make on his soul.

Secondly, in order to be saved it is necessary to commend one's self to God: "Ask, and you shall receive" (Jn.16:24). Now, the members of the confraternities do this continually, and God hears them more graciously, because he has said that he will grant great graces to prayers made in common: "If two of you shall agree upon earth concerning anything, whatsoever they shall ask, it shall be done for them by my Father who is in heaven" (Mt. 18:19). Concerning which St. Ambrose says: "Many who are weak become strong by uniting together; and the prayers cannot but be heard."

Again, in the confraternity the sacraments are more frequently approached on account of the rules, as well as on account of the example of other members. By this means perseverance in divine grace is more easily obtained. "Holy Communion is an antidote by which we are freed from daily sins, and are preserved from mortal sins" (Concil. Trid., Sess. 13, c. 2).

Thirdly, besides the sacraments in the sodalities, there are practiced many exercises of mortification, humility, and charity towards infirm and poor persons. Such exercises of piety also confirm the members more and more in the grace of Almighty God.

Fourthly, all know how much more sure is our salvation if we serve the Mother of God; and do not the members serve her in the confraternity? How many prayers do they offer up to her! How much do they praise her there! There they consecrate themselves from the beginning to her service, choosing her; in a special manner, for their Mother; and they are inscribed in the book of the children of Mary. Hence, as they are distinguished servants and children of the Virgin, she treats them with distinction and protects them in life and in death. Thus a member of the confraternity may say that, with the confraternity, he has received every blessing: "Now all good things come to me together with her" (Wis. 7:11).

About a year ago a brother priest wrote to me the following account of a conversion: "During a mission in which I was engaged in a certain city of the West, a middle-aged man came and told me the following: 'I am,' he said, 'the son of good Catholic parents, who brought me up with great care. When I was about fourteen years of age, I was sent to my uncle, a learned and edifying Catholic priest, to receive the preparatory education for the priesthood. I stayed with my uncle until I was sixteen years old. I then became tired of the kind of life I was leading; I desired to be free and have my own way. One day this desire came stronger than ever before, and, the opportunity being favorable, I ran away from my uncle to seek a home elsewhere. I went from place to place, doing a little work here and there to make a living. When I was at the age of twenty-one, I met with some gentlemen, who were very kind to me. They started me in business and helped me along for a while, apparently from motives of compassion; but, as the sequel showed, it was done only to ruin me the more successfully. They were Freemasons, and after gaining my confidence, and putting me under obligations to them, they induced me to join a lodge. I had neglected my religious duties for several years, and became fit for anything wicked. I became a Mason. I was successful in business, but was not happy. I was always uneasy in my mind. I left this place and began business in another, where I joined another lodge, hoping to find peace and contentment of mind. I married, being now about twenty-four years of age. After a year of married life I ran away from my wife to another city to try my luck there. I failed in business, and became desperate. I now determined to return to my wife. She was a Catholic, and, although my desertion had grieved her deeply, she was willing to live with me again. I now began business with brighter prospects, and succeeded better than ever before; but in spite of this temporal prosperity, I found no peace, no happiness, no contentment of mind. At times I stood on the very verge of despair. About three weeks ago this feeling reached its highest stage, and I determined to put an end to my life. I said nothing of the matter to my wife. Towards evening I left home, and went, as usual, to my place of business. I sat there for a while reflecting on what I could do. Finally I arose, took my pocket book, my watch and chain, and gave them to my clerk, telling him that he might give them to my wife when she would call. I left my place of business, and in these very clothes you see on me I went to the lake and cast myself into the deep waters. For about half an hour I did all I could to get my head under the water, but could not succeed. My efforts to drown myself were all in vain. An invisible power seemed to hold me up, for I cannot swim. Seeing my efforts fruitless, I thought of making my way out of the water. But here was the difficulty. The waves were wild and dashing. The shore of the lake was protected against the water by elevated wood works. Even had I been able to swim, I could not have climbed over those barriers through the foam and fury of the waves. As I was drifting to and fro on the stormy lake, I was all of a sudden thrown upon a small staircase reaching from the shore into the water to serve as a means of descending into the little pleasure boats which are often used for excursion purposes in summer. I took hold of the steps and made my way out of the water. When I stood on the shore and looked back upon the wild, foaming waters, and recalled to mind all my misery, I felt again strongly tempted to cast myself into the lake. But suddenly I changed my mind and went towards my home. My clothes were all soaked with water, and I dreaded being seen in that state by my wife. So I went to the nearest hotel, where I passed the night. Next morning I went home; and now you see me here, Father, with the earnest desire to make my peace with God.'"

The priest now inquired how he came to be saved in so extraordinary a manner. "What devotion have you performed?" said the priest to the gentleman. "Did you wear the scapular or any other article of devotion?" "No, Father," replied he; "only one thing do I remember. Before I cast myself into the water I knelt down and said three Hail Marys and I believe it was this that saved me." Ah! if Mary showed herself compassionate to this miserable wretch because he recommended himself to her, even at the moment when he was determined to commit suicide and go to hell, how much more will she show herself a tender, a most affectionate Mother to those who faithfully persevere in serving her in her sodalities.

Every member, then, should pay particular attention to two things. First, as to the end; that is, to enter the confraternity for no other purpose than to serve God and his holy Mother, and save his own soul. Secondly, not to stay away from the meetings of the confraternity on the appointed days for affairs of the world, since there the most important business in the world is to be transacted – namely, eternal salvation. Endeavor also to draw as many as you can to the confraternity and to say the Rosary.

Albertus Castella relates that in Spain a most learned doctor, from observing the effects of the Rosary upon a certain devout lady who, from her girlhood, had assiduously practiced it, was induced to devote all his efforts to propagate this devotion. After a long conversation with her on the subject, he became thenceforth her disciple, and proceeded to preach everywhere upon the fruits of the Rosary. By his persuasions he induced the people to practice this devotion.

Endeavor especially to induce those members who have left the sodality to return to it again. Oh! what great punishments have befallen those who have abandoned the Confraternity of Our Lady. In Naples a certain member left the Confraternity, and, being exhorted to return, he said: "I will return when my legs are broken and my head cut off." He was, to a certain extent, a prophet, for soon after his legs were broken and his head cut off by some of his enemies ("Glories of Mary," by St. Alphonsus). On the other hand, the members who persevere are favored by Mary with spiritual and temporal blessings. Father Auriemma relates many special graces granted by Mary to the members of the confraternity in life, and especially in death. Father Crasset relates (To. 2, pr. 5) that in 1586 there was a youth who, being near death, fell asleep. On awaking he said to his confessor: "O Father! I have been in great danger of hell, but the Blessed Virgin has rescued me. The devils presented my sins before the tribunal of God, and already they were dragging me to hell. but the holy Virgin came to my aid and said to them: 'Where are you taking this youth? What have you to do with one of my servants, who has so long served me in the confraternity?' The devils fled, and thus I have been saved from their hands." The same author relates also that another member of the confraternity, when on the point of death, had a great conflict with hell; but he conquered, and, full of joy, exclaimed: "Oh! what blessings come from serving well the Blessed Mother of God in her confraternity." Thus, entirely consoled, he died. The Duke of Popoli, when on his death-bed, said to his son "My son, know that the little good I have done in life I owe to the confraternity; and therefore I have no greater good to leave to thee than the Sodality of Mary. I am more proud of having been a member of the confraternity than the Duke of Popoli."

"Let, therefore," says St. Alphonsus, "no one condemn confraternities, saying that they give rise to contention, and that many join them from human motives. The sacraments are also abused by many, yet for that we do not condemn them. The Sovereign Pontiffs, instead of condemning confraternities, have approved and highly commended them and enriched them with indulgences. What did not St. Charles Borromeo do to establish and multiply these sodalities? In his synods he distinctly intimates to confessors that they should endeavor to induce their penitents to join them. And with reason;

for these confraternities, especially those of Our Lady, are like so many arks of Noe, in which the poor people of the world may find refuge from the deluge of temptations and sins which inundate them in it."

"Enter, then," says St. Francis de Sales, "enter willingly, into the confraternities of the place in which you reside, and especially those whose exercises are the most productive of fruit and edification, as in so doing you practice a sort of obedience acceptable to God; for, although these confraternities are not commanded, they are, nevertheless, recommended, by the Church, which, to testify her approbation of them, grants indulgences and other privileges to such as enter them. Besides, it is very laudable to concur and co-operate with many in their good designs; for although we might perform as many good exercises alone as in the company of a confraternity, and perhaps take more pleasure in performing them in private, yet God is more glorified by the union and contribution we make of our good works with those of our brethren and neighbors."

And now let us close this chapter with the beautiful words of St. Bernardine: "O woman blessed among all women! thou art the honor of the human race, the salvation of our people. Thou hast a merit that has no limits, and an entire power over all creatures. Thou art the Mother of God, the mistress of the world, the Queen of Heaven. Thou art the dispenser of all graces, the glory of the holy Church. Thou art the example of the just, the consolation of the saints, and the source of our salvation. Thou art the joy of Paradise, the gate of heaven, the glory of God. Behold, we have published thy praises. We pray thee, then, O Mother of mercy! to strengthen our weakness, to pardon our boldness, to accept our service, to bless our labors, and impress thy love upon the hearts of all, that, after having honored and loved thy Son on earth, we may praise and bless him eternally in heaven. Amen."

CHAPTER 30

ANSWERS TO OBJECTIONS

Before the coming of our Redeemer mankind was groaning under the tyranny of the devil. He was lord, and even caused himself to be worshipped as God, with incense and with sacrifices, not only of animals, but even of children and human lives. And what return did he make them? He tortured their bodies with the most barbarous cruelty, he blinded their minds, and, by a path of pain and misery, led them down to torment everlasting. It was to overthrow this tyrant, and release mankind from its wretched thraldom, that the Son of God came; that the unfortunate creatures, freed from the darkness of death, rescued from the bondage of their eternal enemy, and enlightened to know the true way of salvation, might serve their real and lawful Master, who loved them as a Father, and from slaves of Satan wished to make them his own beloved children. The prophet Isaias had long ago foretold that our Redeemer should destroy the empire which Satan held over mankind: "And the scepter of their oppressor thou hast overcome" (Is. 9:4). Why does the prophet call Satan oppressor? It is because this heartless master exacts from the poor sinners who become his slaves heavy tribute in the shape of passions, hatreds, disorderly affections, by means of which, while he scourges, he binds them in a still faster servitude.

Our Savior came to release us from the slavery of this deadly foe; but in what manner did he effect this release? By offering his sufferings and death in satisfaction to the divine justice for the punishment due to our sins; by the sacrifice of his life upon the cross he overthrew the empire of Satan over mankind. Whenever we offer to God the sacred Blood of Jesus Christ, for ourselves and others, we break the power of Satan over us. Hence the Lord one day said to St. Magdalene of Pazzi: "See, my daughter, how the Christians are in the devil's hands. If my elect did not deliver them by their prayers in offering my Blood for them, they would be devoured." Inflamed with holy zeal by these words, she offered to God the Blood of Christ fifty times a day in behalf of sinners. She did this with so much fervor that God repeatedly showed her multitudes of souls whom she had thus delivered from the power of the devil and reconciled with the Almighty. Now, in the devotion of the Rosary we commemorate the life and Passion of our dear Savior; we offer to the heavenly Father the sacred Blood of his Son, and all he has done for us; and thus at each mystery of the Rosary the devil's power is broken and lessened in proportion as we persevere in this devotion. The devil trembles, we cause him unspeakably great pain, and put him to flight, each time we begin to say the beads. What terror overcomes him at the sacred sign of the cross alone, with which we begin the Rosary! And the very saying of the Creed and "Glory be to the Father," to thank the Blessed Trinity for the divine benefits, is in itself a renunciation of Satan; but when he sees us pray and hears us pronounce the powerful names of Jesus and Mary, he is confounded and takes to flight.

One day, as St. Gregory Thaumaturgus was returning from the city of Neocæsarea to the wilderness, a violent rain obliged him to take shelter in a heathenish temple, the most famous in the country on account of the devilish oracles and divinations delivered there. Knowing that the temple was full of evil spirits, he made, as soon as he entered it, the sign of the cross several times to purify the place, and then passed, with his companions, the night there in prayer. Next morning, when the idolatrous priest performed his usual superstitious practices in the temple, the devils were heard to declare that they had been forced to leave the temple by the sign of the cross made by the man who had passed the night there (Butler's "Lives of the Saints," Vol. 4 p. 356).

When Simon, the great magician, was in Rome, he promised the Emperor Nero and the Roman people to fly in the air, thus pretending to imitate the ascension of our Savior into heaven. Accordingly, he raised himself into the air, by means of the devil, in the presence of the Emperor. When Sts. Peter and Paul saw the delusion, they betook themselves to prayer, and at the name of Jesus the devil lost his power over Simon Magus; the impostor fell to the ground, was bruised, broke a leg, and died a few days after in rage and confusion (Butler's "Lives of the Saints," Vol. 2 p. 463).

It is related in the accounts of the missions of Japan that many demons appeared in the form of wild beasts to a certain Christian of that country to alarm him and threaten him, but he spoke in these words: "I have no arms with which to terrify you; if the Most High permits it, do with me according to your pleasure; meanwhile, I use as my defense the most sweet names of Jesus and Mary." Hardly had he uttered these words when, behold, at the sound of those powerful names the earth opened and those proud spirits were swallowed up ("Glories of Mary," by St. Alphonsus). Let us rest assured that an earthly enemy is not so terrified at a great army as are the powers of hell at the names and protection of Jesus and Mary. At the thunder of those great names the devil flees and hell trembles; for the names are like a tower of strength, by taking refuge in which not only sinners are shielded from punishment and come forth securely defended and saved, but the just also are preserved from the assaults of hell. The Blessed Virgin revealed to St. Bridget that, even from the most abandoned sinners, who had wandered the furthest from God and were most fully possessed by the devil, the enemy departs as soon as he hears her most powerful name invoked by them, if invoked with the intention of true amendment; but she added that, if the soul does not amend and with contrition quit its sin, the demons immediately return to it and hold it in their possession (Lib. 1 Rev. c. 9). And as the rebel angels depart from sinners who invoke the names of Jesus and Mary, so, on the other hand, as Our Lady told St. Bridget, the good angels draw more closely around those just souls who devoutly pronounce them.

When we say the Rosary, we pronounce these powerful names no less than one hundred and fifty-four times; and should we say only five decades of the Rosary, we pronounce them fifty-four times. Imagine, then, what great pain and confusion we cause the devil by saying the Rosary. Next to the holy sacrifice of the Mass, there is, indeed, nothing more terrifying to him, nor does he bear a more implacable hatred to anything than to the devotion of the Rosary.

241

When St. Dominic was preaching at Caucassone, in France, an Albigensian heretic was possessed by demons because he had publicly spoken against the devotion of the most holy Rosary. This person having been brought to St. Dominic, the great servant of the Lord ordered the demons, in the name of God, to declare whether those things which he had said concerning the Rosary were true, and, howling with rage, they said: "Hear, O Christians! all that this our enemy has said of Mary and of the most holy Rosary is true." They added, moreover, that they had no power over the servants of Mary, and that many who at death invoked Mary were saved, contrary to their deserts; and finally they said: "We are constrained to declare that no one is lost who perseveres in devotion to Mary and in the devotion of the most holy Rosary, for Mary obtains for sinners a true repentance before death." St. Dominic made the people immediately say the Rosary; and, wonderful to relate, at every Hail Mary many devils went out from that wretched man in the shape of burning coals, so that when the Rosary was finished he was entirely freed from all evil spirits and many heretics became converted ("Glories of Mary," by St.Alphonsus).

Satan understands but too well all the blessings which God bestows upon the just as well as upon sinners by the devotion of the Rosary. No wonder, therefore, that he bears to it an implacable hatred, and does all in his power to prevent Catholics from saying it. To succeed in his attempt he makes use of his agents – heretics, infidels, and lukewarm Catholics. Protestantism has at all times proscribed the Rosary. Calvin and Bucer, not satisfied with denouncing it from the pulpit, even caused the beads to be sought for in the houses of the Catholics, and woe to him who was found with them in his hands. Jansenism, a branch of Protestantism, could never cherish a devotion so dear to the Blessed Virgin. Infidel philosophers have always scoffed at it, knowing that Catholic faith could never perish so long as the devotion of the Rosary should exist. The devil employs both these enemies of our holy faith and lukewarm Catholics, who call themselves liberal, as his agents, to undermine, and if possible to destroy, this devotion by throwing ridicule and sarcasm on it. They term it " *the vain, tedious repetition of the Rosary.*" Generally speaking, the reverse of what the devil suggests by his agents is true. This may not always be the case, but it is certainly the case in this objection. Now, the reverse of "the vain, tedious repetition of the Rosary" is "the most profitable and delightful repetition of the Rosary." Satan, as we know, is accustomed to misrepresent the truth; he cannot help telling lies. It requires but little reflection to see that the above objection to the Rosary is utterly false, and that its reverse is a great truth.

When there is question about the repetition of sinful acts, the devil or his agents have no objection to make. On the contrary, they delight in seeing them repeated, because the devil knows very well that the oftener a man repeats a sinful act, the more he becomes confirmed in vice, and his conversion is rendered more difficult. What more vain, more tedious, and more abominable, than to repeat the sin of blasphemy, of ridiculing the religious ceremonies and practices of the Church? What more detestable than to repeat the sin of cursing, missing Mass, of disobedience to parents, of drunkenness, of scandal, of child-murder, of impurity, of theft, of slander? To the repetition of these sins no objection is made. But to the repetition of prayer and other good works the devil has every objection, because he knows that by repeating good works we become confirmed in good, and more and more like unto our heavenly Father.

The successful man in every calling, whether literary, scientific or commercial, is he who can say: "This one thing I do constantly." When Michaelangelo was asked why he did not marry, he replied: "Painting is my wife, and my works are my children." He became a great painter because he was a whole man at one thing. He touched and retouched the canvas hundreds of times to produce a good painting. Thousands of men have failed in life by dabbling in too many things. To do anything perfectly, there should be an exclusiveness, a bigotry, a blindness of attachment, to that one object, which shall make all others for the time being seem worthless.

This is the first law of success in worldly pursuits. It also is the first law of success in spiritual pursuits, in the road of perfection. To become virtuous we must constantly repeat the acts of virtue; to become patient we must often repeat the acts of patience; to become strong in faith, in obedience, in holy purity, we must constantly practice the acts of those virtues. In like manner, to become a man of prayer we must often repeat our prayers. This frequent repetition is the law of success. St. Teresa repeated the offering of herself to God fifty times in the day. St. Martha repeated her prayer a hundred times in the day and a hundred times in the night. St. Francis Borgia also repeated his prayer a hundred times in the day. St. Philip Neri made a kind of Rosary of the words, "O God! Come to my aid; O Lord! Make haste to help me." He recited this Rosary sixty times in the day, and taught his penitents to do the same. St. Gertrude repeated the prayer, "Thy will be done on earth as it is in heaven," three hundred and sixty-five times a day. St. Leonard of Port Maurice recommended himself to the Blessed Virgin Mary two hundred times a day; he used to say that we should not let a moment pass without repeating the words, "Have mercy on me, O Jesus! Have mercy on me." He also tells us that he knew a man who repeated this prayer, "Jesus, have mercy on me," one hundred times in less than an hour. St. Bartholomew the Apostle repeated his acts of divine adoration two hundred times every day. St. Patrick, the Apostle of Ireland, made every day three hundred genuflections in adoration of the Blessed Trinity, and he made the sign of the cross one hundred times before each canonical hour. St. Margaret of Cortona repeated the Our Father over a thousand times in the day. St. Alphonsus was accustomed, before going to bed, to repeat his acts of faith, hope, charity, sorrow, etc., ten times. Jesus Christ himself has taught us by his example to repeat our prayers. When the agony and terror of death came upon him in the Garden of Olives, he prayed with the greatest earnestness, and uttered again and again the same prayer. We also learn this practice from the blessed in heaven, who do not cease day and night to sing: "Holy, holy, holy Lord God, who was, who is, and who is to come." The power of prayer does not consist in many words; it consists rather in repeating constantly the same petition with greater fervor. What is more powerless than the scattered cloud of steam as they rise in the sky? They are as impotent as the dewdrops that fall nightly upon the earth. But, concentrated and condensed in a steam boiler, they are able to cut through solid rock, to hurl mountains into the sea, and to bring the antipodes to our doors. If we wish to make our prayer powerful with God, we must continually condense our desires in the boiler of our heart, upon one particular object, one grace that we stand most in need of. And, oh! What a powerful prayer is such a condensed desire with God. Many have become rich by keeping on picking rags. The saints became rich in the grace of God, because they persevered in repeating the same prayer. Oneness of aim and the direction of the energies to a single pursuit, while all others are waived aside as profitless, enable the weariest weakling to make his mark where he strikes. The devil understands this truth too well; applied to the devotion of the Rosary, it enkindles his infernal rage against all those who practice it. He knows that the oftener we say, "Our Father who art in heaven," the more our confidence will be increased in God; he knows that the more earnestly we repeat, "Hallowed be thy name, thy kingdom come, thy will be done on earth as it is in heaven," the more grace God will give us to know him, to love him, and to serve him according to his will; he knows that the oftener we repeat, "Holy Mary, Mother of God, pray for us," the more the Blessed Virgin will show herself a most powerful and merciful mother to us with God. Hence, consistent with his nature, the devil misrepresents the truth. He calls vain what is most profitable to us, and tedious what is most delightful – "The vain, tedious repetition of the Rosary." He who gives utterance to this suggestion of the devil must be his agent. By repeating it he shows that he does not love God, or he would delight in often saying,

" Our Father who art in heaven." He shows that he does not care for knowing God better for being with him in heaven, and serving him according to his will, or he would often pray, "Hallowed be thy name," etc. He shows that he does not care for the prayers of the Blessed Virgin, or he would delight in repeating, "Holy Mary, Mother of God, Pray for us sinners." He shows that he is a most ungrateful wretch, or he would delight in repeating the act of thanksgiving, "Glory be to the Father." These agents of the devil "desire to be the teachers of the law, and understand nothing, neither the things they say, nor whereof they affirm" (1Tim. 1:7).

To keep alive, we must constantly draw breath; to preserve the life of the soul, the grace of God – to increase it in us daily

– we must often repeat our prayer for it. Were a good friend to present us several times with a thousand dollars, we would not object to such a sum, but rather wish the amount to be increased. The good Christian, in like manner, never finds the repetition of the prayers of the Rosary tedious, but rather truly delightful. He knows that one single prayer of the Rosary, which is recited with devotion is of more value than all the money, than all the riches, in the universe. What will money, what will all the riches of this world, avail us after death? But the prayers of the Rosary will then be of more help to us than all the honors and wealth in the world. If we endeavor, by meditation and prayer, to understand fully all the graces which we need to be saved, that we pray for all these graces when we recite the Rosary, and that it is most necessary for us to ask again and again of our Lord to be heard – far from requiring an exhortation to make the same petitions over and over again, the impulse of our own devotion will prompt us to repeat the prayers of the Rosary several times a day, like that good old soldier who, being overcome with fatigue, and suffering from many wounds received in battle, had found a home in the Hospital of the Incurables at Anvers. He had grown old in the camp, says the author of the "Month of the Rosary;' but had preserved his heart pure; consequently, he was easily impressed with piety. A priest who visited him taught him the devotion of the holy Rosary, and the poor soldier found so much consolation in this prayer that he wept at learning it so late. "Had I but known it sooner," he said, "I should have recited it daily"; but, in the ardor of his regret, he endeavored to supply the time lost, and he said his chaplet with the accelerated speed of a traveler who, being exposed to the rays of the burning sun, seeks to gain the shade. Not hoping for his recovery, he said with great simplicity: "If the holy Virgin would but accord me two years more of life, I would recite as many Rosaries as there have been days in my life." He then asked how many days there were in sixty years. He was told twenty-one thousand nine hundred. He then asked how many Rosaries he would have to recite daily to complete the number in two years. He was told thirty! The aged soldier, undaunted, imposed this duty upon himself with alacrity. Night and day he had his Rosary in his hand, and in two years he arrived, enlightened and improved by his piety, at the completion of his pious and self-imposed duty. Death there awaited him; he lived not a day, not even an hour, over the time, and he expired reciting the last Ave Maria. This pure soul went to contemplate in glory her who had been the support and consolation of his old age.

Others, again, will say: "Oh! The Rosary, the beads – that may do for old women or ignorant people, who can neither read nor write. Old people who have lost their eyesight, and have already one foot in the grave may say the beads – that is very becoming and reasonable; but as for people who have received a good education, people who can read and pray for themselves, what need have they of the Rosary? It is quite out of fashion for them to say the beads."

The devil grants that the Rosary is a good devotion for old women, because he cannot so easily prevail upon them to give up this devotion. But knowing that the learned and educated people stand more in need of this devotion than old women, because in too many instances they are greater sinners, Satan tries to prevent them from embracing this devotion by treating it with contempt.

There is a proverb which says: "A little learning is a dangerous thing." And verily, only with persons gifted with a very moderate share of learning can such a silly objection hold. Is, indeed, the devotion of the Rosary fit only for the old and the ignorant? What, then, is the Rosary? We have seen that the Rosary is one of the most ancient devotions in the Church; that it is a devotion from heaven; that the prayers which compose it have been in part inspired, in part taught us directly by God himself.

Let us examine the first of these prayers – the Apostles' Creed. It is to be hoped that all those who object to the Rosary know it by heart. The Creed, as shown already, is a short compendium of all the mysteries of our holy religion. It is a creed in defense of which so many Fathers and doctors of the Church have written and preached, for which so many tender virgins have quitted everything that was dear to them on earth; a creed for which so many noble martyrs have poured out their hearts' blood like water. And persons have the imprudence to tell us that such a creed is fit only for the old and the ignorant!

What is the Our Father? The Our Father was, as we know, taught us by our Blessed Savior himself. It is a prayer so truly sublime, so heavenly, so full of the deepest wisdom, that the most eloquent preachers, the most learned theologians, the most enlightened saints, have preached on it, have paraphrased it, have explained it, and still its meaning has not been exhausted. Now, can anyone assert without manifest blasphemy that such a prayer is fit only for the ignorant?

We have already seen that the Hail Mary was in part inspired, in part taught us by God himself through his holy angel. It is a prayer so full of power, of sweetness, and of the most sublime mysteries that, next to Our Father, there is, perhaps, no prayer on earth to be compared to it. And yet such a prayer, too, is said to be fit only for the ignorant! If, then, the prayers that compose the Rosary are so holy and so sublime, must not the Rosary itself be holy and sublime?

This is what truly great, learned, and saintly men have ever known and felt. The great and zealous prelate St. Charles Borromeo recited the Rosary daily. The saintly Bishop of Geneva, St. Francis de Sales, even made a vow to say the Rosary daily, and he kept it till the day of his death. The learned and venerable Bishop of St.Agatha, St.Alphonsus de Liguori, the founder of the Society of the Most Holy Redeemer, who, by his rank, his learning, and his labors as a missionary and a prelate and doctor of the Church, stands second to none, not only said the Rosary daily himself, but also left it as a sweet obligation to all his children, the Redemptorist Fathers. Moreover, he ordered it to be recited daily during every mission.

But not merely ecclesiastics and saints, who especially loved prayer, have recited the Rosary; orators, generals, nobles, and even kings, queens, and emperors, have considered it an honor to wear the Rosary, to recite it in public as well as in private. The renowned Emperor of Germany, Charles V, said the Rosary with great fervor and devotion. He considered the devotion of the Rosary as a most sure means to obtain the protection of Almighty God. Hence he used to say the beads whenever he had to transact an affair of importance. "I will say the Rosary," said he, "and then attend to this affair." Edward III, King of England, observed the same practice. Alfonso

V, King of Portugal, used to say to his officers: "Let us say the Rosary, in order to be sure that the Blessed Virgin will assist us by her prayers in the government of the kingdom." The Emperor Frederic III requested the Pope to re-establish the Archconfraternity of the Rosary in Cologne, whereupon he had himself, the Empress Eleanore, and his son Maximilian enrolled as members of the Archconfraternity. Henry II, Francis II, and Charles IX, kings of France, were members.

In 1775, Ferdinand, Duke of Parma, wrote a little book on the Rosary, many copies of which he circulated among his subjects in order to make them love and practice this devotion.

The famous Catholic musician Haydn confessed that he had conceived his finest musical ideas whilst telling his beads. Doctor Récamier, who was celebrated in Europe for his medical skill, said the beads with the devotion of a fervent Christian. "When I am uneasy about some patient," said he, "when I find medicine powerless, and have exhausted my resources, I address myself to the Blessed Virgin; and, going on sick calls, I say a decade or two of my Rosary. The beads are like a door bell. To get admission to the great of this world, and ask a favor, we have to wait long; but to speak to the Holy Virgin is the simplest thing in the world: we just ring the bell by saying a decade on the beads, and, behold, the door opens, and Mary is so very kind that, unless there are good reasons why it should not be, the prayer is granted at once."

It is tedious to enumerate all the great and learned personages who have recited the Rosary. But I will cite yet a single instance of one whose name is, no doubt, familiar to all – the eloquent Irish orator, the unflinching champion of Catholic freedom – Daniel O'Connell. Whilst the important question of Catholic emancipation was being agitated in England and Ireland, O'Connell was the only one who stood up boldly for the rights of the Irish Catholics. He was, it is true, an eloquent speaker, but he had powerful and eloquent opponents – men who hated Catholicism as Satan hates the cross. O'Connell knew that his cause was just, that Heaven was on his side; he therefore prayed fervently that God would at length free his holy

Church from the galling yoke of English Protestant tyranny. He prayed especially to the Mother of God, Mary Immaculate, whom he knew to be the seat of wisdom, the fountain of eloquence. When the day came on which the question was to be ultimately decided, such an immense multitude had assembled that the speakers had to come out in the open air. O'Connell's Protestant opponent first arose and spoke with such eloquence that he won the applause of all. During this harangue O'Connell sat quietly in his place, and, unobserved by any one save the blessed eye of God, kept his hand in his bosom and recited his beads. We may be sure that he prayed with devotion, for he saw that the moment had come which was to decide the future destiny of his dear Catholic Church in Ireland, and that faith for which his forefathers had bled and died. He prayed to Mary, the Help of Christians, and his prayer was heard. His opponent took his seat, and O'Connell arose. He spoke with such eloquence and such fire, such boldness and freedom, that he carried all before him, and completely silenced his opponents. He won the day, for Our Lady of the Rosary had assisted him, and the Catholic Church in Ireland was free. With such examples before us, I ask, What are we to think of him who asserts that the devotion of the Rosary is fit only for the old and the ignorant? Most assuredly "he is not of the seed of those men by whom salvation was brought to Israel" (1 Mach. 5:62). He cannot say, in truth, with St. Paul: "I think that I also have the Spirit of God" (1 Cor. 8:40). It is dangerous to follow his sentiments.

When St. Dominic introduced the devotion of the Rosary there were many who despised and ridiculed it. Among them was a certain clergyman of Toulouse. When he heard the Rosary preached by St. Dominic, he spoke of it afterwards with contempt, saying it was only fit for women or children. But he was soon convinced of his error. By a particular permission of God he was persecuted and calumniated in a most atrocious manner, and during the time of this persecution he had a vision. It seemed to him that he was plunged in deep mire, out of which he could not extricate himself. Suddenly he saw above him the forms of Our Blessed Lady and St. Dominic, who let down to him a chain of one hundred and fifty rings, fifteen of which were of gold. No sooner had he taken hold of this chain than he found himself placed safe on dry land. From this vision he understood that by means of the devotion of the Rosary he should be delivered from his enemies. So he began to say the Rosary quite devoutly, and soon afterwards the Blessed Virgin delivered him from his enemies ("Life of St. Dominic").

About the same time a noble lady bitterly opposed the new confraternities of the Rosary. But she was soon converted. She saw, in a vision, a large number of men and women surrounded by a heavenly light, who devoutly recited the Rosary; and for every Hail Mary which they said a beautiful star came forth from their mouths, and the prayers were written in a book in letters of gold. Then the blessed Virgin spoke to her and said: "In this book are written the names of the brothers and sisters of my Rosary, but thy name is not written; and because thou hast persuaded many not to enter this confraternity thou shalt fall sick, but thy sickness will be thy salvation." Soon after the lady was taken sick, and, recognizing the truth of the prediction, on her recovery she had her name entered among the members of the confraternity.

"Very true," some one may say; "but where shall I find time for saying the Rosary? I am a father of a family, and must work hard the whole day to support my wife and children, and in the evening I need a little rest." "And I," says the mother, "I have to take care of the children; I have to keep the house in order; and in the evening I am too fatigued to think of the Rosary."

"You are too fatigued to kneel so long?" Why, then, you may stand, or even sit down, during the Rosary, though of course it is far more becoming to kneel.

"You cannot meditate on the mysteries?" Then, at least, pay attention to the words of each prayer. And if the father and mother are too tired to say the Rosary themselves, why, let one of the children read it aloud. He will be proud of such an office.

"But you have no time." Such an objection betrays a bad will. What! You have time to read the newspaper, time to chat with a friend, time to visit your neighbor, you find time even to step into the grog shop, and you cannot find time to say the Rosary? How much time, then, is required for the beads? At the most about twenty minutes. What! Can you not spare twenty minutes to draw down the blessing of God upon your family? And should you not have even twenty minutes to spare, why, then you may say the beads even whilst at work, at home, or when going to your work or returning home from it. To gain the indulgences it is sufficient if one of the family says the Rosary aloud, while the others join with him in reciting it. The mother, for instance, can sew or knit while the Rosary is being recited, and yet gain all the indulgences.

A certain young lady, whilst at her work, was seen with ten small pieces of paper before her, which she shifted forward and backward. Being asked why she did so, she said: "I thus count my Rosary prayers.'

"But I have no beads," says another one. Why, then, you have a natural pair of beads on your fingers, till you can procure one; or can you not do what a Protestant young lady in a city of Iowa did about a year ago? She took peas and made a pair of beads of them, and thus began to practice the devotion of the Rosary. She came to one of our Fathers, who gave a mission in that city, to be received into the Church. She made her confession with such great contrition that it seemed she would die of sorrow for her sins. Ah! How this example confounds the lukewarm Catholic!

Dear Christian, there is no valid excuse for not practicing the daily devotion of the Rosary, and, for the most part, those who make these objections and excuses are influenced by a secret unwillingness to lead a Christian life in good earnest. They are unwilling to practice retirement, detachment from creatures, and self-denial. They omit saying the beads in order to avoid the rebuke of their conscience for their sensuality, pride, vanity, uncharitableness, and sloth. Miserable are the consequences of such a course of conduct. Not being willing to seek true peace of heart in religion, such men try to find their consolation in exterior things; they multiply faults and imperfections in proportion as they withdraw from God. And what is most lamentable is that not infrequently their venial sins lead them into mortal sins, and they live in such a state for months, remaining in constant danger of being overtaken by a sudden and unprovided death, the just punishment of their ingratitude and indifference toward Jesus Christ and the Blessed Virgin.

There are cases in which reluctance to practice the devotion of the Rosary may proceed from a want of instruction on the great treasures hidden in and derived from this devotion. Enough has been said here to show the groundlessness of the objections commonly made to it; to show that, though simple and within the scope of every one, yet this devotion contains a depth of holy science and blessings, spiritual and temporal, that is unfathomable, for the greatest saints and most enlightened persons who, on that account, showed the deepest attachment for this devotion. Only give it a trial, if you have hitherto neglected it, and you will not only find time enough for it, but you will also experience how many graces and blessings are attached to the devout recital of the Rosary. If you are asked why you say the beads so often, answer that two classes of persons should say them every day: the perfect to persevere in perfection, and the imperfect to attain perfection; the strong not to become weak, and the weak to grow strong; the sick to be cured, and the healthy to prevent sickness. And as to yourself, say that, because you are imperfect, weak, and infirm, you stand in need of the devotion of the Rosary. Tell those Who ask that you wish to become patient, and therefore you must, by this devotion, honor your patient Savior, and beg patience of him; that you wish to become meek, and that, therefore, you must remember, by this devotion, the example of your meek Savior; that you wish to love contempt, and therefore you must, by the Rosary, have recourse to your despised Savior; that you wish to love crosses, and therefore you must, by the Rosary, implore grace to bear them; that you wish to become strong against the temptations of the devil, the flesh, and the world, and therefore you must make use of the Rosary to obtain strength from your comforting Savior. Tell them that the Blessed Virgin said to St. Dominic: "This devotion is most dear to my Son and to me. The faithful shall obtain by it numberless benefits, and shall always find me ready to aid them in all their wants." She, in whose words you put your trust will justify you; your soul will continually grow stronger in virtue; your heart will become more and more pure; your passions will grow weaker; your faith more lively, your hope more firm, your charity more ardent; you will receive an abundance of graces to live in the world as an heir of heaven; and when at your last hour the priest comes to administer the Holy Viaticum, you will, like St. Teresa, exclaim with a holy confidence: "My Lord and my Bridegroom! So, then, the hour is come at last for which my heart has longed so much. Now is the time that we shall see each other face to face. Blessed be this hour! Thy will be done! O happy hour! in which my exile has an end, and my soul takes its flight to thee, for whom I have always longed so much!"

CHAPTER 31

THE DEVOTION OF THE SCAPULAR

The Blessed Mother of God, our loving Mother Mary, is ever rich in graces. Not satisfied with having given her children the holy devotion of the Rosary, she has given us likewise another devotion as simple as it is powerful, a devotion as universal as it is dear to every Catholic heart – the holy devotion of the Scapular.

The Scapular consists of two or more pieces of cloth worn over the shoulders. There are five Scapulars approved of in the Church. The first is the brown Scapular, or the Scapular of Our Lady of Mount Carmel. The Carmelites are one of the oldest orders in the Church. They trace their descent from the great prophet Elias, who lived more than eight hundred years before the coming of the Redeemer. At the coming of our Lord and Savior the pious disciples of the prophet became Christians. They entertained a great love and devotion to the Blessed Virgin Mary, in whose honor they had erected an altar in one of the many grottoes of Mount Carmel, and thus the devotion of Our Lady of Mount Carmel has continued to the present day.

The Order of the Carmelites has produced many great and learned men, one of the most illustrious of whom was St. Simon Stock, an Englishman by birth. From his early childhood this holy man cherished a tender devotion to the Immaculate Mother of God, and he received from Mary in return many extraordinary graces. It is now about 600 years ago since the saint was one day kneeling before a statue of Mary. He besought her with all the fervor of his soul to protect himself and his order from the many dangers that threatened them. On a sudden a brilliant light surrounded him. He beheld a great multitude of angels, in the midst of whom, was the Queen of Angels, the Blessed Mother of God herself. She was radiant with glory and unutterable beauty, and she held in her hand a Scapular; which she presented to the saint, saying: "My son, receive this Scapular; it is a pledge of salvation, a safeguard. He that dies and wears this Scapular shall not burn in the flames of hell." This is the origin of the brown Scapular.

II. The black Scapular, or, as it is called, the Scapular of Our Lady of Dolors, originated in the following manner: There lived a few centuries ago in the fair city of Florence seven pious noblemen; they were members of a confraternity of Our Lady, and often met together to celebrate the praises of the Mother of God. While they were once assembled on the Feast of the Assumption of the Blessed Virgin, in order to celebrate devoutly that glorious festival, they felt their hearts filled with an extraordinary love for God and his Holy Mother. They were on a sudden wrapt into an ecstasy, and all beheld a globe of fire, from which issued seven brilliant rays that penetrated their hearts and filled them with an unutterable yearning after heaven. They then beheld the ever Blessed Virgin Mary crowned with a crown of glory, beaming with heavenly light, and surrounded by a multitude of angels. The Blessed Virgin gazed on them with the utmost affection, called each of them by his name, and commanded them to quit the world. The vision passed away, and the noblemen agreed together to obey the voice of their heavenly Queen. They then distributed their wealth to the poor, and retired to a wild mountainous district some distance from the city, where they led a life of prayer and penance, meditating daily on the suffering of our Savior and on the sorrows of his beloved Mother. Whenever they entered the city the people flocked around them and craved their blessing, and even the children were heard to cry out as these holy men passed: "See the servants of Mary! These are the servants of Mary!" On Good Friday evening, as they were meditating on the sorrows of the Mother of God, they were again wrapt into an ecstasy, and beheld the Blessed Virgin descending from heaven, accompanied by a great multitude of angels carrying with them the instruments of our Savior's Passion. One of them bore a palm branch, the emblem of victory. Another carried a shield, on which the words "Servants of Mary" were written in letters of gold. The Blessed Virgin herself held in her hand a religious habit of black cloth. Her beautiful countenance bore an expression of unutterable compassion and love. She presented the habit to the pious religious, saying: "My children, receive this habit, and with it the name of my servants; persevere as you have begun, and this palm of victory shall one day be yours." As the faithful were now desirous of sharing in the merits and good works of this pious order, these good religions instituted the black Scapular, which was approved of by the Church and enriched with many indulgences.

III.   The next is the blue Scapular, or the Scapular of the Immaculate Conception. It was on the Feast of Candlemas, a few centuries ago, that Our Blessed Lady appeared to a pious maiden named Ursula Benincasa. Our Lady was clad in a robe of dazzling whiteness, over which she wore a mantle of heavenly blue. A troop of beautiful virgins, clad in the same attire, surrounded their Virgin Queen, who bore her Divine Infant in her arms. The Holy Mother of God smiled graciously upon the pious maiden, who was at the time bitterly bewailing her sins, and consoled her. "My daughter," said she, "dry up thy tears; thy sorrow shall now be changed into pure and heavenly joy. Hearken to the words of my Divine Son, whom thou hast chosen for the Spouse." The infant Jesus now commanded Ursula to found a new order bearing the name of the Immaculate Conception. This order was to be composed of thirty virgins, who were to wear a habit similar to that in which the Blessed Virgin Mary appeared. The Divine Infant promised special graces to all those who would join this order. The pious maiden was rejoiced beyond measure at these happy tidings. In her great charity she wished that these gracious promises might be extended to all the faithful. She therefore besought fervently the Mother of Mercy to extend these graces to all those who would wear a blue Scapular, honor the Immaculate Conception, and fulfil the duties of their state of life. Her prayer was granted, and she immediately beheld a great multitude of angels busily engaged in distributing this Scapular among the faithful.

IV.   The next is the Scapular of the Most Holy Trinity. Its color is white, with a cross of red and blue in the center. About seven or eight centuries ago the Moors were very powerful; they often landed on the coast of southern Europe, seized upon many defenseless Christians, and sold them as slaves. They also attacked Christian vessels, plundered them, and sold the crew into bondage. There lived at this time in Paris a holy priest named John de Matha. During his first Mass he was honored by a heavenly vision. He beheld a bright angel, clad in a robe of snowy whiteness; on his breast shimmered a cross of blue and crimson. He held his hands extended over a Moor and a Christian who stood beside him. The saint understood from this vision that he was called by God to ransom the Christian captives. In order, then, to prepare himself for this generous undertaking, he quitted Paris and retired to a wilderness, where he sought the company of St. Felix, a holy intermit, who was heir to the crown of France, but had quitted all to secure his salvation. As these holy men were one day seated near a cool spring that gushed forth beside their hermitage, and were discoursing of heavenly things, they suddenly beheld a snow white stag. Between its antlers glittered a brilliant cross of blue and crimson. St. John de Matha now told his astonished companion the vision he had seen during his first Mass. The two holy men then agreed to obey the voice of Heaven and to found an order for the redemption of the Christian captives. They therefore set out for Rome to receive the approbation of the Pope. On their arrival they were graciously received, and on the following morning the Pope also, during Mass, had the same vision which John de Matha beheld in Paris. The Holy Father then approved the new order, and gave it the name of the Order of the Most Holy Trinity. As the faithful were desirous of partaking in the merits and good works of this order, the Scapular of the Most Holy Trinity was instituted and approved of and enriched by the Church with many indulgences.

V.   The last is the red Scapular, or the Scapular of the Passion and of the Sacred Hearts of Jesus and Mary. It was about the year 1846 that a Sister of Charity was praying one evening before the Blessed Sacrament. Our Blessed Savior appeared to her holding in his hand the red Scapular. On one part of the Scapular was represented the Crucifixion. At the foot of the cross lay the instruments of our Lord's Passion, the scourge, the hammer, and the robe that had covered his bleeding body. Around the cross were the words, "Holy Passion of our Lord Jesus Christ, save us." On the other part of the Scapular were represented the Sacred Hearts of Jesus and Mary. Between these Hearts arose a cross, and around them were the words, "Sacred Hearts of Jesus and Mary, protect us." This apparition was renewed several times. One day our Lord revealed to the Sister that all those who wear this Scapular shall receive every Friday a great increase of faith, hope, and clarity. At another time, while this religious was meditating on the Passion during the holy Mass, she had another apparition, which she relates as follows: "I thought," said she, "I saw our Lord Jesus hanging on the cross. The ghastly paleness of his countenance made a deep impression on me, and my whole body became covered with a cold sweat. Our Lord's head was bowed down. His brow was pierced by long and sharp thorns. On a sudden he raised his head, and the thorns were violently forced into his eyes and temples. Never can I forget that sight. There was something terrible in the pain he must have endured in the rude shock of his adorable head against the wood of the cross. I was filled with anguish and trembling. From that moment the Passion of our Lord has always been before my eyes."

One evening this Sister was making the Way of the Cross. It seemed to her, at the thirteenth station, that the Blessed Virgin Mary put into her arms the mangled body of her Divine Son. The Blessed Mother of God then uttered these remarkable words: "The world is going to ruin because it does not think of the Passion of Jesus Christ. Do all you can to get men to think of the Passion, do all you can for the world's salvation."

One Sunday our Divine Savior showed this religious a beautiful river, clearer than crystal. Many persons were on its banks. Those that plunged in became all resplendent with brilliancy. Diamonds and gold seem to fall from their hands. Those that fled away became enveloped in a black smoke which made them hideous to the sight. Our Savior then told her that this beautiful river represented his mercy, always ready to receive the repentance of the sinner and to give it a value.

From these well authenticated facts we see that the Scapular is a badge of our love and veneration of the holy Mother of God. It is, at the same time, a sweet pledge of her powerful protection; it is a devotion most ancient and venerable – a devotion descended from heaven. The most learned theologians, among them the renowned Cardinal Bellarmine, concur in asserting its heavenly origin. The popes have approved of it in various bulls; the holy Catholic Church has instituted a special feast, a Mass, and office to celebrate the devotion of the Scapular. Every nation into which the one saving Church has yet penetrated, every rank and class of men, from the layman to the Pope, all honor and practice the devotion of the Scapular. But, more than all this, God himself, who is the living truth, who alone can suspend the laws of nature, has confirmed the heavenly origin of the Scapular by numberless miracles. Father Crasset, S.J., relates that a military officer told him that he saw with his own eyes how a trumpeter of his company received a pistol shot from some one near, and that, when he examined his breast, where he said that he had been hit, he found that the ball had been stopped by the Scapular of the Virgin which the man wore, and that it had not even troubled the flesh. He took it and exhibited it to the whole company. Louis XIII, King of France, on witnessing this miracle, immediately put on the heavenly armor of the Scapular. (Crasset, tom. 2, tr. 6, pr. 14.)

The Savannah (GA) *Republician* says: "A letter has been sent from Key West to Bishop Verot, describing the wonderful escape from death of Sister M. Theophilus, who was struck down by lightning in the convent at that place. She was laid upon her bed insensible, froth flowing from her mouth, her countenance black and distorted. On removing her collar the lightning flash was found depicted on her neck and breast. It formed a red line about a finger's width, burnt into the skin and flesh, but stopped just under the Scapular she wore. The Sister recovered, and the physician was so impressed that he had his entire family baptized."

In 1656 some missionaries were preaching a mission at Saint Aulay, a town in Saintonge. About ten o'clock a fire broke out in a house, and raged with such violence that a great number of the inhabitants collected on the spot to give all the help possible under the circumstances. Among the crowd was a worthy clergyman, who (recollecting that at Perigueux, about twenty years before, a great fire had been miraculously extinguished by a Scapular, which event had been inquired into and attested by the magistrate of the town) desired a young man, remarkable for his faith and piety, and who happened to be on the spot, to take off his Scapular, and to throw it into the midst of the flames, "and you will find," he added, "that they will be soon extinguished through the intercession of the Blessed Virgin." The young man hastened to obey, and, making his way through the crowd, threw his Scapular into that part of the fire where it was raging most violently. At the same moment the flames seemed to ascend like a whirlwind, and the fire ceased burning. The Scapular was found intact on the following day in the midst of the burnt remains of the house. The miracle was so apparent that some Calvinists who were present said among themselves, "That young man is a sorcerer," while the Catholics, on the other hand, praised God and admired the virtue of the Scapular."

"These are the very words of the attestation," says the missionary, Pére le Jeune, of the Congregation of the Oratory of Jesus, who relates the fact, "which I received from the Rev. Fathers of the mission of Perigueux."

In the year 1719 the hamlet of Ballon, in the Diocese of Metz, was threatened with destruction by fire, which had suddenly broken out, when the confidence of the inhabitants in the protection of Our Lady of Mount Carmel induced them to cast a Scapular into the flames; the fire instantly abated, and the Scapular was found miraculously preserved on a burning rafter. The Bishops of Metz had an attestation of the above drawn up, which was signed and sealed by him; in this document, after relating the miracle, he says: "All the circumstances of this event plainly prove that the Almighty intended to reward the faith and confidence which had been shown in the Blessed Virgin by a public and well authenticated miracle; therefore we ordain, in order to preserve the remembrance of so signal a favor, as well as to promote the edification of the faithful, and an increase of devotion to Our Blessed Lady, which is grounded on the tradition of the whole Church, that on the second Sunday of July, every year, in perpetuity, there shall be added to the pious ceremonies and devotions practiced by the members of the Confraternity of the Scapular a procession round the hamlet of Ballon, after which the 'Te Deum' shall be sung in thanksgiving for the miracle with which it has pleased the Divine Goodness to honor the said place, as well as to encourage the faith and devotion of those who have recourse to God, by a praiseworthy confidence in the intercession of the Blessed Mary."

"Given in our palace of Metz, signed, countersigned, and sealed with our arms, the 12th of January, 1820."

HENRY CHARLES DU CAMBOUT,
"Bishop of Metz, Duc de Coislin."

Let, then, the infidel and wiseacre ridicule the devotion of the Scapular, but let them beware of the malediction which the inspired apostle uttered against those carnal men who blaspheme what they ignore.

The Blessed Virgin Mary has promised that he who dies wearing the Scapular will not burn in the flames of hell. There are many individuals, believing themselves to be enlightened, who smile at those simple souls that put faith in such a promise. Why, even some Catholics try to explain it away. But where is there anything really absurd in believing this? Is it not the Blessed Virgin Mary herself who has made this promise, and is she not the Mother of God? Are not all the treasures of God's mercy placed in her hands? Is she not truly, as the Holy Church calls her, the Mother of Mercy? Is she, then, not willing, and is she not able also, to fulfil her promise? Can Mary not obtain for the sinner in his last moments a grace so powerful as to change his heart and to move him to contrition? Cannot her prayers produce the same effect on the dying sinner as they produced on the thief on the cross, who, from a robber and murderer, became in a moment a child of God and an heir of heaven?

But let us not be misunderstood on this point. If one tends a life of sin up to the last hour, he cannot enter heaven unless he be sincerely sorry for his sins. Our good Mother Mary can obtain for him this sorrow in his last moments. When it is least expected, she can enlighten his soul with a ray of supernatural light; she can show him the vanity of the world, the hell that awaits the impenitent sinner, and the dread fate of falling unprepared into the hands of the living and long enduring God. Mary has power over the demons, and she can send legions of angels to protect the sinner against their attacks. By her prayer she is all powerful, and she can obtain even, if necessary, a prolongation of the sinner's life, as she has so often done.

Father Crasset, S.J., relates that an officer was sent out one day to the battlefield to superintend the transport of the wounded soldiers. In the midst of a great heap of the slain he found a soldier, still alive, who held in his hand a Scapular of Mary, and asked for a priest, as he wished to make his confession. On approaching, the officer noticed that this soldier had received a deep saber gash on his head, and that his forehead had been pierced by a bullet, so that his brains were oozing out. He ordered his men to leave the soldier among the dead, as there could be no hopes of his recovery. The poor soldier, hearing this, entreated for God's sake to be placed in the wagon with the wounded soldiers. "Only bring me to a priest," said he, "that I may make my confession; after that you may throw me where you will and let me die." His request was granted, and after they had gone almost a mile they met the chaplain. The dying soldier now made his confession with the utmost presence of mind. As soon as he had received absolution he raised his eyes to heaven, murmured the sweet names of Jesus and Mary, and immediately expired. This is but one example out of thousands of the kind that might be cited.

In 1636 Mousieur de Cuge, cornet of a company of horse, was wounded at Tefia by a cannon ball, which, passing through his left side, had torn his heart to pieces, so that naturally he could not live a moment. Nevertheless, Almighty God, through the intercession of the Blessed Virgin Mary, gave him time to repent; for he was in mortal sin, as he afterwards declared. His life was prolonged for about four hours. During this time he made his confession, and with his own hands wrote down his last will. When the surgeon examined his wounds, he found that the bullet had driven the Scapular into his heart. He died as soon as it was drawn out, making continual acts of thanksgiving for this great miracle.

But the Blessed Virgin not only saves the souls of her servants by prolonging their life; she often obtains for them the happiness of dying in the state of grace before falling into mortal sin. There is a proverb which says: "Those Whom God loves die young"; and the Holy Ghost says expressly of an innocent youth who died in the flower of his age: "God loved the youth and so he took him away from the earth; God snatched him away from the midst of sinners before his soul could be defiled by sin."

This great grace the Blessed Virgin Mary obtains also for her servants. The superior of a certain college went around one night in the dormitories to see whether all the students had retired to rest. He found a young student still kneeling at his bedside. The superior asked him why he did not go to sleep. "O Rev. Father!" said the boy, "I gave my Scapular this morning to the door keeper to mend it, and he has not returned it to me yet. I am afraid to go to sleep, for, perhaps, I might die tonight, and then I would die without the Scapular." The superior told him to fear nothing; he said he should go to sleep, and that he would get his Scapular next morning. "But, Rev. Father, said the little fellow, "I cannot sleep; I am afraid I might die tonight," etc.; and as he said this he burst into tears. The superior, touched by his earnestness went and got the Scapular from the door keeper, and gave it back to the student. The boy kissed his Scapular devoutly as he put it on, and soon fell asleep whilst murmuring the sweet names of Jesus and Mary. Next morning the superior went around again to see if all the students had arisen punctually. He came to the bed of the little tudent and found him still asleep. He called him by his name, but no answer; he shook him, and found to his horror that the boy was dead! Yes, he had died during the night; his sleep was the sleep of death; but his hand, stiff and cold in death, still grasped his Scapular. How many sick have been healed, how many lives have been saved, how many fires have been extinguished, how many tempests stilled, how many remarkable conversions have been wrought, by means of this simple devotion!

But there may be some who will object: "Can the Blessed Virgin save me from hell, if I reject all these graces, if I do not wish to change my life, if I wish to die in sin?" The answer is clear. if you wish to die in sin, then die in sin; God himself, though he is almighty, cannot, and will not, *force* a will that is once confirmed in sin and resolved to persevere in it. The Blessed Virgin Mary can obtain graces sufficient to change the most hardened sinner, but he always remains free to reject or to accept these graces. God will never force a soul into heaven. One, then, may die impenitent in his sins, bereft of God;

but not in the Scapular. No! no! The Blessed Virgin Mary cannot tear a sinner from his sins, but she will find means to tear away from the impenitent her holy Scapular. Nay, such a one himself will cast it aside before dying a reprobate. A young girl who had received a sound Catholic education had the misfortune to neglect all the good advice she had received in her youth. She spent the greater part of her time in reading novels, going to balls, parties, theaters, and the like. In a short time the novels and the gay company corrupted her heart. She was watched; the hour of temptation came; she forgot to pray, and fell. Then followed shame and bitter remorse. The demon who had tempted her whispered into her ear that there was no happiness for her any more in this life – no hope, no forgiveness. Instead of casting herself at the wounded feet of Jesus – feet wounded for her sake – instead of casting herself into the arms of her loving Mother Mary, the unhappy girl now gave herself up to despair. Her life was a burden to her, and she resolved to put an end to it. She hastened to the river. It was night, and the stars looked sadly down, and seemed to reproach that erring, unhappy soul. She shuddered as she gazed upon the cold, dark flood before her; she hesitated, but it was only for a moment. Shame and despair urged her on; she cast herself into the river, and sank, but soon rose again. She made every effort to drown herself, but, strange to say, she could not succeed. A fisherman happened to be near, and, seeing a person falling into the water, he hastened to rescue her. He was soon near, and made an effort to save her; but just too late! Seeing that she was about to be rescued, the evil one inspired her with the thought that it was the Scapular she wore that hindered her from drowning. Immediately the unhappy girl took off her Scapular and flung it from her, and that very instant she sank beneath the cold, dark waves, and her murdered soul sank for ever into the dark, burning waves of hell.

There lived a few years ago, in Belgium, a very wicked man; still, he wore the Scapular. He was taken ill, and grew worse. His last agony came on him, but he did not die. The doctor expected him to die every moment, but he lived on. His agony continued two, even three, days; every moment seemed to be his last. The doctor expressed his astonishment that he could remain alive so long.

265

"Ah!" said the man, "I understand it; I can tell you how it is. I wear the Scapular. I feel that as long as I have it on the Blessed Virgin, by her prayers, keeps me alive that I may repent. If I were to take off the Scapular, she would no longer pray for me, and I should die. But I do not want to repent; I will die as I have lived. What I have said is true, as you will see. The moment I take off the Scapular I shall die."

He then raised his hand, took the Scapular off his neck, and that very instant he died.

Hundreds of similar examples might be related, but these are sufficient to show that the promise of the Blessed Virgin is not only possible, but that it has been really fulfilled. But we shall see still more clearly how it is that those who wear the Scapular until death shall not burn in the flames of hell.

He that wears the Scapular declares thereby that he is a servant of Mary, and consequently has a claim to her special protection. One of the most consoling doctrines of the church is that of the Communion of Saints. This doctrine is exemplified especially in the confraternities of the Scapular. Those who wear the Scapular have a share in all the Masses, almsdeeds, penance, and other good works continually offered to God by the various religious orders represented by the Scapular. Their satisfaction for sin becomes ours; their prayers for heavenly blessings belong to us. The holy Scapular is the key to the rich treasure of graces that has been for centuries accumulating in the Church. All the missionary labors, the studies and toils, the prayers and watching, the fasting, and other works of penance of so many holy servants of God, belong to those who wear the Scapular. But this is not all. Those who wear the Scapular and fulfil the conditions required gain, in addition, the numerous indulgences annexed to this devotion, and thus they share, not only the merits of the pious members of the religious orders and confraternities of the Scapular, but also the merits of all the saints, the merits of the Blessed Virgin Mary, and even the infinite merits of Jesus Christ himself.

The other devotions to Our Lady last only for a certain time, but he who wears the Scapular honors Our Lady at all times and in all places. The Scapular is, as the Blessed Virgin herself has declared, "a safeguard in danger," and the demon fears to attack a soul whom he sees invested with the holy Scapular.

During a mission at Wexford the children were invested with the holy Scapular. Some time afterwards one of those children, together with its father and mother, left Wexford and went to Liverpool. They had to cross the sea between Ireland and England. The night was dark and stormy, the wind blew hard, the waves of the sea rose up like mountains. There were many ships lost on that stormy night. It was an old ship in which the child and its parents were sailing, and the people in it were expecting to be drowned. The little child was in a room below, very sick. Its father came downstairs and told it to get ready to die, for it was expected that the ship would soon sink. Now, the little child remembered the words of the Blessed Virgin: *"This Scapular is a sign of safety in dangers."* So the child quietly raised its hand and took off the Scapular. It said: "Please, father, take this Scapular and let it drop into the sea." The father took the Scapular and went to the side of the ship. Then he stretched his hand out, and let it drop into the sea. It was soon swallowed up by the waves. A few minutes after the people in the ship felt that there was a great change in the weather; the wind did not blow so hard; the waves became more quiet. In half an hour the sea was quite calm and the ship was safe. The people wondered at such a change in the weather, and did not know what had brought the change. But the little child knew the promise of the Blessed Virgin, "that the Scapular should bring safety in danger," and, believing this, was saved from death.

A little boy in Ireland had been invested with the holy Scapular. One day he was in a small boat on the sea, with two other boys bigger than himself. These two boys began to shake the boat, wanting to frighten the little boy and make him think that he would fall into the sea. He did not seem frightened, for he remembered that he was wearing the Scapular – *"a sign of safety in danger."* It happened, however, that the little boy did fall out of the boat into the sea. He was soon out of sight of the other boys, and he sank. The poor little fellow went down, and in another minute or two he would have been drowned. At this moment he felt something pulling at his neck. It was the Scapular! He felt himself drawn upwards, and was soon out of the water on the dry land. All this became known very soon. A great many people came to examine the little boy. They took off his Scapular and looked at it. They found that the strings were wet through and through with the salt water; but not a drop of water had touched the cloth. It is the cloth which receives the blessing. The cloth was quite dry, and the Scapular is still kept by one of the missionaries.

A young man in Perugia once promised the devil that if he would help him to commit a sinful act which he desired to do, he would give him his soul, and he gave him a writing to that effect, signed with his blood. The evil deed was committed, and the devil demanded the performance of the promise. He led the young man to a well, and threatened to take him body and soul to hell, if he would not cast himself into it. The wretched youth, thinking that it would be impossible for him to escape from his enemy, climbed the well-side in order to cast himself into it, but, terrified at the thought of death, he said to the devil that he had not the courage to throw himself in, and that, if he wished to see him dead, he himself should thrust him in. The young man wore about his neck the Scapular of the Blessed Virgin Mary; and the devil said to him: "Take off that Scapular, and I will thrust you in." But the youth, seeing the protection which the Divine Mother still gave him through that Scapular, refused to take it off, and, after much altercation, the devil departed in confusion. The sinner repented, and grateful to the Blessed Virgin, went to thank her, and presented a picture of this case as an offering at her altar in the new church of Santa Maria, in Perugia ("Glories of Mary," by St. Alphonsus, on the Fifth Dolor).

We have seen some of the many advantages, some of the many graces and blessings, obtained by wearing the Scapular. And now what are the obligations? The obligations are, strictly speaking, none whatever. You can be good members of the confraternity, you can have a share in all the merits and good works of the various religious orders, you have a right to a great many personal indulgences, merely by wearing the Scapular. The custom of saying seven Our Fathers and Hail Marys once a day, or, as some do, once a week, is very good, because we can gain thereby more indulgences; but it is not obligatory. The custom of abstaining on Wednesdays and Saturdays is not obligatory, unless we desire to gain the Sabbatine Indulgence; and even this obligation of abstaining on Wednesdays and Saturdays can be changed into any other good work by a priest empowered to do so. This so-called Sabbatine indulgence was first promulgated by Pope John XXII. The Blessed Virgin appeared to this Pope, and promised him that all those who wear the Scapular, practice chastity according to their state, and will abstain from meat on Wednesdays and Saturdays, will be delivered from Purgatory on the Saturday after their death. There is nothing unreasonable in this promise; for God can, by increasing the intensity of the torments, completely purify a soul in a few hours, though it might otherwise take several years. Moreover, the great number of suffrages and indulgences these souls receive soon satisfy God's justice and greatly shorten the duration of their sufferings.

The advantages of wearing the holy Scapular are, then innumerable, whilst the obligations are strictly none whatever. We have in the holy Scapular so easy and so powerful a means of securing our salvation that who will hesitate to wear it? Let the welfare of our immortal soul not be the last and least important affair in our eyes. Mary offers us her Scapular; she promises to make us eternally happy if we accept her gift. How can we remain indifferent? To acquire the special protection of the Blessed Virgin will not cost us half the trouble we take to gain the goodwill of some great personage on earth. Mary does not wait until we pray to her. No! she offers us her graces of her own accord. she opens her loving arms to receive us as her children. She seems to consider it a sacred duty to make us forever happy. Let no one reject this loving Mother; let no one repay her affection only by coldness and indifference. Were Mary to require of us all our worldly goods in return for the goods of heaven; were she to require of us all that her most fervent servants have most gladly done to honor her; were she to require us to wear, not a Scapular but the rough penitential garb of some religious order, even then we should not hesitate a moment, but receive with joy and press to our lips such a pledge of our salvation. Nay, were Mary to require one of the greatest and most painful sacrifices, even then we should obey promptly; for heaven is worth every sacrifice. Each Christian has but one soul – an immortal soul; if it be lost, all is lost forever; if it be gained, all is gained, and gained for all eternity. And now the Blessed Virgin offers us a pledge of our salvation – her holy Scapular. The Queen of Heaven and Earth invites us to wear it. Our loving Mother, the Mother of God, wishes to make us forever happy, and she requires so little in return. She only asks us to wear her Scapular. She promises us, if we do so, our eternal salvation, and she promises it in language so clear that it cannot be twisted into another meaning. She has attested her promises by the most extraordinary miracles – miracles which are renewed every day to strengthen our confidence; and even if the Blessed Virgin Mary had not bound herself to help us, the fact of our always wearing her holy Scapular would force her grateful heart to assist us, to love us, and protect us in danger of soul and body. In the "Life of St Alphonsus" (Vol. 1. book 2 Ch. 16 p. 185) we read the following "In the year 1743 the saint vent to Augri, a town in Italy, to give a mission in the church of St. Matthew. To inspire the people with devotion towards the Blessed Virgin, he exhorted the faithful of the parish of St. Matthew to erect a statue to Our Lady of Dolors in the church. Immediately the women brought to the church everything they had most precious in gold and silver. The offerings were so numerous that a considerable sum remained, which was given to the poor. Alphonsus was so devoted to Mary that this most glorious Virgin testified her love for him by operating the most extraordinary conversions at his intercession. The evening he arrived an unfortunate young man arose during the night to engage in a sinful transaction. He had a repugnance, however, to commit a sin with the Scapular about his neck. So he took it off to place it in a hole in the wall; but when he extended his hand he felt himself drawn back, and fled from the spot in terror. The following night the Blessed Virgin, willing to recompense the slight homage paid to her Scapular, appealed to him in a dream. 'miserable being!' she said, 'thou hadst respect for my Scapular, and thou hadst no horror for offending my Son! Tomorrow Father Alphonsus will come here to give a mission; go, confess to him, and amend thy life.' The young man had never heard of Alphonsus, and knew nothing of the mission. Next morning he went to find a fortune teller to have his dream interpreted; but before he could open his mouth this person addressed him with: 'Do you not know that Father Alphonsus has arrived today to give a mission?' When the young man heard the words 'Alphonsus' and 'mission,' he was thunderstruck; he ran in haste to the dwelling of Alphonsus, found him, and recounted to him the whole story. 'So, then,' said Alphonsus, his eyes filling with tears, 'our good Mother has sent you to me.' He heard his confession, reconciled him with God, and his life ever after was most edifying."

The following example is related by St. Alphonsus as having happened to a priest, a companion of his. While this priest was hearing confessions in a certain church (for sufficient reasons he did not mention the place where this occurred, although the penitent gave him permission to publish the fact), a youth stood before him who seemed to wish and not to wish to come to confession. The Father, after looking at him several times, at length called him, and asked him whether he wished to make his confession. The youth answered, "Yes"; but as he required a long time for it, the confessor took him into a retired room. There the young man began by telling him that he was a foreigner and of noble birth, but he could not believe that it was possible for God to pardon him after the life he had led. Besides innumerable sins of impurity, homicide, etc., which he had committed, he said that, being entirely in despair of salvation, he set about committing sins, not so much for his own gratification as to defy God and manifest the hatred he bore him. He said, among other things, that he had with him a crucifix which he had beaten out of contempt, and that just before, on that very morning, he had made a sacrilegious communion for no other purpose than that he might put under his feet the consecrated wafer; and that, in fact, he had actually received, and was about to put in execution his horrible intention, but was prevented by the people who observed him. He then consigned to the confessor the consecrated Host, wrapped in paper, and told him that as he was passing by that church he had a great desire to enter. He could not resist this desire, and had entered. That then he felt great remorse of conscience, together with a certain confused and irresolute desire to make his confession. For this reason he had placed himself before the confessional, but while there he felt so confused and timid that he wished to go away, but it seemed as if some one had retained him by force, "Until you, Father," said he, "called me. And now I find myself here; I find myself making my confession, but know not how to do it." The Father then asked him if he had practiced any act of devotion towards the most Holy Mother during that time; for such sudden conversions only come through the powerful hands of the Blessed Virgin. "None, Father; what devotion could I offer," answered the youth, "when I believed myself lost?" "But try to remember more carefully," replied the Father. "Father, nothing." But accidentally putting his hand to his breast, he remembered that he wore the Scapular of the Seven Dolors of Mary. "Ah! my son," said the confessor to him, "do you not see that Our Blessed Lady has bestowed this grace upon you? And know," he added, "that this church is a church of Our Blessed Lady." Hearing this, the youth was moved to contrition and began to weep. He confessed his sins, and his compunction increased to such a degree that, bursting into tears, he fell, overcome with grief, as it seemed, at the feet of the Father, who, having restored him by a cordial, finally finished hearing his confession, and absolved him with the greatest consolation, as he was entirely contrite and resolved to amend his life. The Father sent him back to his own country, after having obtained from him full liberty to preach and publish everywhere the great mercy exercised by Mary towards him ("Glories of Mary," disc. 6 p. 471).

Let us, then, take pride in wearing the holy Scapular as men take pride in having others wear their livery; but, at the same time, let us show to the world, by virtuous lives, that we are "servants" of Mary. To wear the holy habit of the Queen of Virgins and to lead the life of a brute is to dishonor Mary, to act the part of a vile and detestable hypocrite. Mary will obtain for us innumerable graces, but we, on our part, must correspond with these graces. Mary will enlighten our souls and touch our hearts, but we must follow these divine inspirations. Mary will show herself a watchful and tender Mother, but we also must prove ourselves dutiful and loving children. Let us, then, persevere in our devotion to Mary, and Mary will guard us during life, will assist us at the dread hour of death. She will console our suffering souls in Purgatory, and will finally lead us into the never-ending joys of heaven.

Plenary Indulgences granted to those who wear the five Scapulars.

Besides the innumerable graces and indulgences annexed to this devotion, the Popes have granted many plenary and partial indulgences to those who wear the four Scapulars. The following are the principal indulgences, to obtain which no special visit to any particular church is required:

Paul V. by his briefs of the 30th October, 1606, 31st August, 1609, and 19th July, 1614;

Clement X. in his Constitution of 8th May, 1673;

Clement XI. in his Constitution of 12th May, 1710;

Innocent XI. by his Constitution of the 10th February, 1680, 1st September, 1681, and 24th October, 1682, have granted the following indulgences:

1. Four Plenary Indulgences on the day of reception, when they have the four Scapulars, provided they go to confession and receive Holy Communion, and pray for the intention of the Church.

2. Four Plenary Indulgences at the hour of death, if they receive the Sacraments.

3. A Plenary Indulgence on the principal feast of Our Lady of the Seven Dolors, on the usual conditions.

4. A Plenary Indulgence on Passion Sunday, if they meditate for some time on the sufferings of our Lord and of His Blessed Mother, receive the Sacraments, and pray for the intention of the Church.

5. A Plenary Indulgence on the Festival of Our Lady of Mount Carmel, July 16; also whenever other confraternities have a Plenary Indulgence, and on all the festivals of our Lord, of the Blessed Virgin, and of the Apostles; on any two days of every week, at their option; and on every Friday, if they devoutly meditate for some time on the Passion of our Lord, receive the Sacraments, and pray for the intention of the Church.

All these indulgences are applicable to the souls in Purgatory.

"And let it be remembered," says St. Alphonsus, "that, besides many particular indulgences, there are annexed to the Scapular of the Immaculate Conception all the indulgences which are granted to any religious order, pious place, or person. And particularly by reciting the Our Father, Hail Mary, and Glory be to the Father six times, in honor of the Most Holy Trinity and of the Immaculate Mary, are gained each time all the indulgences of Rome, Portiuncula, Jerusalem, Galicia, which reach the number of four hundred and thirty-three Plenary Indulgences, besides the temporal, which are innumerable" ("Glories of Mary").

MY ROSARY

Some twenty years ago or more,
When famine wasted Erin's shore,
And children's wails made mothers sore,
    'Twas then I got my Rosary.

With tears I stood upon the strand,
And bade adieu to native land;
My mother then, with trembling hand,
    Put into mine this Rosary.

"My child, it almost breaks my heart
To think that you and I must part;
But promise me, no human art
    Will wean you from your Rosary.

"But if some brighter day should dawn,
And some one ask my colleen bawn
To wed him, say your all is gone
    Except your mother's Rosary

"And now, my dearest child adieu!
God's angels will watch over you,
If to your promise you keep true-
    to Him and to your Rosary."

Through all the wildness of the storm,
'Wid women's shrieks and men's alarm,
I still was calm; I feared no harm,
    For me or for my Rosary.

I reach the country of "the free;"
Whither, oh! wither, shall I flee?
A chapel with a cross I see:
    I go and say my Rosary.

A stranger among strangers thrown,
I work for bread, without a groan,
Save when a scornful mien was shown,
    Not me, but my brown Rosary.

Years passed and then a gay young man-
l blush to tell it-said, "You can
Of me, dear, make a happy man;"
    I went and said my Rosary.

He knew th'advice my mother gave,
Ere I had crossed the stormy wave:
Tho'she lies in the dark, cold grave,
    Her memory's in my Rosary.

He smiled, and coldly turned away,
Nor e'en a parting word did say;
I sought my room, and then did pray
    To God, on mother's Rosary.

At length a nobler suitor came,
For whom I gladly changed my name;
His little bride I knew he'd blame
    If she forgot her Rosary.

Now oft beneath the shady tree,
As children clamber up his knee,
He often says, "Come in, till we
    Recite our daily Rosary."

Then, let life's fortunes ebb or flow
Come joy or sadness, weal or woe
Poor sinner, to this refuge go,
    And fervent say thy Rosary.

And when Death's voice at last is come,
To summon exiles to their home,
May we, beyond yon starry dome,
    Find God thro' Mary's Rosary!

        From Rev. Buckley's Sermons.

THE GREAT COMMENTARY on THE FOUR GOSPELS by Cornelius aLapide, S.J.

QUOTES FROM THE REVIEW by SCOTT HAHN

Cornelius aLapide, S.J. (1568-1637) is a giant figure in the history of Catholic biblical interpretation. Born in a tiny Catholic enclave in the Calvinist Netherlands in the bloody generation after the Reformation, Lapide grew to be one of the Church's most gifted scholars and spiritual interpreters of the sacred page.

Between 1614 and 1645, Lapide wrote commentaries on every book of Scripture except Job and Psalms.

To read Lapide four hundred years later is to enter a nearly forgotten world of biblical interpretation ...more striking – the sheer breadth and density of Lapide's interpretative matrix or his audacity in summoning all these resources to the interpretation of the sacred text.

Lapide himself takes a breathtaking high view of Scripture's purpose: Lapide prefaces his commentary with thirty-eight "canons of interpretation," which reflect a wise and prayerful method. "

It is clear that the Fathers hold pride of place for Lapide in his interpretative work.

- *6"x 9" Book format*
- *2900+ Pages in four volumes*
- *First complete English translation*
- *Sewn Binding & Headbands*
- *Bonded Leather Covers &*
  Satin Ribbons
- *Greatest Catholic Bible*
  Commentary ever
- *Extensive discussion of Greek and Hebrew words*
- *$199. Per four volume set*